Handbook on Impact Evaluation

Handbook on Impact Evaluation

Quantitative Methods and Practices

Shahidur R. Khandker
Gayatri B. Koolwal
Hussain A. Samad

THE WORLD BANK
Washington, D.C.

© 2010 The International Bank for Reconstruction and Development / The World Bank
1818 H Street NW
Washington DC 20433
Telephone: 202-473-1000
Internet: www.worldbank.org
E-mail: feedback@worldbank.org

ISBN: 978-0-8213-8028-4
eISBN: 978-0-8213-8029-1
DOI: 10.1596/978-0-8213-8028-4

Library of Congress Cataloging-in-Publication Data
Khandker, Shahidur R. Handbook on impact evaluation : quantitative methods and practices / Shahidur R. Khandker, Gayatri B. Koolwal, Hussain A. Samad.
    p. cm.
 Includes bibliographical references and index.
 ISBN 978-0-8213-8028-4 — ISBN 978-0-8213-8029-1 (electronic)
 1. Economic development projects—Evaluation. 2. Economic assistance—Evaluation.
 I. Koolwal, Gayatri B. II. Samad, Hussain A., 1963- III. Title.
 HD75.9.K52 2009
 338.90072—dc22
                             2009020886

Cover design by Patricia Hord.Graphik Design.

Contents

Boxes

Figures

Table

Foreword

Identifying the precise effects of a policy is a complex and challenging task. This issue is particularly salient in an uncertain economic climate, where governments are under great pressure to promote programs that can recharge growth and reduce poverty. At the World Bank, our work is centered on aid effectiveness and how to improve the targeting and efficacy of programs that we support. As we are well aware, however, times of crisis as well as a multitude of other factors can inhibit a clear understanding of how interventions work—and how effective programs can be in the long run.

Handbook on Impact Evaluation: Quantitative Methods and Practices makes a valuable contribution in this area by providing, for policy and research audiences, a comprehensive overview of steps in designing and evaluating programs amid uncertain and potentially confounding conditions. It draws from a rapidly expanding and broad-based literature on program evaluation—from monitoring and evaluation approaches to experimental and nonexperimental econometric methods for designing and conducting impact evaluations.

Recent years have ushered in several benefits to policy makers in designing and evaluating programs, including improved data collection and better forums to share data and analysis across countries. Harnessing these benefits, however, depends on understanding local economic environments by using qualitative as well as quantitative approaches. Although this *Handbook* has a quantitative emphasis, several case studies are also presented of methods that use both approaches in designing and assessing programs.

The vast range of ongoing development initiatives at institutions such as the World Bank, as well as at other research and policy institutions around the world, provide an (albeit wieldy) wealth of information on interpreting and measuring policy effects. This *Handbook* synthesizes the spectrum of research on program evaluation, as well as the diverse experiences of program officials in the field. It will be of great interest to development practitioners and international donors, and it can be used in training and building local capacity. Students and researchers embarking on work in this area will also find it a useful guide for understanding the progression and latest methods on impact evaluation.

I recommend this *Handbook* for its relevance to development practitioners and researchers involved in designing, implementing, and evaluating programs and policies for better results in the quest of poverty reduction and socioeconomic development.

Justin Yifu Lin
Senior Vice President and Chief Economist
Development Economics
The World Bank

Preface

Evaluation approaches for development programs have evolved considerably over the past two decades, spurred on by rapidly expanding research on impact evaluation and growing coordination across different research and policy institutions in designing programs. Comparing program effects across different regions and countries is also receiving greater attention, as programs target larger populations and become more ambitious in scope, and researchers acquire enough data to be able to test specific policy questions across localities. This progress, however, comes with new empirical and practical challenges.

The challenges can be overwhelming for researchers and evaluators who often have to produce results within a short time span after the project or intervention is conceived, as both donors and governments are keen to regularly evaluate and monitor aid effectiveness. With multiple options available to design and evaluate a program, choosing a particular method in a specific context is not always an easy task for an evaluator, especially because the results may be sensitive to the context and methods applied. The evaluation could become a frustrating experience.

With these issues in mind, we have written the *Handbook on Impact Evaluation* for two broad audiences—researchers new to the evaluation field and policy makers involved in implementing development programs worldwide. We hope this book will offer an up-to-date compendium that serves the needs of both audiences, by presenting a detailed analysis of the quantitative research underlying recent program evaluations and case studies that reflect the hands-on experience and challenges of researchers and program officials in implementing such methods.

The *Handbook* is based on materials we prepared for a series of impact evaluation workshops in different countries, sponsored by the World Bank Institute (WBI). In writing this book, we have benefitted enormously from the input and support of a number of people. In particular, we would like to thank Martin Ravallion who has made far-reaching contributions to research in this area and who taught with Shahid Khandker at various WBI courses on advanced impact evaluation; his work has helped shape this book. We also thank Roumeen Islam and Sanjay Pradhan for their support, which was invaluable in bringing the *Handbook* to completion.

We are grateful to Boniface Essama-Nssah, Jonathan Haughton, Robert Moffitt, Mark Pitt, Emmanuel Skoufias, and John Strauss for their valuable conversations and input into the conceptual framework for the book. We also thank several researchers at the country institutions worldwide who helped organize and participate in the WBI workshops, including G. Arif Khan and Usman Mustafa, Pakistan Institute for Development Economics (PIDE); Jirawan Boonperm and Chalermkwun Chiemprachanarakorn, National Statistics Office of Thailand; Phonesaly Souksavath, National Statistics Office of Lao PDR; Jose Ramon Albert and Celia Reyes, Philippine Institute for Development Economics; Matnoor Nawi, Economic Planning Unit of Malaysia; and Zhang Lei, International Poverty Reduction Center in China. We would also like to thank the participants of various WBI-sponsored workshops for their comments and suggestions.

Finally, we thank the production staff of the World Bank for this book, including Denise Bergeron, Stephen McGroarty, Erin Radner, and Dina Towbin at the World Bank Office of the Publisher, and Dulce Afzal and Maxine Pineda at the WBI. Putting together the different components of the book was a complex task, and we appreciate their support.

About the Authors

Shahidur R. Khandker (PhD, McMaster University, Canada, 1983) is a lead economist in the Development Research Group of the World Bank. When this *Handbook* was written, he was a lead economist at the World Bank Institute. He has authored more than 30 articles in peer-reviewed journals, including the *Journal of Political Economy, The Review of Economic Studies*, and the *Journal of Development Economics*; authored several books, including *Fighting Poverty with Microcredit: Experience in Bangladesh*, published by Oxford University Press; co-authored with Jonathan Haughton, the *Handbook on Poverty and Inequality*, published by the World Bank; and, written several book chapters and more than two dozen discussion papers at the World Bank on poverty, rural finance and microfinance, agriculture, and infrastructure. He has worked in close to 30 countries. His current research projects include seasonality in income and poverty, and impact evaluation studies of rural energy and microfinance in countries in Africa, Asia, and Latin America.

Gayatri B. Koolwal (PhD, Cornell University, 2005) is a consultant in the Poverty Reduction and Economic Management Network, Gender and Development, at the World Bank. Her current research examines the distributional impacts of rural infrastructure access and the evolution of credit markets in developing countries. She recently taught an impact evaluation workshop at the Pakistan Institute of Development Economics (PIDE) through the World Bank Institute. Her research has been published in *Economic Development and Cultural Change* and in the *Journal of Development Studies*.

Hussain A. Samad (MS, Northeastern University, 1992) is a consultant at the World Bank with about 15 years of experience in impact assessment, monitoring and evaluation, data analysis, research, and training on development issues. He has been involved in various aspects of many World Bank research projects—drafting proposals, designing projects, developing questionnaires, formulating sampling strategies and planning surveys, as well as data analysis. His research interests include energy and rural electrification, poverty, micro-credit, infrastructure, and education. Mr. Samad designed course materials for training and conducted hands-on training in workshops in several countries.

Abbreviations

2SLS	two-stage least squares
AEPC	Alternative Energy Promotion Center (Nepal)
ATE	average treatment effect
ATT	average treatment of the treated
BRAC	Bangladesh Rural Advancement Committee
CO	community organization
DD	double-difference (methods)
FAQs	frequently asked questions
FFS	farmer-field-school
FONCODES	Fondo de Cooperación para el Desarrollo Social, or Cooperation Fund for Social Development (Peru)
GPS	global positioning system
GSS	girls' secondary schools
IA	Income Assistance (program) (Canada)
IE	impact evaluation
ITT	intention-to-treat (impact)
IV	instrumental variable
JSIF	Jamaica Social Investment Fund
KDP	Kecamatan Development Program (Indonesia)
LATE	local average treatment effect
LLM	local linear matching
M&E	monitoring and evaluation
MTE	marginal treatment effect
NN	nearest-neighbor (matching)
OLS	ordinary least squares
PACES	Plan de Ampliación de Cobertura de la Educación Secundaria, or Plan for Increasing Secondary Education Coverage (Colombia)
PC	Patwar Circle (Pakistan)
PROGRESA	Programa de Educación, Salud y Alimentación, or Education, Health, and Nutrition Program (Mexico)
PRS	Poverty Reduction Strategy
PSM	propensity score matching
QDD	quantile difference-in-difference (approach)
QTE	quantile treatment effect

RD	regression discontinuity
REDP	Rural Electrification Development Program (Nepal)
SEECALINE	Surveillance et Éducation d'Écoles et des Communautés en Matière d'Alimentation et de Nutrition Élargie, or Expanded School and Community Food and Nutrition Surveillance and Education (program) (Madagascar)
SIIOP	Sistema Integral de Información para la Operación de Oportunidades, or Complete Information System for the Operation of Oportunidades (Mexico)
SSP	Self-Sufficiency Project (Canada)
SWP	Southwest China Poverty Reduction Project
TOT	treatment effect on the treated
TUP	Targeting the Ultra-Poor Program (Bangladesh)

PART 1

Methods and Practices

1. Introduction

Public programs are designed to reach certain goals and beneficiaries. Methods to understand whether such programs actually work, as well as the level and nature of impacts on intended beneficiaries, are main themes of this book. Has the Grameen Bank, for example, succeeded in lowering consumption poverty among the rural poor in Bangladesh? Can conditional cash-transfer programs in Mexico and other Latin American countries improve health and schooling outcomes for poor women and children? Does a new road actually raise welfare in a remote area in Tanzania, or is it a "highway to nowhere"? Do community-based programs like the Thailand Village Fund project create long-lasting improvements in employment and income for the poor?

Programs might appear potentially promising before implementation yet fail to generate expected impacts or benefits. The obvious need for impact evaluation is to help policy makers decide whether programs are generating intended effects; to promote accountability in the allocation of resources across public programs; and to fill gaps in understanding what works, what does not, and how measured changes in well-being are attributable to a particular project or policy intervention.

Effective impact evaluation should therefore be able to assess precisely the mechanisms by which beneficiaries are responding to the intervention. These mechanisms can include links through markets or improved social networks as well as tie-ins with other existing policies. The last link is particularly important because an impact evaluation that helps policy makers understand the effects of one intervention can guide concurrent and future impact evaluations of related interventions. The benefits of a well-designed impact evaluation are therefore long term and can have substantial spillover effects.

This book reviews quantitative methods and models of impact evaluation. The formal literature on impact evaluation methods and practices is large, with a few useful overviews (for example, Blundell and Dias 2000; Duflo, Glennerster, and Kremer 2008; Ravallion 2008). Yet there is a need to put the theory into practice in a hands-on fashion for practitioners. This book also details challenges and goals in other realms of evaluation, including monitoring and evaluation (M&E), operational evaluation, and mixed-methods approaches combining quantitative and qualitative analyses.

Broadly, the question of *causality* makes impact evaluation different from M&E and other evaluation approaches. In the absence of data on counterfactual outcomes (that is, outcomes for participants had they not been exposed to the program), impact evaluations can be rigorous in identifying program effects by applying different models to survey data to construct comparison groups for participants. The main question of impact evaluation is one of attribution—isolating the effect of the program from other factors and potential selection bias.

Impact evaluation spans qualitative and quantitative methods, as well as ex ante and ex post methods. Qualitative analysis, as compared with the quantitative approach, seeks to gauge potential impacts that the program may generate, the mechanisms of such impacts, and the extent of benefits to recipients from in-depth and group-based interviews. Whereas quantitative results can be generalizable, the qualitative results may not be. Nonetheless, qualitative methods generate information that may be critical for understanding the mechanisms through which the program helps beneficiaries.

Quantitative methods, on which this book focuses, span ex ante and ex post approaches. The ex ante design determines the possible benefits or pitfalls of an intervention through simulation or economic models. This approach attempts to predict the outcomes of intended policy changes, given assumptions on individual behavior and markets. Ex ante approaches often build structural models to determine how different policies and markets interlink with behavior at the beneficiary level to better understand the mechanisms by which programs have an impact. Ex ante analysis can help in refining programs before they are implemented, as well as in forecasting the potential effects of programs in different economic environments. Ex post impact evaluation, in contrast, is based on actual data gathered either after program intervention or before and after program implementation. Ex post evaluations measure actual impacts accrued by the beneficiaries because of the program. These evaluations, however, sometimes miss the mechanisms underlying the program's impact on the population, which structural models aim to capture. These mechanisms can be very important in understanding program effectiveness (particularly in future settings).

Although impact evaluation can be distinguished from other approaches to evaluation, such as M&E, impact evaluation can or should not necessarily be conducted independently of M&E. M&E assesses how an intervention evolves over time, evaluating data available from the project management office in terms of initial goals, indicators, and outcomes associated with the program. Although M&E does not spell out whether the impact indicators are a *result* of program intervention, impact evaluations often depend on knowing how the program is designed, how it is intended to help the target audience, and how it is being implemented. Such information is often available only through operational evaluation as part of M&E. M&E is necessary to understand the goals of a project, the ways an intervention can take place, and the potential metrics to measure effects on the target beneficiaries. Impact evaluation provides a framework sufficient to understand whether the beneficiaries are truly benefiting from the program—and not from other factors.

This book is organized as follows. Chapter 2 reviews the basic issues pertaining to an evaluation of an intervention to reach certain targets and goals. It distinguishes impact evaluation from related concepts such as M&E, operational evaluation, qualitative versus quantitative evaluation, and ex ante versus ex post impact evaluation. This chapter focuses on the basic issues of quantitative ex post impact evaluation that concern evaluators.

Two major veins of program design exist, spanning experimental (or randomized) setups and nonexperimental methods. Chapter 3 focuses on the experimental design of an impact evaluation, discussing its strengths and shortcomings. Various nonexperimental methods exist as well, each of which are discussed in turn through chapters 4 to 7. Chapter 4 examines matching methods, including the propensity score matching technique. Chapter 5 deals with double-difference methods in the context of panel data, which relax some of the assumptions on the potential sources of selection bias. Chapter 6 reviews the instrumental variable method, which further relaxes assumptions on self-selection. Chapter 7 examines regression discontinuity and pipeline methods, which exploit the design of the program itself as potential sources of identification of program impacts.

This book also covers methods to shed light on the mechanisms by which different participants are benefiting from programs. Given the recent global financial downturn, for example, policy makers are concerned about how the fallout will spread across economic sectors, and the ability of proposed policies to soften the impact of such events. The book, therefore, also discusses how macro- and micro-level distributional effects of policy changes can be assessed. Specifically, chapter 8 presents a discussion of how distributional impacts of programs can be measured, including new techniques related to quantile regression. Chapter 9 discusses structural approaches to program evaluation, including economic models that can lay the groundwork for estimating direct and indirect effects of a program. Finally, chapter 10 discusses the strengths and weaknesses of experimental and nonexperimental methods and also highlights the usefulness of impact evaluation tools in policy making.

The framework presented in this book can be very useful for strengthening local capacity in impact evaluation—in particular—among technicians and policy makers in charge of formulating, implementing, and evaluating programs to alleviate poverty and underdevelopment. Building on the impact evaluation literature, this book extends discussions of different experimental and nonexperimental quantitative models, including newer variants and combinations of ex ante and ex post approaches. Detailed case studies are provided for each of the methods presented, including updated examples from the recent evaluation literature.

For researchers interested in learning how to use these models with statistical software, this book also provides data analysis and statistical software exercises for Stata in the context of evaluating major microcredit programs in Bangladesh, including the Grameen Bank. These exercises, presented in chapters 11 to 16, are based on data from Bangladesh that have been collected for evaluating microcredit programs for the poor. The exercises demonstrate how different evaluation approaches (randomization, propensity score matching, etc.) would be applied had the microcredit programs and survey been designed to accommodate that method. The exercises therefore provide a hypothetical view of how program impacts could be calculated in Stata, and do not imply that the Bangladesh data actually follow the same design. These exercises will help researchers formulate and solve problems in the context of evaluating projects in their countries.

References

Blundell, Richard, and Monica Costa Dias. 2000. "Evaluation Methods for Non-experimental Data." *Fiscal Studies* 21 (4): 427–68.

Duflo, Esther, Rachel Glennerster, and Michael Kremer. 2008. "Using Randomization in Development Economics Research: A Toolkit." In *Handbook of Development Economics*, vol. 4, ed. T. Paul Schultz and John Strauss, 3895–962. Amsterdam: North-Holland.

Ravallion, Martin. 2008. "Evaluating Anti-poverty Programs." In *Handbook of Development Economics*, vol. 4, ed. T. Paul Schultz and John Strauss, 3787–846. Amsterdam: North-Holland.

2. Basic Issues of Evaluation

Summary

Several approaches can be used to evaluate programs. *Monitoring* tracks key indicators of progress over the course of a program as a basis on which to evaluate outcomes of the intervention. *Operational evaluation* examines how effectively programs were implemented and whether there are gaps between planned and realized outcomes. *Impact evaluation* studies whether the changes in well-being are indeed due to the program intervention and not to other factors.

These evaluation approaches can be conducted using quantitative methods (that is, survey data collection or simulations) before or after a program is introduced. *Ex ante evaluation* predicts program impacts using data before the program intervention, whereas *ex post evaluation* examines outcomes after programs have been implemented. Reflexive comparisons are a type of ex post evaluation; they examine program impacts through the difference in participant outcomes before and after program implementation (or across participants and nonparticipants). Subsequent chapters in this handbook provide several examples of these comparisons.

The main challenge across different types of impact evaluation is to find a good counterfactual—namely, the situation a participating subject would have experienced had he or she not been exposed to the program. Variants of impact evaluation discussed in the following chapters include randomized evaluations, propensity score matching, double-difference methods, use of instrumental variables, and regression discontinuity and pipeline approaches. Each of these methods involves a different set of assumptions in accounting for potential selection bias in participation that might affect construction of program treatment effects.

Learning Objectives

After completing this chapter, the reader will be able to discuss and understand

- Different approaches to program evaluation
- Differences between quantitative and qualitative approaches to evaluation, as well as ex ante versus ex post approaches
- Ways selection bias in participation can confound the treatment effect
- Different methodologies in impact evaluation, including randomization, propensity score matching, double differences, instrumental variable methods, and regression discontinuity and pipeline approaches

Introduction: Monitoring versus Evaluation

Setting goals, indicators, and targets for programs is at the heart of a monitoring system. The resulting information and data can be used to evaluate the performance of program interventions. For example, the World Bank Independent Evaluation Group weighs the progress of the World Bank–International Monetary Fund Poverty Reduction Strategy (PRS) initiative against its objectives through monitoring; many countries have also been developing monitoring systems to track implementation of the PRS initiative and its impact on poverty. By comparing program outcomes with specific targets, monitoring can help improve policy design and implementation, as well as promote accountability and dialogue among policy makers and stakeholders.

In contrast, evaluation is a systematic and objective assessment of the results achieved by the program. In other words, evaluation seeks to prove that changes in targets are due only to the specific policies undertaken. Monitoring and evaluation together have been referred to as *M&E*. For example, M&E can include *process evaluation*, which examines how programs operate and focuses on problems of service delivery; *cost-benefit analysis*, which compares program costs against the benefits they deliver; and *impact evaluations*, which quantify the effects of programs on individuals, households, and communities. All of these aspects are part of a good M&E system and are usually carried out by the implementing agency.

Monitoring

The challenges in monitoring progress of an intervention are to

- Identify the *goals* that the program or strategy is designed to achieve, such as reducing poverty or improving schooling enrollment of girls. For example, the Millennium Development Goals initiative sets eight broad goals across themes such as hunger, gender inequalities, schooling, and poverty to monitor the performance of countries and donors in achieving outcomes in those areas.
- Identify key *indicators* that can be used to monitor progress against these goals. In the context of poverty, for example, an indicator could be the proportion of individuals consuming fewer than 2,100 calories per day or the proportion of households living on less than a dollar a day.
- Set *targets*, which quantify the level of the indicators that are to be achieved by a given date. For instance, a target might be to halve the number of households living on less than a dollar a day by 2015.
- Establish a *monitoring system* to track progress toward achieving specific targets and to inform policy makers. Such a system will encourage better management of and accountability for projects and programs.

Setting Up Indicators within an M&E Framework

Indicators are typically classified into two major groups. First, *final indicators* measure the outcomes of poverty reduction programs (such as higher consumption per capita) and the impact on dimensions of well-being (such as reduction of consumption poverty). Second, *intermediate indicators* measure inputs into a program (such as a conditional cash-transfer or wage subsidy scheme) and the outputs of the program (such as roads built, unemployed men, and women hired). Target indicators can be represented in four clusters, as presented in figure 2.1. This so-called logic framework spells out the inputs, outputs, outcomes, and impacts in the M&E system. Impact evaluation, which is the focus of this handbook, spans the latter stages of the M&E framework.

Viewed in this framework, monitoring covers both implementation and performance (or results-based) monitoring. Intermediate indicators typically vary more quickly than final indicators, respond more rapidly to public interventions, and can be measured more easily and in a more timely fashion. Selecting indicators for monitoring against goals and targets can be subject to resource constraints facing the project management authority. However, it is advisable to select only a few indicators that can be monitored properly rather than a large number of indicators that cannot be measured well.

One example of a monitoring system comes from PROGRESA (Programa de Educación, Salud y Alimentación, or Education, Health, and Nutrition Program) in Mexico (discussed in more detail in box 2.1). PROGRESA (now called Oportunidades) is one of the largest randomized interventions implemented by a single country. Its aim was

Figure 2.1   Monitoring and Evaluation Framework

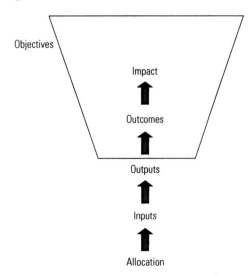

Source: Authors' representation.

> ### BOX 2.1   Case Study: PROGRESA (Oportunidades) in Mexico
>
> Monitoring was a key component of the randomized program PROGRESA (now called Oportunidades) in Mexico, to ensure that the cash transfers were directed accurately. Program officials foresaw several potential risks in implementing the program. These risks included the ability to ensure that transfers were targeted accurately; the limited flexibility of funds, which targeted households instead of communities, as well as the nondiscretionary nature of the transfers; and potential intrahousehold conflicts that might result because transfers were made only to women.
>
> Effective monitoring therefore required that the main objectives and intermediate indicators be specified clearly. Oportunidades has an institutional information system for the program's operation, known as SIIOP (Sistema Integral de Información para la Operación de Oportunidades, or Complete Information System for the Operation of Oportunidades), as well as an audit system that checks for irregularities at different stages of program implementation. These systems involved several studies and surveys to assess how the program's objectives of improving health, schooling, and nutrition should be evaluated. For example, to determine schooling objectives, the systems ran diagnostic studies on potentially targeted areas to see how large the educational grants should be, what eligibility requirements should be established in terms of grades and gender, and how many secondary schools were available at the local, municipal, and federal levels. For health and nutrition outcomes, documenting behavioral variation in household hygiene and preparation of foods across rural and urban areas helped to determine food supplement formulas best suited for targeted samples.
>
> These systems also evaluated the program's ability to achieve its objectives through a design that included randomized checks of delivery points (because the provision of food supplements, for example, could vary substantially between providers and government authorities); training and regular communication with stakeholders in the program; structuring of fieldwork resources and requirements to enhance productivity in survey administration; and coordinated announcements of families that would be beneficiaries.
>
> The approaches used to address these issues included detailed survey instruments to monitor outcomes, in partnership with local and central government authorities. These instruments helped to assess the impact of the program on households and gave program officials a sense of how effectively the program was being implemented. The surveys included, for example, a pilot study to better understand the needs of households in targeted communities and to help guide program design. Formal surveys were also conducted of participants and nonparticipants over the course of the program, as well as of local leaders and staff members from schools and health centers across the localities. Administrative data on payments to households were also collected.

to target a number of health and educational outcomes including malnutrition, high infant mortality, high fertility, and school attendance. The program, which targeted rural and marginal urban areas, was started in mid-1997 following the macroeconomic crisis of 1994 and 1995. By 2004, around 5 million families were covered, with a budget of about US$2.5 billion, or 0.3 percent of Mexico's gross domestic product.

The main thrust of Oportunidades was to provide conditional cash transfers to households (specifically mothers), contingent on their children attending school and visiting health centers regularly. Financial support was also provided directly to these institutions. The average benefit received by participating households was about 20 percent of the value of their consumption expenditure before the program, with roughly equal weights on the health and schooling requirements. Partial participation was possible; that is, with respect to the school subsidy initiative, a household could receive a partial benefit if it sent only a proportion of its children to school.

Results-Based Monitoring

The actual execution of a monitoring system is often referred to as *results-based monitoring*. Kusek and Rist (2004) outline 10 steps to results-based monitoring as part of an M&E framework.

First, a readiness assessment should be conducted. The assessment involves understanding the needs and characteristics of the area or region to be targeted, as well as the key players (for example, the national or local government and donors) that will be responsible for program implementation. How the effort will respond to negative pressures and information generated from the M&E process is also important.

Second, as previously mentioned, program evaluators should agree on specific outcomes to monitor and evaluate, as well as key performance indicators to monitor outcomes. Doing so involves collaboration with recipient governments and communities to arrive at a mutually agreed set of goals and objectives for the program. Third, evaluators need to decide how trends in these outcomes will be measured. For example, if children's schooling were an important outcome for a program, would schooling achievement be measured by the proportion of children enrolled in school, test scores, school attendance, or another metric? Qualitative and quantitative assessments can be conducted to address this issue, as will be discussed later in this chapter. The costs of measurement will also guide this process.

Fourth, the instruments to collect information need to be determined. Baseline or preprogram data can be very helpful in assessing the program's impact, either by using the data to predict outcomes that might result from the program (as in ex ante evaluations) or by making before-and-after comparisons (also called *reflexive comparisons*). Program managers can also engage in frequent discussions with staff members and targeted communities.

Fifth, targets need to be established; these targets can also be used to monitor results. This effort includes setting periodic targets over time (for example, annually or every two years). Considering the duration of the likely effects of the program, as well as other factors that might affect program implementation (such as political considerations), is also important. Monitoring these targets, in particular, embodies the sixth step in this results-based framework and involves the collection of good-quality data.

The seventh step relates to the timing of monitoring, recognizing that from a management perspective the timing and organization of evaluations also drive the extent to which evaluations can help guide policy. If actual indicators are found to be diverging rapidly from initial goals, for example, evaluations conducted around that time can help program managers decide quickly whether program implementation or other related factors need to be adjusted.

The eighth step involves careful consideration of the means of reporting, including the audience to whom the results will be presented. The ninth step involves using the results to create avenues for feedback (such as input from independent agencies, local authorities, and targeted and nontargeted communities). Such feedback can help evaluators learn from and update program rules and procedures to improve outcomes.

Finally, successful results-based M&E involves sustaining the M&E system within the organization (the 10th step). Effective M&E systems will endure and are based on, among other things, continued demand (a function of incentives to continue the program, as well as the value for credible information); transparency and accountability in evaluation procedures; effective management of budgets; and well-defined responsibilities among program staff members.

One example of results-based monitoring comes from an ongoing study of microhydropower projects in Nepal under the Rural Electrification Development Program (REDP) administered by the Alternative Energy Promotion Center (AEPC). AEPC is a government institute under the Ministry of Environment, Science, and Technology. The microhydropower projects began in 1996 across five districts with funding from the United Nations Development Programme; the World Bank joined the REDP during the second phase in 2003. The program is currently in its third phase and has expanded to 25 more districts. As of December 2008, there were about 235 microhydropower installations (3.6 megawatt capacity) and 30,000 beneficiary households. Box 2.2 describes the monitoring framework in greater detail.

Challenges in Setting Up a Monitoring System

Primary challenges to effective monitoring include potential variation in program implementation because of shortfalls in capacity among program officials, as well as ambiguity in the ultimate indicators to be assessed. For the microhydropower projects in Nepal, for example, some challenges faced by REDP officials in carrying out the M&E framework included the following:

- Key performance indicators were not well defined and hence not captured comprehensively.
- Limited human resources were available for collecting and recording information.

BOX 2.2 **Case Study: Assessing the Social Impact of Rural Energy Services in Nepal**

REDP microhydropower projects include six community development principles: organizational development, skill enhancement, capital formation, technology promotion, empowerment of vulnerable communities, and environment management. Implementation of the REDP microhydropower projects in Nepal begins with community mobilization. Community organizations (COs) are first formed by individual beneficiaries at the local level. Two or more COs form legal entities called *functional groups*. A management committee, represented by all COs, makes decision about electricity distribution, tariffs, operation, management, and maintenance of microhydropower projects.

A study on the social impact of rural energy services in Nepal has recently been funded by Energy Sector Management Assistance Program and is managed by the South Asia Energy Department of the World Bank. In implementing the M&E framework for the microhydropower projects, this study seeks to (a) improve management for the program (better planning and reporting); (b) track progress or systematic measurement of benefits; (c) ensure accountability and results on investments from stakeholders such as the government of Nepal, as well as from donors; and (d) provide opportunities for updating how the program is implemented on the basis of continual feedback on how outcomes overlap with key performance indicators.

Box figure 2.A describes the initial monitoring framework set up to disseminate information about how inputs, outputs, and outcomes were measured and allocated. Information is collected at each of the community, district, and head office (AEPC) levels. Community mobilizers relay field-level information to coordinators at the district level, where additional information is also collected. At the district level, information is verified and sent to AEPC, where reports are prepared and then sent to various stakeholders. Stakeholders, in particular, can include the government of Nepal, as well as donors.

BOX Figure 2.A   Levels of Information Collection and Aggregation

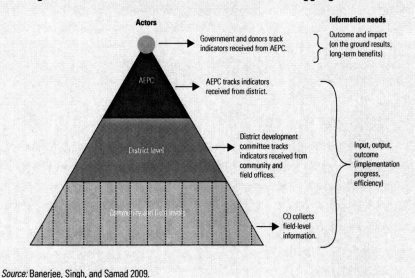

Source: Banerjee, Singh, and Samad 2009.

(Box continues on the following page.)

13

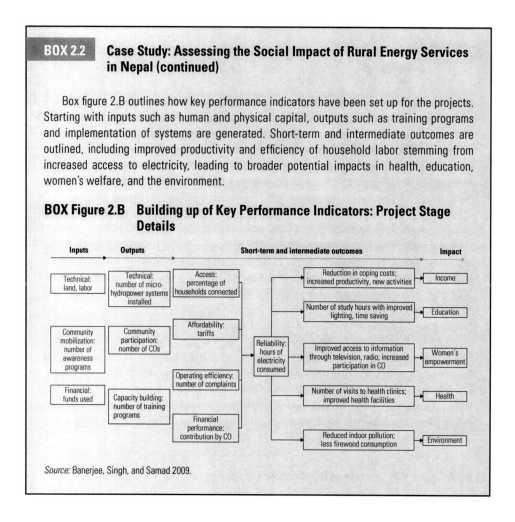

BOX 2.2 **Case Study: Assessing the Social Impact of Rural Energy Services in Nepal (continued)**

Box figure 2.B outlines how key performance indicators have been set up for the projects. Starting with inputs such as human and physical capital, outputs such as training programs and implementation of systems are generated. Short-term and intermediate outcomes are outlined, including improved productivity and efficiency of household labor stemming from increased access to electricity, leading to broader potential impacts in health, education, women's welfare, and the environment.

BOX Figure 2.B **Building up of Key Performance Indicators: Project Stage Details**

Source: Banerjee, Singh, and Samad 2009.

- M&E personnel had limited skills and capacity, and their roles and responsibilities were not well defined at the field and head office levels.
- AEPC lacked sophisticated tools and software to analyze collected information.

Weaknesses in these areas have to be addressed through different approaches. Performance indicators, for example, can be defined more precisely by (a) better understanding the inputs and outputs at the project stage, (b) specifying the level and unit of measurement for indicators, (c) frequently collecting community- and beneficiary-level data to provide periodic updates on how intermediate outcomes are evolving and whether indicators need to be revised, and (d) clearly identifying the people and entities responsible for monitoring. For data collection in particular, the survey timing (from a preproject baseline, for example, up to the current period); frequency (monthly or semiannually, for example); instruments (such as interviews or bills); and level of collection (individual, household, community, or a broader administrative unit such as district) need to defined and set up explicitly within the M&E framework. Providing the staff with training and tools for data collection and analysis, as well as for data verification at different levels of the monitoring structure (see box figure 2.A in box 2.2 for an example), is also crucial.

Policy makers might also need to establish how microlevel program impacts (at the community or regional level) would be affected by country-level trends such as increased trade, inflation, and other macroeconomic policies. A related issue is heterogeneity in program impacts across a targeted group. The effects of a program, for example, may vary over its expected lifetime. Relevant inputs affecting outcomes may also change over this horizon; thus, monitoring long-term as well as short-term outcomes may be of interest to policy makers. Also, although program outcomes are often distinguished simply across targeted and nontargeted areas, monitoring variation in the program's implementation (measures of quality, for example) can be extremely useful in understanding the program's effects. With all of these concerns, careful monitoring of targeted and nontargeted areas (whether at the regional, household, or individual level) will help greatly in measuring program effects. Presenting an example from Indonesia, box 2.3 describes some techniques used to address M&E challenges.

BOX 2.3   **Case Study: The Indonesian Kecamatan Development Project**

The Kecamatan Development Program (KDP) in Indonesia, a US$1.3 billion program run by the Community Development Office of the Ministry of Home Affairs, aims to alleviate poverty by strengthening local government and community institutions as well as by improving local governance. The program began in 1998 after the financial crisis that plagued the region, and it works with villages to define their local development needs. Projects were focused on credit and infrastructural expansion. This program was not ultimately allocated randomly.

A portion of the KDP funds were set aside for monitoring activities. Such activities included, for example, training and capacity development proposed by the communities and local project monitoring groups. Technical support was also provided by consultants, who were assigned to sets of villages. They ranged from technical consultants with engineering backgrounds to empowerment consultants to support communication within villages.

Governments and nongovernmental organizations assisted in monitoring as well, and villages were encouraged to engage in self-monitoring through piloted village-district parliament councils and cross-village visits. Contracts with private banks to provide village-level banking services were also considered. As part of this endeavor, financial supervision and training were provided to communities, and a simple financial handbook and checklist were developed for use in the field as part of the monitoring initiative. District-level procurement reforms were also introduced to help villages and local areas buy technical services for projects too large to be handled by village management.

Project monitoring combined quantitative and qualitative approaches. On the quantitative side, representative sample surveys helped assess the poverty impact of the project across different areas. On the qualitative side, consultants prepared case studies to highlight lessons learned

(Box continues on the following page.)

15

> **BOX 2.3** **Case Study: The Indonesian Kecamatan Development Project (continued)**
>
> from the program, as well as to continually evaluate KDP's progress. Some issues from these case studies include the relative participation of women and the extreme poor, conflict resolution, and the role of village facilitators in disseminating information and knowledge.
>
> Given the wide scope of the program, some areas of improvement have been suggested for KDP monitoring. Discussions or sessions conducted with all consultants at the end of each evaluation cycle can encourage feedback and dialogue over the course of the program, for example. Focus groups of consultants from different backgrounds (women, for example) might also elicit different perspectives valuable to targeting a diverse population. Suggestions have also been made to develop themes around these meetings, such as technical issues, transparency and governance, and infrastructure. Consultants were also often found to not regularly report problems they found in the field, often fearing that their own performance would be criticized. Incentives to encourage consultants to accurately report developments in their areas have also been discussed as part of needed improvements in monitoring.

Operational Evaluation

An operational evaluation seeks to understand whether implementation of a program unfolded as planned. Specifically, operational evaluation is a retrospective assessment based on initial project objectives, indicators, and targets from the M&E framework. Operation evaluation can be based on interviews with program beneficiaries and with officials responsible for implementation. The aim is to compare what was planned with what was actually delivered, to determine whether there are gaps between planned and realized outputs, and to identify the lessons to be learned for future project design and implementation.

Challenges in Operational Evaluation

Because operational evaluation relates to how programs are ultimately implemented, designing appropriate measures of implementation quality is very important. This effort includes monitoring how project money was ultimately spent or allocated across sectors (as compared to what was targeted), as well as potential spillovers of the program into nontargeted areas. Collecting precise data on these factors can be difficult, but as described in subsequent chapters, it is essential in determining potential biases in measuring program impacts. Box 2.4, which examines FONCODES (Fondo de Cooperación para el Desarrollo Social, or Cooperation Fund for Social Development), a poverty alleviation program in Peru, shows how operational evaluation also often involves direct supervision of different stages of program implementation. FONCODES has both educational and nutritional objectives. The nutritional

---

> **BOX 2.4**   **Case Study: Monitoring the Nutritional Objectives of the FONCODES Project in Peru**
>
> Within the FONCODES nutrition initiative in Peru, a number of approaches were taken to ensure the quality of the nutritional supplement and efficient implementation of the program. At the program level, the quality of the food was evaluated periodically through independent audits of samples of communities. This work included obtaining and analyzing random samples of food prepared by targeted households. Every two months, project officials would randomly visit distribution points to monitor the quality of distribution, including storage. These visits also provided an opportunity to verify the number of beneficiaries and to underscore the importance of the program to local communities.
>
> Home visits were also used to evaluate beneficiaries' knowledge of the project and their preparation of food. For example, mothers (who were primarily responsible for cooking) were asked to show the product in its bag, to describe how it was stored, and to detail how much had been consumed since the last distribution. They were also invited to prepare a ration so that the process could be observed, or samples of leftovers were taken for subsequent analysis.
>
> The outcomes from these visits were documented regularly. Regular surveys also documented the outcomes. These data allowed program officials to understand how the project was unfolding and whether any strategies needed to be adjusted or reinforced to ensure program quality. At the economywide level, attempts were made at building incentives within the agrifood industry to ensure sustainable positioning of the supplement in the market; companies were selected from a public bidding process to distribute the product.
>
> The operational efforts aimed at ultimately reducing poverty in these areas, however, did vary from resulting impact estimates. FONCODES was not allocated randomly, for example, and Schady (1999) found that the flexibility of allocation of funds within FONCODES, as well as in the timing and constitution of expenditures, made the program very vulnerable to political interference. Paxson and Schady (2002) also used district-level data on expenditures from the schooling component of the program to find that though the program did reach the poorest districts, it did not necessarily reach the poorest households in those districts. They did find, however, that the program increased school attendance, particularly that of younger children. Successful program implementation therefore requires harnessing efforts over all of the program's objectives, including effective enforcement of program targeting.

component involves distributing precooked, high-nutrition food, which is currently consumed by about 50,000 children in the country. Given the scale of the food distribution initiative, a number of steps were taken to ensure that intermediate inputs and outcomes could be monitored effectively.

Operational Evaluation versus Impact Evaluation

The rationale of a program in drawing public resources is to improve a selected outcome over what it would have been without the program. An evaluator's main problem is to measure the impact or effects of an intervention so that policy makers can decide whether the program intervention is worth supporting and whether the program should be continued, expanded, or disbanded.

Operational evaluation relates to ensuring effective implementation of a program in accordance with the program's initial objectives. *Impact evaluation* is an effort to understand whether the changes in well-being are indeed due to project or program intervention. Specifically, impact evaluation tries to determine whether it is possible to identify the program effect and to what extent the measured effect can be attributed to the program and not to some other causes. As suggested in figure 2.1, impact evaluation focuses on the latter stages of the log frame of M&E, which focuses on outcomes and impacts.

Operational and impact evaluation are complementary rather than substitutes, however. An operational evaluation should be part of normal procedure within the implementing agency. But the template used for an operational evaluation can be very useful for more rigorous impact assessment. One really needs to know the context within which the data was generated and where policy effort was directed. Also, the information generated through project implementation offices, which is essential to an operational evaluation, is also necessary for interpretation of impact results.

However, although operational evaluation and the general practice of M&E are integral parts of project implementation, impact evaluation is not imperative for each and every project. Impact evaluation is time and resource intensive and should therefore be applied selectively. Policy makers may decide whether to carry out an impact evaluation on the basis of the following criteria:

- The program intervention is innovative and of strategic importance.
- The impact evaluation exercise contributes to the knowledge gap of what works and what does not. (Data availability and quality are fundamental requirements for this exercise.)

Mexico's Oportunidades program is an example in which the government initiated a rigorous impact evaluation at the pilot phase to determine whether to ultimately roll out the program to cover the entire country.

Quantitative versus Qualitative Impact Assessments

Governments, donors, and other practitioners in the development community are keen to determine the effectiveness of programs with far-reaching goals such as lowering poverty or increasing employment. These policy quests are often possible only through impact evaluations based on hard evidence from survey data or through related quantitative approaches.

This handbook focuses on quantitative impact methods rather than on qualitative impact assessments. Qualitative information such as understanding the local sociocultural and institutional context, as well as program and participant details, is, however, essential to a sound quantitative assessment. For example, qualitative information can help identify mechanisms through which programs might be having an impact; such surveys can also identify local policy makers or individuals who would be important in determining the course of how programs are implemented, thereby aiding operational evaluation. But a qualitative assessment on its own cannot assess outcomes against relevant alternatives or *counterfactual* outcomes. That is, it cannot really indicate what might happen in the absence of the program. As discussed in the following chapters, quantitative analysis is also important in addressing potential statistical bias in program impacts. A mixture of qualitative and quantitative methods (a *mixed-methods approach*) might therefore be useful in gaining a comprehensive view of the program's effectiveness.

Box 2.5 describes a mixed-methods approach to examining outcomes from the Jamaica Social Investment Fund (JSIF). As with the Kecamatan Development Program in Indonesia (see box 2.3), JSIF involved community-driven initiatives, with communities making cash or in-kind contributions to project development costs (such as construction). The qualitative and quantitative evaluation setups both involved comparisons of outcomes across matched treated and untreated pairs of communities, but with different approaches to matching communities participating and not participating in JSIF.

BOX 2.5   Case Study: Mixed Methods in Quantitative and Qualitative Approaches

Rao and Ibáñez (2005) applied quantitative and qualitative survey instruments to study the impact of Jamaica Social Investment Fund. Program evaluators conducted semistructured in-depth qualitative interviews with JSIF project coordinators, local government and community leaders, and members of the JSIF committee that helped implement the project in each community. This information revealed important details about social norms, motivated by historical and cultural influences that guided communities' decision making and therefore the way the program ultimately played out in targeted areas. These interviews also helped in matching communities, because focus groups were asked to identify nearby communities that were most similar to them.

Qualitative interviews were not conducted randomly, however. As a result, the qualitative interviews could have involved people who were more likely to participate in the program, thereby leading to a bias in understanding the program impact. A quantitative component to the study was therefore also included. Specifically, in the quantitative component, 500 households (and, in turn, nearly 700 individuals) were surveyed, split equally across communities participating and not participating in the fund. Questionnaires covered a range of variables, including socioeconomic characteristics, details of participation in the fund and other local programs, perceived priorities for community development, and social networks, as well as ways a number of their outcomes had changed relative to five years ago (before JSIF began). Propensity score matching, discussed in

(Box continues on the following page.)

> **BOX 2.5** **Case Study: Mixed Methods in Quantitative and Qualitative Approaches (continued)**
>
> greater detail in chapter 4, was used to compare outcomes for participating and nonparticipating households. Matching was conducted on the basis of a poverty score calculated from national census data. Separate fieldwork was also conducted to draw out additional, unmeasured community characteristics on which to conduct the match; this information included data on local geography, labor markets, and the presence of other community organizations. Matching in this way allowed better comparison of targeted and nontargeted areas, thereby avoiding bias in the treatment impacts based on significant observed and unobserved differences across these groups.
>
> The qualitative data therefore revealed valuable information on the institutional context and norms guiding behavior in the sample, whereas the quantitative data detailed trends in poverty reduction and other related indicators. Overall, when comparing program estimates from the qualitative models (as measured by the difference-in-differences cross-tabulations of survey responses across JSIF and non-JSIF matched pairs—see chapter 5 for a discussion of difference-in-differences methods) with the quantitative impact estimated from nearest-neighbor matching, Rao and Ibáñez found the pattern of effects to be similar. Such effects included an increased level of trust and an improved ability of people from different backgrounds to work together. For the latter outcome, for example, about 21 percent of the JSIF sample said it was "very difficult" or "difficult" for people of different backgrounds to work together in the qualitative module, compared with about 32 percent of the non-JSIF sample. Similarly, the nearest-neighbor estimates revealed a significant positive mean benefit for this outcome to JSIF areas (about 0.33).
>
> The quantitative impacts were also broken down by household socioeconomic characteristics. They tended to show, however, that JSIF may have created better outcomes in terms of increased collective action for wealthier and better-educated participants; qualitative evidence also revealed that these groups tended to dominate the decision-making process.

Quantitative Impact Assessment: Ex Post versus Ex Ante Impact Evaluations

There are two types of quantitative impact evaluations: ex post and ex ante. An ex ante impact evaluation attempts to measure the intended impacts of future programs and policies, given a potentially targeted area's current situation, and may involve simulations based on assumptions about how the economy works (see, for example, Bourguignon and Ferreira 2003; Todd and Wolpin 2006). Many times, ex ante evaluations are based on structural models of the economic environment facing potential participants (see chapter 9 for more discussion on structural modeling). The underlying assumptions of structural models, for example, involve identifying the main economic agents in the development of the program (individuals, communities, local or national governments), as well as the links between the agents and the different markets in determining outcomes from the program. These models predict program impacts.

Ex post evaluations, in contrast, measure actual impacts accrued by the beneficiaries that are attributable to program intervention. One form of this type of evaluation is the treatment effects model (Heckman and Vytlacil, 2005). Ex post evaluations have immediate benefits and reflect reality. These evaluations, however, sometimes miss the mechanisms underlying the program's impact on the population, which structural models aim to capture and which can be very important in understanding program effectiveness (particularly in future settings). Ex post evaluations can also be much more costly than ex ante evaluations because they require collecting data on actual outcomes for participant and nonparticipant groups, as well as on other accompanying social and economic factors that may have determined the course of the intervention. An added cost in the ex post setting is the failure of the intervention, which might have been predicted through ex ante analysis.

One approach is to combine both analyses and compare ex post estimates with ex ante predictions (see Ravallion 2008). This approach can help explain how program benefits emerge, especially if the program is being conducted in different phases and has the flexibility to be refined from added knowledge gained from the comparison. Box 2.6 provides an example of this approach, using a study by Todd and Wolpin (2006) of a school subsidy initiative under PROGRESA.

The case studies discussed in the following chapters primarily focus on ex post evaluations. However, an ex post impact exercise is easier to carry out if the researchers have an ex ante design of impact evaluation. That is, one can plan a design for

---

BOX 2.6   Case Study: An Example of an Ex Ante Evaluation

Todd and Wolpin (2006) applied an ex ante approach to evaluation, using data from the PROGRESA (now Oportunidades) school subsidy experiment in Mexico. Using an economic model of household behavior, they predicted impacts of the subsidy program on the proportion of children attending school. The predictions were based only on children from the control group and calculated the treatment effect from matching control group children from households with a given wage and income with children from households where wages and income would be affected by the subsidy. See chapter 4 for a detailed discussion on matching methods; chapter 9 also discusses Todd and Wolpin's model in greater detail.

Predictions from this model were then compared with ex post experimental impacts (over the period 1997–98) measured under the program. Todd and Wolpin (2006) found that the predicted estimates across children 12 to 15 were similar to the experimental estimates in the same age group. For girls between 12 and 15, they found the predicted increase in schooling to be 8.9 percentage points, compared with the actual increase of 11.3 percentage points; for boys, the predicted and experimental estimates were 2.8 and 2.1 percentage points, respectively.

The ex ante evaluation they conducted also allowed them to evaluate how outcomes might change if certain parameters were altered. An ex ante assessment could also describe the potential range of impacts from the program, which could help in ultimate targeting ex post.

an impact evaluation before implementing the intervention. Chapter 9 provides more case studies of ex ante evaluations.

The Problem of the Counterfactual

The main challenge of an impact evaluation is to determine what would have happened to the beneficiaries if the program had not existed. That is, one has to determine the per capita household income of beneficiaries in the absence of the intervention. A beneficiary's outcome in the absence of the intervention would be its *counterfactual.*

A program or policy intervention seeks to alter changes in the well-being of intended beneficiaries. Ex post, one observes outcomes of this intervention on intended beneficiaries, such as employment or expenditure. Does this change relate directly to the intervention? Has this intervention caused expenditure or employment to grow? Not necessarily. In fact, with only a point observation after treatment, it is impossible to reach a conclusion about the impact. At best one can say whether the objective of the intervention was met. But the result after the intervention cannot be attributed to the program itself.

The problem of evaluation is that while the program's impact (independent of other factors) can truly be assessed only by comparing actual and counterfactual outcomes, the counterfactual is not observed. So the challenge of an impact assessment is to create a convincing and reasonable comparison group for beneficiaries in light of this missing data. Ideally, one would like to compare how the same household or individual would have fared with and without an intervention or "treatment." But one cannot do so because at a given point in time a household or an individual cannot have two simultaneous existences—a household or an individual cannot be in the treated and the control groups at the same time. Finding an appropriate counterfactual constitutes the main challenge of an impact evaluation.

How about a comparison between treated and nontreated groups when both are eligible to be treated? How about a comparison of outcomes of treated groups before and after they are treated? These potential comparison groups can be "counterfeit" counterfactuals, as will be discussed in the examples that follow.

Looking for a Counterfactual: With-and-Without Comparisons

Consider the case of Grameen Bank's beneficiaries in Bangladesh. Grameen Bank offers credit to poor women to improve their food consumption. Data, however, show that the per capita consumption among program participants is lower than that of nonparticipants prior to program intervention. Is this a case of failure of Grameen Bank? Not necessarily. Grameen Bank targeted poor families because they had lower per capita food consumption to begin with, so judging the program's impact by comparing the

Figure 2.2 Evaluation Using a With-and-Without Comparison

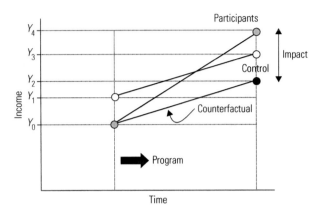

Source: Authors' representation.

food consumption of program participants with that of nonparticipants is incorrect. What is needed is to compare what would have happened to the food consumption of the participating women had the program not existed. A proper comparison group that is a close counterfactual of program beneficiaries is needed.

Figure 2.2 provides an illustration. Consider the income of Grameen Bank participants after program intervention as Y_4 and the income of nonparticipants or control households as Y_3. This with-and-without group comparison measures the program's effect as $Y_4 - Y_3$. Is this measure a right estimate of program effect? Without knowing why some households participated while others did not when a program such as Grameen Bank made its credit program available in a village, such a comparison could be deceptive. Without such information, one does not know whether Y_3 is the right counterfactual outcome for assessing the program's effect. For example, incomes are different across the participant and control groups before the program; this differential might be due to underlying differences that can bias the comparison across the two groups. If one knew the counterfactual outcomes (Y_0, Y_2), the real estimate of program effect is $Y_4 - Y_2$, as figure 2.2 indicates, and not $Y_4 - Y_3$. In this example, the counterfeit counterfactual yields an underestimate of the program's effect. Note, however, that depending on the preintervention situations of treated and control groups, the counterfeit comparison could yield an over- or underestimation of the program's effect.

Looking for a Counterfactual: Before-and-After Comparisons

Another counterfeit counterfactual could be a comparison between the pre- and postprogram outcomes of participants. One might compare ex post outcomes for beneficiaries with data on their outcomes before the intervention, either with comparable survey data before the program was introduced or, in the absence of a proper evaluation design, with retrospective data. As shown in figure 2.3, one then has two points of observations for the beneficiaries of an intervention: preintervention income (Y_0) and postintervention income (Y_2). Accordingly, the program's effect might be estimated as ($Y_2 - Y_0$). The literature refers to this approach as the *reflexive method* of impact, where resulting participants' outcomes before the intervention function as comparison or control outcomes. Does this method offer a realistic estimate of the program's effect? Probably not. The time series certainly makes reaching better conclusions easier, but it is in no way conclusive about the impact of a program. Looking at figure 2.3, one sees, for example, that the impact might be ($Y_2 - Y_1$). Indeed, such a simple difference method would not be an accurate assessment because many other factors (outside of the program) may have changed over the period. Not controlling for those other factors means that one would falsely attribute the participant's outcome in absence of the program as Y_0, when it might have been Y_1. For example, participants in a training program may have improved employment prospects after the program. Although this improvement may be due to the program, it may also be because the economy is recovering from a past crisis and employment is growing again. Unless they are carefully done, reflexive comparisons cannot distinguish between the program's effects and other external effects, thus compromising the reliability of results.

Reflexive comparisons may be useful in evaluations of full-coverage interventions such as nationwide policies and programs in which the entire population participates and there is no scope for a control group. Even when the program is not as far reaching, if outcomes for participants are observed over several years, then structural changes in outcomes could be tested for (Ravallion 2008).

In this context, therefore, a broad baseline study covering multiple preprogram characteristics of households would be very useful so that one could control for as

Figure 2.3 Evaluation Using a Before-and-After Comparison

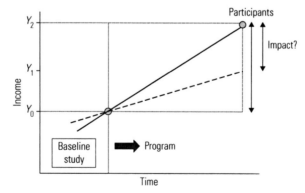

Source: Authors' representation.

many other factors as might be changing over time. Detailed data would also be needed on participation in existing programs before the intervention was implemented. The following chapters discuss several examples of before-and-after comparisons, drawing on a reflexive approach or with-and-without approach.

Basic Theory of Impact Evaluation: The Problem of Selection Bias

An impact evaluation is essentially a problem of missing data, because one cannot observe the outcomes of program participants had they not been beneficiaries. Without information on the counterfactual, the next best alternative is to compare outcomes of treated individuals or households with those of a comparison group that has not been treated. In doing so, one attempts to pick a comparison group that is very similar to the treated group, such that those who received treatment would have had outcomes similar to those in the comparison group in absence of treatment.

Successful impact evaluations hinge on finding a good comparison group. There are two broad approaches that researchers resort to in order to mimic the counter-factual of a treated group: (a) create a comparator group through a statistical design, or (b) modify the targeting strategy of the program itself to wipe out differences that would have existed between the treated and nontreated groups before comparing outcomes across the two groups.

Equation 2.1 presents the basic evaluation problem comparing outcomes Y across treated and nontreated individuals i:

$$Y_i = \alpha X_i + \beta T_i + \varepsilon_i. \qquad (2.1)$$

Here, T is a dummy equal to 1 for those who participate and 0 for those who do not participate. X is set of other observed characteristics of the individual and perhaps of his or her household and local environment. Finally, ε is an error term reflecting unobserved characteristics that also affect Y. Equation 2.1 reflects an approach commonly used in impact evaluations, which is to measure the direct effect of the program T on outcomes Y. Indirect effects of the program (that is, those not directly related to participation) may also be of interest, such as changes in prices within program areas. Indirect program effects are discussed more extensively in chapter 9.

The problem with estimating equation 2.1 is that treatment assignment is not often random because of the following factors: (a) purposive program placement and (b) self-selection into the program. That is, programs are placed according to the need of the communities and individuals, who in turn self-select given program design and placement. Self-selection could be based on observed characteristics (see chapter 4), unobserved factors, or both. In the case of unobserved factors, the error term in the estimating equation will contain variables that are also correlated with the treatment dummy T. One cannot measure—and therefore account for—these unobserved characteristics in equation 2.1, which leads to *unobserved selection bias*. That is, cov $(T, \varepsilon) \neq 0$ implies the violation of one of the key assumptions of ordinary least squares in obtaining unbiased estimates: independence of regressors from the disturbance term ε. The correlation between T and ε naturally biases the other estimates in the equation, including the estimate of the program effect β.

This problem can also be represented in a more conceptual framework. Suppose one is evaluating an antipoverty program, such as a credit intervention, aimed at raising household incomes. Let Y_i represent the income per capita for household i. For participants, $T_i = 1$, and the value of Y_i under treatment is represented as $Y_i(1)$. For nonparticipants, $T_i = 0$, and Y_i can be represented as $Y_i(0)$. If $Y_i(0)$ is used across nonparticipating households as a comparison outcome for participant outcomes $Y_i(1)$, the average effect of the program might be represented as follows:

$$D = E(Y_i(1) \mid T_i = 1) - E(Y_i(0) \mid T_i = 0). \tag{2.2}$$

The problem is that the treated and nontreated groups may not be the same prior to the intervention, so the expected difference between those groups may not be due entirely to program intervention. If, in equation 2.2, one then adds and subtracts the expected outcome for nonparticipants had they participated in the program—$E(Y_i(0) / T_i = 1)$, or another way to specify the counterfactual—one gets

$$\begin{aligned} D = E(Y_i(1) \mid T_i = 1) - E(Y_i(0) \mid T_i = 0) \\ + [E(Y_i(0) \mid T_i = 1) - E(Y_i(0) \mid T_i = 1)]. \end{aligned} \tag{2.3}$$

$$\Rightarrow D = ATE + [E(Y_i(0) \mid T_i = 1) - E(Y_i(0) \mid T_i = 0)]. \tag{2.4}$$

$$\Rightarrow D = ATE + B. \tag{2.5}$$

In these equations, ATE is the average treatment effect $[E(Y_i(1) \mid T_i = 1) - E(Y_i(0) \mid T_i = 1)]$, namely, the average gain in outcomes of participants relative to nonparticipants, as if nonparticipating households were also treated. The ATE corresponds to a situation in which a randomly chosen household from the population is assigned to participate in the program, so participating and nonparticipating households have an equal probability of receiving the treatment T.

The term B, $[E(Y_i(0) \mid T_i = 1) - E(Y_i(0) \mid T_i = 0)]$, is the extent of selection bias that crops up in using D as an estimate of the ATE. Because one does not know $E(Y_i(0) \mid T_i = 1)$, one cannot calculate the magnitude of selection bias. As a result, if one does not know the extent to which selection bias makes up D, one may never know the exact difference in outcomes between the treated and control groups.

The basic objective of a sound impact assessment is then to find ways to get rid of selection bias ($B = 0$) or to find ways to account for it. One approach, discussed in chapter 3, is to randomly assign the program. It has also been argued that selection bias would disappear if one could assume that whether or not households or individuals receive treatment (conditional on a set of covariates, X) were independent of the outcomes that they have. This assumption is called the *assumption of unconfoundedness*, also referred to as the *conditional independence assumption* (see Lechner 1999; Rosenbaum and Rubin 1983):

$$(Y_i(1), Y_i(0)) \perp T_i \mid X_i. \tag{2.6}$$

One can also make a weaker assumption of *conditional exogeneity of program placement.* These different approaches and assumptions will be discussed in the following chapters. The soundness of the impact estimates depends on how justifiable the assumptions are on the comparability of participant and comparison groups, as well as the exogeneity of program targeting across treated and nontreated areas. However, without any approaches or assumptions, one will not be able to assess the extent of bias B.

Different Evaluation Approaches to Ex Post Impact Evaluation

As discussed in the following chapters, a number of different methods can be used in impact evaluation theory to address the fundamental question of the missing counterfactual. Each of these methods carries its own assumptions about the nature of potential selection bias in program targeting and participation, and the assumptions are crucial to developing the appropriate model to determine program impacts. These methods, each of which will be discussed in detail throughout the following chapters, include

1. Randomized evaluations
2. Matching methods, specifically propensity score matching (PSM)
3. Double-difference (DD) methods
4. Instrumental variable (IV) methods
5. Regression discontinuity (RD) design and pipeline methods
6. Distributional impacts
7. Structural and other modeling approaches

These methods vary by their underlying assumptions regarding how to resolve selection bias in estimating the program treatment effect. Randomized evaluations involve a randomly allocated initiative across a sample of subjects (communities or individuals, for example); the progress of treatment and control subjects exhibiting similar preprogram characteristics is then tracked over time. Randomized experiments have the advantage of avoiding selection bias at the level of randomization. In the absence of an experiment, PSM methods compare treatment effects across participant and matched nonparticipant units, with the matching conducted on a range of observed characteristics. PSM methods therefore assume that selection bias is based only on observed characteristics; they cannot account for unobserved factors affecting participation.

DD methods assume that unobserved selection is present and that it is time invariant—the treatment effect is determined by taking the difference in outcomes across treatment and control units before and after the program intervention. DD methods can be used in both experimental and nonexperimental settings. IV models can be used with cross-section or panel data and in the latter case allow for selection bias on unobserved characteristics to vary with time. In the IV approach, selection bias on unobserved characteristics is corrected by finding a variable (or instrument) that is correlated with participation but not correlated with unobserved characteristics affecting the outcome; this instrument is used to predict participation. RD and pipeline methods are extensions of IV and experimental methods; they exploit exogenous program rules (such as eligibility requirements) to compare participants and nonparticipants in a close neighborhood around the eligibility cutoff. Pipeline methods, in particular, construct a comparison group from subjects who are eligible for the program but have not yet received it.

Finally, the handbook covers methods to examine the distributional impacts of programs, as well as modeling approaches that can highlight mechanisms (such as intermediate market forces) by which programs have an impact. These approaches cover a mix of different quantitative methods discussed in chapters 3 to 7, as well as ex ante and ex post methods.

The handbook also draws examples and exercises from data on microfinance participation in Bangladesh over two periods (1991/92 and 1998/99) to demonstrate how ex post impact evaluations are conducted.

Overview: Designing and Implementing Impact Evaluations

In sum, several steps should be taken to ensure that impact evaluations are effective and elicit useful feedback. During project identification and preparation, for example, the importance and objectives of the evaluation need to be outlined clearly. Additional concerns include the nature and timing of evaluations. To isolate the effect of the program on outcomes, independent of other factors, one should time and structure impact evaluations beforehand to help program officials assess and update targeting, as well as other guidelines for implementation, during the course of the intervention.

Data availability and quality are also integral to assessing program effects; data requirements will depend on whether evaluators are applying a quantitative or qualitative approach—or both—and on whether the framework is ex ante, ex post, or both. If new data will be collected, a number of additional concerns need to be addressed, including timing, sample design and selection, and selection of appropriate survey instruments. Also, pilot surveys will need to be conducted in the field so that interview questions can be revised and refined. Collecting data on relevant socioeconomic characteristics at both the beneficiary level and the community level can also help in better understanding the behavior of respondents within their economic and social environments. Ravallion (2003) also suggests a number of guidelines to improving data collection in surveys. These guidelines include understanding different facets and stylized facts of the program and of the economic environments of participants and nonparticipants to improve sampling design and flesh out survey modules to elicit additional information (on the nature of participation or program targeting, for example) for understanding and addressing selection bias later on.

Hiring and training fieldwork personnel, as well as implementing a consistent approach to managing and providing access to the data, are also essential. During project implementation, from a management perspective, the evaluation team needs to be formed carefully to include enough technical and managerial expertise to ensure accurate reporting of data and results, as well as transparency in implementation so that the data can be interpreted precisely. Ongoing data collection is important to keep program officials current about the progress of the program, as well as, for example, any parameters of the program that need to be adapted to changing circumstances or trends accompanying the initiative. The data need to be analyzed carefully and presented to policy makers and other major stakeholders in the program to allow potentially valuable feedback. This input, in addition to findings from the evaluation itself, can help guide future policy design as well.

Questions

1. The purpose of impact evaluation (IE) is to
    A. determine if a project benefits intended beneficiaries and, if so, how much.
    B. help policy makers decide if a project is worth supporting.
    C. determine resource allocation in different stages of the project.
       (a) All of the above
       (b) A and B
       (c) A and C
       (d) A only

2. In the M&E project cycle, which stage(s) is (are) covered by IE?
    A. Inputs
    B. Outputs
    C. Outcomes
    D. Impacts.
       (a) All of the above
       (b) A and B
       (c) A, B, and C
       (d) C and D

3. Which of the following statement(s) is (are) true for ex post IE?
   A. Ex post IE is done few months before a project starts its operation.
   B. Ex post IE cannot be done using panel data.
   C. Ex post IE is more common than ex ante evaluation.
      (a) All of the above
      (b) A and B
      (c) B and C
      (d) C only

4. Which of the following statement(s) is (are) true about counterfactual?
   A. *Counterfactual* is a hypothetical situation that says what would have happened to participants had they not participated in a program.
   B. Taking care of counterfactual is key to IE.
   C. Different IE methodologies handle counterfactual differently.
      (a) All of the above
      (b) A and B
      (c) B and C
      (d) C only

5. Which statement is true about the design of an ex post evaluation?
   A. Evaluators are part of the program management.
   B. Evaluators are engaged at early stage.
   C. An ex ante design is better than an ex post design of program evaluation.
      (a) All of the above
      (b) A and B only
      (c) B and C only
      (d) C only

6. Which IE methodology typically assumes that differences in outcomes between participants and nonparticipants stem from differences in the participation decision?
      (a) Double difference (DD)
      (b) Propensity score matching (PSM)
      (c) Randomization
      (d) Instrumental variable (IV)

References

Banerjee, Sudeshna, Avjeet Singh, and Hussain Samad. 2009. "Developing Monitoring and Evaluation Frameworks for Rural Electrification Projects: A Case Study from Nepal." Draft, World Bank, Washington, DC.

Bourguignon, François, and Francisco H. G. Ferreira. 2003. "Ex Ante Evaluation of Policy Reforms Using Behavioral Models." In *The Impact of Economic Policies on Poverty and Income Distribution: Evaluation Techniques and Tools*, ed. François Bourguignon and Luiz A. Pereira da Silva, 123–41. Washington, DC: World Bank and Oxford University Press.

Heckman, James J., and Edward Vytlacil. 2005. "Structural Equations, Treatment Effects, and Econometric Policy Evaluation." *Econometrica* 73 (3): 669–738.

Kusek, Jody Zall, and Ray C. Rist. 2004. *A Handbook for Development Practitioners: Ten Steps to a Results-Based Monitoring and Evaluation System.* Washington, DC: World Bank.

Lechner, Michael. 1999. "Earnings and Employment Effects of Continuous Off-the-Job Training in East Germany after Unification." *Journal of Business Economic Statistics* 17 (1): 74–90.

Paxson, Christina, and Norbert Schady. 2002. "The Allocation and Impact of Social Funds: Spending on School Infrastructure in Peru." *World Bank Economic Review* 16 (2): 297–319.

Rao, Vjayendra, and Ana María Ibáñez. 2005. "The Social Impact of Social Funds in Jamaica: A 'Participatory Econometric' Analysis of Targeting, Collective Action, and Participation in Community-Driven Development." *Journal of Development Studies* 41 (5): 788–838.

Ravallion, Martin. 2003. "Assessing the Poverty Impact of an Assigned Program." In *The Impact of Economic Policies on Poverty and Income Distribution: Evaluation Techniques and Tools*, ed. François Bourguignon and Luiz A. Pereira da Silva, 103–22. Washington, DC: World Bank and Oxford University Press.

———. 2008. "Evaluating Anti-Poverty Programs." In *Handbook of Development Economics*, vol. 4, ed. T. Paul Schultz and John Strauss, 3787–846. Amsterdam: North-Holland.

Rosenbaum, Paul R., and Donald B. Rubin. 1983. "The Central Role of the Propensity Score in Observational Studies for Causal Effects." *Biometrika* 70 (1): 41–55.

Schady, Norbert. 1999. "Seeking Votes: The Political Economy of Expenditures by the Peruvian Social Fund (FONCODES), 1991–95." Policy Research Working Paper 2166, World Bank, Washington, DC.

Todd, Petra, and Kenneth Wolpin. 2006. "Ex Ante Evaluation of Social Programs." PIER Working Paper 06-122, Penn Institute for Economic Research, University of Pennsylvania, Philadelphia.

3. Randomization

Summary

Allocating a program or intervention randomly across a sample of observations is one solution to avoiding selection bias, provided that program impacts are examined at the level of randomization. Careful selection of control areas (or the counterfactual) is also important in ensuring comparability with participant areas and ultimately calculating the treatment effect (or difference in outcomes) between the two groups. The treatment effect can be distinguished as the *average treatment effect* (ATE) between participants and control units, or the *treatment effect on the treated* (TOT), a narrower measure that compares participant and control units, conditional on participants being in a treated area.

Randomization could be conducted purely randomly (where treated and control units have the same expected outcome in absence of the program); this method requires ensuring external and internal validity of the targeting design. In actuality, however, researchers have worked in partial randomization settings, where treatment and control samples are chosen randomly, conditional on some observable characteristics (for example, landholding or income). If these programs are exogenously placed, conditional on these observed characteristics, an unbiased program estimate can be made.

Despite the clarity of a randomized approach, a number of factors still need to be addressed in practice. They include resolving ethical issues in excluding areas that share similar characteristics with the targeted sample, accounting for spillovers to nontargeted areas as well as for selective attrition, and ensuring heterogeneity in participation and ultimate outcomes, even if the program is randomized.

Learning Objectives

After completing this chapter, the reader will be able to discuss

- How to construct an appropriate counterfactual
- How to design a randomized experiment, including external and internal validity
- How to distinguish the ATE from the TOT
- How to address practical issues in evaluating randomized interventions, including accounting for spillovers, selective attrition, ethical issues, and selective heterogeneity in program impacts among the treated sample

Setting the Counterfactual

As argued in chapter 2, finding a proper counterfactual to treatment is the main challenge of impact evaluation. The counterfactual indicates what would have happened to participants of a program had they not participated. However, the same person cannot be observed in two distinct situations—being treated and untreated at the same time.

The main conundrum, therefore, is how researchers formulate counterfactual states of the world in practice. In some disciplines, such as medical science, evidence about counterfactuals is generated through randomized trials, which ensure that outcomes in the control group really do capture the counterfactual for a treatment group.

Figure 3.1 illustrates the case of randomization graphically. Consider a random distribution of two "similar" groups of households or individuals—one group is treated and the other group is not treated. They are similar or "equivalent" in that both groups prior to a project intervention are observed to have the same level of income (in this case, Y_0). After the treatment is carried out, the observed income of the treated group is found to be Y_2 while the income level of the control group is Y_1. Therefore, the effect of program intervention can be described as $(Y_2 - Y_1)$, as indicated in figure 3.1. As discussed in chapter 2, extreme care must be taken in selecting the control group to ensure comparability.

Statistical Design of Randomization

In practice, however, it can be very difficult to ensure that a control group is very similar to project areas, that the treatment effects observed in the sample are generalizable, and that the effects themselves are a function of only the program itself.

Statisticians have proposed a two-stage randomization approach outlining these priorities. In the first stage, a sample of potential participants is selected randomly

Figure 3.1   The Ideal Experiment with an Equivalent Control Group

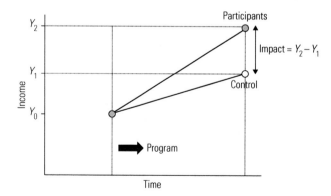

Source: Authors' representation.

from the relevant population. This sample should be representative of the population, within a certain sampling error. This stage ensures *external validity* of the experiment. In the second stage, individuals in this sample are randomly assigned to treatment and comparison groups, ensuring *internal validity* in that subsequent changes in the outcomes measured are due to the program instead of other factors. Conditions to ensure external and internal validity of the randomized design are discussed further later.

Calculating Treatment Effects

Randomization can correct for the selection bias B, discussed in chapter 2, by randomly assigning individuals or groups to treatment and control groups. Returning to the setup in chapter 2, consider the classic problem of measuring treatment effects (see Imbens and Angrist 1994): let the treatment, T_i, be equal to 1 if subject i is treated and 0 if not. Let $Y_i(1)$ be the outcome under treatment and $Y_i(0)$ if there is no treatment.

Observe Y_i and T_i, where $Y_i = [T_i \cdot Y_i(1) + (1 - T_i) \cdot Y_i(0)]$.[1] Strictly speaking, the treatment effect for unit i is $Y_i(1) - Y_i(0)$, and the ATE is ATE $= E[Y_i(1) - Y_i(0)]$, or the difference in outcomes from being in a project relative to control area for a person or unit i randomly drawn from the population. This formulation assumes, for example, that everyone in the population has an equally likely chance of being targeted.

Generally, however, only $E[Y_i(1)|T_i = 1]$, the average outcomes of the treated, conditional on being in a treated area, and $E[Y_i(0)|T_i = 0]$, the average outcomes of the untreated, conditional on not being in a treated area, are observed. With non-random targeting and observations on only a subsample of the population, $E[Y_i(1)]$ is not necessarily equal to $E[Y_i(1)|T_i = 1]$, and $E[Y_i(0)]$ is not necessarily equal to $E[Y_i(0)|T_i = 0]$.

Typically, therefore, alternate treatment effects are observed in the form of the TOT: TOT $= E[Y_i(1) - Y_i(0)|T_i = 1]$, or the difference in outcomes from receiving the program as compared with being in a control area for a person or subject i randomly drawn from the treated sample. That is, the TOT reflects the average gains for participants, conditional on these participants receiving the program. Suppose the area of interest is the TOT, $E[Y_i(1) - Y_i(0)|T_i = 1]$. If T_i is nonrandom, a simple difference between treated and control areas, $D = E[Y_i(1)|T_i = 1] - E[Y_i(0)|T_i = 0]$ (refer to chapter 2), will not be equal to the TOT. The discrepancy between the TOT and this D will be $E[Y_i(0)|T_i = 1] - E[Y_i(0)|T_i = 0]$, which is equal to the bias B in estimating the treatment effect (chapter 2):

$$\text{TOT} = E[Y_i(1) - Y_i(0)|T_i = 1] \tag{3.1}$$

$$= E[Y_i(1)|T_i = 1] - E[Y_i(0)|T_i = 1] \tag{3.2}$$

$$= D = E[Y_i(1)|T_i = 1] - E[Y_i(0)|T_i = 0] \quad \text{if } E[Y_i(0)|T_i = 0] = E[Y_i(0)|T_i = 1] \quad (3.3)$$

$$\Rightarrow \text{TOT} = D \quad \text{if } B = 0. \tag{3.4}$$

Although in principle the counterfactual outcome $E[Y_i(0)|T_i = 1]$ in equation 3.2 cannot be directly observed to understand the extent of the bias, still some intuition about it might exist. Duflo, Glennerster, and Kremer (2008), for example, discuss this problem in the context of a program that introduces textbooks in schools. Suppose one were interested in the effect of this program on students' learning, but the program was nonrandom in that schools that received textbooks were already placing a higher value on education. The targeted sample would then already have higher schooling achievement than the control areas, and $E[Y_i(0)|T_i = 1]$ would be greater than $E[Y_i(0)|T_i = 0]$, so that $B > 0$ and an upward bias exists in the program effect. If groups are randomly targeted, however, $E[Y_i(0)|T_i = 1]$ and $E[Y_i(0)|T_i = 0]$ are equal, and there is no selection bias in participation ($B = 0$).

In an effort to unify the literature on treatment effects, Heckman and Vytlacil (2005) also describe a parameter called the *marginal treatment effect* (MTE), from which the ATE and TOT can be derived. Introduced into the evaluation literature by Björklund and Moffitt (1987), the MTE is the average change in outcomes Y_i for individuals who are at the margin of participating in the program, given a set of observed characteristics X_i and conditioning on a set of unobserved characteristics U_i in the participation equation: $\text{MTE} = E(Y_i(1) - Y_i(0)|X_i = x, U_i = u)$. That is, the MTE is the average effect of the program for individuals who are just indifferent between participating and not participating. Chapter 6 discusses the MTE and its advantages in more detail.

Treatment Effect with Pure Randomization

Randomization can be set up in two ways: pure randomization and partial randomization. If treatment were conducted purely randomly following the two-stage procedure outlined previously, then treated and untreated households would have the same expected outcome in the absence of the program. Then, $E[Y_i(0)|T_i = 1]$ is equal to $E[Y_i(0)|T_i = 0]$. Because treatment would be random, and not a function of unobserved characteristics (such as personality or other tastes) across individuals, outcomes would not be expected to have varied for the two groups had the intervention not existed. Thus, selection bias becomes zero under the case of randomization.

Consider the case of pure randomization, where a sample of individuals or households is randomly drawn from the population of interest. The experimental sample is then divided randomly into two groups: (a) the treatment group that is exposed to the program intervention and (b) the control group that does not receive the program. In terms of a regression, this exercise can be expressed as

$$Y_i = \alpha + \beta T_i + \varepsilon_i, \tag{3.5}$$

where T_i is the treatment dummy equal to 1 if unit i is randomly treated and 0 otherwise. As above, Y_i is defined as

$$Y_i \equiv [Y_i(1) \cdot T_i] + [Y_i(0) \cdot (1 - T_i)]. \tag{3.6}$$

If treatment is random (then T and ε are independent), equation 3.5 can be estimated by using ordinary least squares (OLS), and the treatment effect $\hat{\beta}_{OLS}$ estimates the difference in the outcomes of the treated and the control group. If a randomized evaluation is correctly designed and implemented, an unbiased estimate of the impact of a program can be found.

Treatment Effect with Partial Randomization

A pure randomization is, however, extremely rare to undertake. Rather, *partial randomization* is used, where the treatment and control samples are chosen randomly, conditional on some observable characteristics X (for example, landholding or income). If one can make an assumption called *conditional exogeneity of program placement,* one can find an unbiased estimate of program estimate.

Here, this model follows Ravallion (2008). Denoting for simplicity $Y_i(1)$ as Y_i^T and $Y_i(0)$ as Y_i^C, equation 3.5 could be applied to a subsample of participants and nonparticipants as follows:

$$Y_i^T = \alpha^T + X_i \beta^T + \mu_i^T \ \text{ if } T_i = 1, i = 1, ..., n \tag{3.7}$$

$$Y_i^C = \alpha^C + X_i \beta^C + \mu_i^C \ \text{ if } T_i = 0, \ i = 1, ..., n^\cdot \tag{3.8}$$

It is common practice to estimate the above as a single regression by pooling the data for both control and treatment groups. One can multiply equation 3.7 by T_i and multiply equation 3.8 by $(1 - T_i)$, and use the identity in equation 3.6 to get

$$Y_i = \alpha^C + (\alpha^T - \alpha^C) T_i + X_i \beta^C + X_i (\beta^T - \beta^C) T_i + \varepsilon_i, \tag{3.9}$$

where $\varepsilon_i = T_i(\mu_i^T - \mu_i^C) + \mu_i^C$. The treatment effect from equation 3.9 can be written as $A^{TT} = E(Y_i | T_i = 1, X) = E[\alpha^T - \alpha^C + X_i(\beta^T - \beta^C)]$. Here, A^{TT} is just the treatment effect on the treated, TOT, discussed earlier.

For equation 3.9, one can get a consistent estimate of the program effect with OLS if one can assume $E(\mu_i^T | X, T = t) = E(\mu_i^C | X, T = t) = 0$, $t = \{0,1\}$. That is, there is no selection bias because of randomization. In practice, a common-impact model is often used that assumes $\beta^T = \beta^C$. The ATE is then simply $\alpha^T - \alpha^C$.

Randomization in Evaluation Design: Different Methods of Randomization

If randomization were possible, a decision would have to be made about what type of randomization (oversubscription, randomized phase-in, within-group randomization, or encouragement design) would be used. These approaches, detailed in Duflo, Glennerster, and Kremer (2008), are discussed in turn below:

- *Oversubscription.* If limited resources burden the program, implementation can be allocated randomly across a subset of eligible participants, and the remaining eligible subjects who do not receive the program can be considered controls. Some examination should be made of the budget, assessing how many subjects could be surveyed versus those actually targeted, to draw a large enough control group for the sample of potential beneficiaries.
- *Randomized phase-in.* This approach gradually phases in the program across a set of eligible areas, so that controls represent eligible areas still waiting to receive the program. This method helps alleviate equity issues and increases the likelihood that program and control areas are similar in observed characteristics.
- *Within-group randomization.* In a randomized phase-in approach, however, if the lag between program genesis and actual receipt of benefits is large, greater controversy may arise about which area or areas should receive the program first. In that case, an element of randomization can still be introduced by providing the program to some subgroups in each targeted area. This approach is therefore similar to phased-in randomization on a smaller scale. One problem is that spillovers may be more likely in this context.
- *Encouragement design.* Instead of randomizing the treatment, researchers randomly assign subjects an announcement or incentive to partake in the program. Some notice of the program is given in advance (either during the time of the baseline to conserve resources or generally before the program is implemented) to a random subset of eligible beneficiaries. This notice can be used as an instrument for take-up in the program. Spillovers might also be measured nicely in this context, if data are also collected on the social networks of households that receive the notice, to see how take-up might differ across households that are connected or not connected to it. Such an experiment would require more intensive data collection, however.

Concerns with Randomization

Several concerns warrant consideration with a randomization design, including ethical issues, external validity, partial or lack of compliance, selective attrition, and spillovers. Withholding a particular treatment from a random group of people and providing access to another random group of people may be simply unethical. Carrying out randomized design is often politically unfeasible because justifying such a design to people who might benefit from it is hard. Consequently, convincing potential partners to carry out randomized designs is difficult.

External validity is another concern. A project of small-scale job training may not affect overall wage rates, whereas a large-scale project might. That is, impact measured by the pilot project may not be an accurate guide of the project's impact on a national scale. The problem is how to generalize and replicate the results obtained through randomized evaluations.

Compliance may also be a problem with randomization, which arises when a fraction of the individuals who are offered the treatment do not take it. Conversely, some members of the comparison group may receive the treatment. This situation is referred to as partial (or imperfect) compliance. To be valid and to prevent selection bias, an analysis needs to focus on groups created by the initial randomization. The analysis cannot exclude subjects or cut the sample according to behavior that may have been affected by the random assignment. More generally, interest often lies in the effect of a given treatment, but the randomization affects only the *probability* that the individual is exposed to the treatment, rather than the treatment itself.

Also, potential spillover effects arise when treatment helps the control group as well as the sample participants, thereby confounding the estimates of program impact. For example, people outside the sample may move into a village where health clinics have been randomly established, thus contaminating program effects. The chapter now examines how such concerns about randomization have actually been addressed in practice.

Randomized Impact Evaluation in Practice

Randomization has been growing in popularity in some parts of the world, in part because if it can be implemented properly, randomization can give a robust indication of program impact. Also, once the survey has been designed and the data collected, the empirical exercises to infer impacts from randomized experiments are quite straightforward. Typically, justifying or initiating a randomized experiment is easiest at the inception of a program, during the pilot phase. This phase offers a natural opportunity to introduce randomization before the program is scaled up. It presents an occasion for the implementation partner to rigorously assess the effectiveness of the program. It can also provide a chance to improve the program's design. One can also introduce an element of randomization into existing programs in many different ways with minimal disruption. Whereas the earlier sections in this chapter have discussed in theory the concerns with randomization, the following sections discuss various practical issues and case studies in the implementation of randomized studies.

Ethical Issues

Implementing randomized experiments in developing countries often raises ethical issues. For example, convincing government officials to withhold a particular program from a randomly selected contingent that shares the same poverty status and limits on earning opportunities as a randomly targeted group may be difficult. Carrying out randomized designs is often politically unfeasible because of the difficulty in justifying such a design to people who might benefit from it.

One counterargument is that randomization is a scientific way of determining the program's impact. It would therefore ultimately help decide, among a set of different programs or paths available to policy makers, which ones really work and hence deserve investment. Thus, in the long run, randomization can help a greater number of people in addition to those who were initially targeted. A randomly phased-in design such as that used by Mexico's PROGRESA (Programa de Educación, Salud y Alimentación, or Education, Health, and Nutrition Program; see box 3.1) can also allow nontargeted, similarly featured areas ultimately to benefit from the program as well as provide a good comparison sample.

BOX 3.1   Case Study: PROGRESA (Oportunidades)

PROGRESA (now called Oportunidades), described in box 2.1 of chapter 2, combined regional and village-level targeting with household-level targeting within these areas. Only the extreme poor were targeted, using a randomized targeting strategy that phased in the program over time across targeted localities. One-third of the randomly targeted eligible communities were delayed entry into the program by 18 months, and the remaining two-thirds received the program at inception. Within localities, households were chosen on the basis of a discriminant analysis that used their socioeconomic characteristics (obtained from household census data) to classify households as poor or nonpoor. On average, about 78 percent of households in selected localities were considered eligible, and about 93 percent of households that were eligible enrolled in the program.

Regarding potential ethical considerations in targeting the program randomly, the phased-in treatment approach allowed all eligible samples to be targeted eventually, as well as the flexibility to adjust the program if actual implementation was more difficult than initially expected. Monitoring and operational evaluation of the program, as discussed in chapter 2, were also key components of the initiative, as was a detailed cost-benefit analysis.

A number of different evaluations have examined the impact of Oportunidades on health and educational outcomes among the treated sample. They include examinations of the program's benefits to health (Gertler 2004); labor-market outcomes for adults and youth (Behrman, Parker, and Todd 2009; Skoufias and di Maro 2007); schooling (de Janvry and others 2006; Schultz 2004; Todd and Wolpin 2006); and nutrition (Behrman and Hoddinott 2005; Hoddinott and Skoufias 2004). Interest in the design and outcomes of Oportunidades has fostered similar conditional cash-transfer programs in South America and Central America, as well as in Bangladesh and Turkey.

Also, in the presence of limited resources, not all people can be targeted by a program—whether experimental or nonexperimental. In that case, randomized targeting is not unethical. The bottom line is that, in practice, convincing potential partners to carry out randomized designs is often difficult; thus, the first challenge is to find suitable partners to carry out such a design. Governments, nongovernmental organizations, and sometimes private sector firms might be potential partners.

Internal versus External Validity

Different approaches in implementing randomized studies reflect the need to adapt the program intervention and survey appropriately within the targeted sample. These concerns are embedded in a broader two-stage process guiding the quality of experimental design. In the first stage, policy makers should define clearly not only the random sample that will be selected for analysis but also the population from which that sample will be drawn. Specifically, the experiment would have external validity, meaning that the results obtained could be generalized to other groups or settings (perhaps through other program interventions, for example). Using the notation discussed earlier, this approach would correspond to the conditions $E[Y_i(0)|T_i = 1] = E[Y_i(0)|T_i = 0]$ and $E[Y_i(1)|T_i = 1] = E[Y_i(1)|T_i = 0]$.

Second, steps should be taken when randomly allocating this sample across treatment and control conditions to ensure that the treatment effect is a function of the intervention only and not caused by other confounding elements. This criterion is known as *internal validity* and reflects the ability to control for issues that would affect the causal interpretation of the treatment impact. Systematic bias (associated with selection of groups that are not equivalent, selective sample attrition, contamination of targeted areas by the control sample, and changes in the instruments used to measure progress and outcomes over the course of the experiment), as well as the effect of targeting itself on related choices and outcomes of participants within the targeted sample, provides an example of such issues. Random variation in other events occurring while the experiment is in progress, although not posing a direct threat to internal validity, also needs to be monitored within data collection because very large random variation can pose a threat to the predictability of data measurement. The following section discusses some approaches that, along with a randomized methodology, can help account for these potentially confounding factors.

Although following the two-stage approach will lead to a consistent measure of the ATE (Kish 1987), researchers in the behavioral and social sciences have almost never implemented this approach in practice. More specifically, the only assumption that can be made, given randomization, is that $E[Y_i(0)|T_i = 1] = E[Y_i(0)|T_i = 0]$. Even maintaining the criterion for internal validity in an economic setting is very difficult, as will be described. At best, therefore, policy makers examining the effect of randomized program interventions can consistently estimate the TOT or effect on a given subpopulation: TOT $= E[Y_i(1) - Y_i(0)|T_i = 1]$, as opposed to ATE $= E[Y_i(1) - Y_i(0)]$.

Intent-to-Treat Estimates and Measuring Spillovers

Ensuring that control areas and treatment areas do not mix is crucial in measuring an unbiased program impact. In the experimental design, a number of approaches can help reduce the likelihood of contamination of project areas. Project and control areas that are located sufficiently far apart, for example, can be selected so that migration across the two areas is unlikely. As a result, contamination of treatment areas is more likely with projects conducted on a larger scale.

Despite efforts to randomize the program intervention ex ante, however, actual program participation may not be entirely random. Individuals or households in control areas may move to project areas, ultimately affecting their outcomes from exposure to the program. Likewise, targeted individuals in project areas may not ultimately participate but may be indirectly affected by the program as well. If a program to target the treated helps the control group too, it would confound the estimates of program impact. In some cases, projects cannot be scaled up without creating general equilibrium effects. For example, a project of small-scale job training may not affect overall wage rates, whereas a large-scale project might. In the latter case, impact measured by the pilot project would be an inaccurate guide of the project's impact on a national scale. Often the Hawthorne effect might plague results of a randomized experiment, where the simple fact of being included in an experiment may alter behavior nonrandomly.[2]

These partial treatment effects may be of separate interest to the researcher, particularly because they are likely to be significant if the policy will be implemented on a large scale. They can be addressed through measuring *intention-to-treat* (ITT) impacts (box 3.2) or by instrumenting actual program participation by the randomized assignment strategy (box 3.3).

Specifically, in cases where the actual treatment is distinct from the variable that is randomly manipulated, call Z the variable that is randomly assigned (for example, the letter inviting university employees to a fair and offering them US\$20 to attend), while T remains the treatment of interest (for example, attending the fair). Using the same notation as previously, one knows because of random assignment that $E[Y_i(0)|Z_i = 1] - E[Y_i(0)|Z_i = 0]$ is equal to zero and that the difference $E[Y_i(1)|Z_i = 1] - E[Y_i(0)|Z_i = 0]$ is equal to the causal effect of Z. However, it is not equal to the effect of the treatment, T, because Z is not equal to T. Because Z has been chosen to at least influence the treatment, this difference is the ITT impact.

Because the ITT is in principle random, it can also act as a valid instrumental variable to identify the treatment impact, given that people who were initially assigned for treatment are in general more likely to have ultimately participated in the program. The ITT estimate would then be the estimated coefficient on the variable describing initial

---

> **BOX 3.2**   **Case Study: Using Lotteries to Measure Intent-to-Treat Impact**
>
> The PACES (Plan de Ampliación de Cobertura de la Educación Secundaria, or Plan for Increasing Secondary Education Coverage) school voucher program, established by the Colombian government in late 1991, granted private secondary school vouchers to 125,000 children from poor neighborhoods who were enrolled in public primary schools. These vouchers covered about half of entering students' schooling expenses and were renewable depending on student performance. However, the program faced oversubscription because the number of eligible households (living in neighborhoods falling in the lowest two of six socioeconomic strata spanning the population) exceeded the number of available vouchers. Many vouchers were therefore allocated through a randomized lottery.
>
> To measure the impact of this school voucher program, Angrist and others (2002) surveyed lottery winners and losers from three groups of applicants. They administered an academic test to both groups, initially finding limited differences in performance for voucher recipients. One reason for this outcome, they suggest, is that about 10 percent of lottery winners did not end up using the voucher or other scholarship, whereas about 25 percent of nonrecipients obtained other scholarships or funding. Angrist and others (2002) therefore used the lottery receipt as an instrument for participation, calculating an intention-to-treat estimate that revealed much larger (50 percent greater) program effects on grade completion and reduced repetitions for lottery winners than in a simple comparison of winners and losers.

assignment. The impact on those whose treatment status is changed by the instrument is also known as the *local average treatment effect* (Abadie, Angrist, and Imbens 2002).

Selective attrition is also a potential problem: people drop out of a program. Box 3.4 describes an example from a schooling program in India, where potential attrition of weaker students could bias the program effect upward.

If measuring the extent of spillovers is of interest to policy makers, randomization can allow this phenomenon to be measured more precisely. The accuracy, of course, depends on the level of spillovers. If spillovers occur at the aggregate or global economy, for example, any methodology—be it randomization or a nonexperimental approach—will have difficulties in capturing the program impact. Local spillovers can, however, be measured with a randomized methodology (Miguel and Kremer 2004; see box 3.5).

Selecting the level of randomization on the basis of the level at which spillovers are expected to occur (that is, whether over individuals, communities, or larger units) is therefore crucial in understanding the program impact. A substantive amount of data measuring factors that might lead to contamination and spillovers (migration, for example) would also need to be examined during the course of the evaluation to be able to estimate the program's impact precisely.

> **BOX 3.3** **Case Study: Instrumenting in the Case of Partial Compliance**
>
> Abadie, Angrist, and Imbens (2002) discussed an approach that introduces instrumental variables to estimate the impact of a program that is randomized in intent but for which actual take-up is voluntary. The program they examined involves training under the U.S. Job Training Partnership Act of 1982. Applicants were randomly assigned to treatment and control groups; those in the treated sample were immediately offered training, whereas training programs for the control sample were delayed by 18 months. Only 60 percent of the treated sample actually received training, and the random treatment assignment was used as an instrumental variable.
>
> The study examined a sample of about 6,100 women and 5,100 men, with earnings data for each individual spanning 30 months. Using the instrumental variables estimates, Abadie, Angrist, and Imbens found that the average rise in earnings for men was about US$1,600 (a 9 percent increase), about half as large as the OLS estimate. For women, the average increase was about US$1,800 (growth of about 15 percent) and was not very different from the corresponding OLS estimate.

> **BOX 3.4** **Case Study: Minimizing Statistical Bias Resulting from Selective Attrition**
>
> Banerjee and others (2007) examined the impact of two randomized educational programs (a remedial education program and computer-assisted learning) across a sample of urban schools in India. These programs were targeted toward students who, relative to students in other schools, were not performing well in basic literacy and other skills. Government primary schools were targeted in two urban areas, with 98 schools in the first area (Vadodara) and 77 schools in the second area (Mumbai).
>
> With respect to the remedial program in particular, half the schools in each area sample were randomly selected to have the remedial program introduced in grade 3, and the other half received the program in grade 4. Each treated group of students was therefore compared with untreated students from the same grade within the same urban area sample. Tests were administered to treated and untreated students to evaluate their performance.
>
> In the process of administering the program, however, program officials found that students were dropping out of school. If attrition was systematically greater among students with weaker performance, the program impact would suffer from an upward bias. As a result, the testing team took efforts to visit students in all schools across the sample multiple times, tracking down children who dropped out of school to have them take the test. Although the attrition rate among students remained relatively high, it was ultimately similar across the treated and untreated samples, thereby lowering the chance of bias in direct comparisons of test scores across the two groups.
>
> Ultimately, Banerjee and others (2007) found that the remedial education program raised average test scores of all children in treatment schools by 0.14 standard deviations in the first year and 0.28 standard deviations in the second year, driven primarily from improvements at the lower end of the distribution of test scores (whose gains were about 0.40 standard deviations relative to the control group sample).

| BOX 3.5 | **Case Study: Selecting the Level of Randomization to Account for Spillovers** |

Miguel and Kremer (2004) provided an evaluation of a deworming program across a sample of 75 schools in western Kenya, accounting for treatment externalities that would have otherwise masked the program impact. The program, called the Primary School Deworming Project, involved randomized phase-in of the health intervention at the school level over the years 1998 to 2000.

Examining the impact at the individual (child) level might be of interest, because children were ultimately recipients of the intervention. However, Miguel and Kremer (2004) found that since infections spread easily across children, strong treatment externalities existed across children randomly treated as part of the program and children in the comparison group. Not accounting for such externalities would therefore bias the program impact, and randomizing the program within schools was thus not possible.

Miguel and Kremer (2004) therefore examined impacts at the school level, because the deworming program was randomized across schools, and treatment and comparison schools were located sufficiently far apart that the likelihood of spillovers across schools was much smaller. They measured the size of the externality by comparing untreated students in treated schools with the comparison group. Their study found that treated schools exhibited significantly (about 25 percent) lower absenteeism rates, although academic test scores did not improve relative to comparison schools. Their analysis also found substantial treatment externalities, in that untreated children in treatment schools exhibited significantly improved health and school participation rates compared with children in nontreated schools. Including the externality benefits, Miguel and Kremer found the cost per additional year of school participation was just US$3.50, making deworming more cost-effective than subsidies in reducing absenteeism.

Heterogeneity in Impacts: Estimating Treatment Impacts in the Treated Sample

The level at which the randomized intervention occurs (for example, the national, regional, or community level) therefore affects in multiple ways the treatment effects that can be estimated. Randomization at an aggregate (say, regional) level cannot necessarily account for individual heterogeneity in participation and outcomes resulting from the program.

One implication of this issue is that the ultimate program or treatment impact at the individual level cannot necessarily be measured accurately as a binary variable (that is, $T = 1$ for an individual participant and $T = 0$ for an individual in a control area). Although a certain program may be randomized at a broader level, individual selection may still exist in the response to treatment. A mixture of methods can be used, including instrumental variables, to account for unobserved selection at the individual level. Interactions between the targeting criteria and the treatment indicator can also be introduced in the regression.

Quantile treatment effects can also be estimated to measure distributional impacts of randomized programs on outcomes such as per capita consumption and expenditure (Abadie, Angrist, and Imbens 2002). Chapter 8 discusses this approach in more detail. Dammert (2007), for example, estimates the distributional impacts on expenditures from a conditional cash-transfer program in rural Nicaragua. This program, Red de Protección Social (or Social Protection Network), was a conditional cash-transfer program created in 2000. It was similar to PROGRESA in that eligible households received cash transfers contingent on a few conditions, including that adult household members (often mothers) attended educational workshops and sent their children under 5 years of age for vaccinations and other health appointments and sent their children between the ages of 7 and 13 regularly to school. Some aspects of the evaluation are discussed in box 3.6. Djebbari and Smith (2008) also provide a similar discussion using data from PROGRESA (Oportunidades).

BOX 3.6 **Case Study: Measuring Impact Heterogeneity from a Randomized Program**

Dammert (2007) examined distributional impacts of the Nicaraguan social safety net program Red de Protección Social, where 50 percent of 42 localities identified as sufficiently poor for the program (according to a marginality index) were randomly selected for targeting. The evaluation survey covered 1,359 project and control households through a baseline, as well as two follow-up surveys conducted one year and two years after program intervention.

Because the cash transfers depended on regular school attendance and health visits, however, whether a household in a targeted locality was already meeting these requirements before the intervention (which correlated heavily with the household's preexisting income and education levels) could result in varying program impacts across households with different socioeconomic backgrounds. For households whose children were already enrolled in school and sent regularly for health checkups, the cash transfer would provide a pure income effect, whereas for households not meeting the criteria, the cash transfer would induce both an income and substitution effect.

As one approach, Dammert (2007) therefore interacted the program variable with household characteristics on which targeting was based, such as education of the household head, household expenditures, and the marginality index used for targeting. Children in poorer localities were found to have greater improvements in schooling, for example. Also, to examine variation in program impacts not driven by observable characteristics, Dammert calculated quantile treatment effects separately for 2001 and 2002. The results show that growth in total per capita expenditures as well as per capita food expenses was lower for households at the bottom of the expenditure distribution. Specifically, in 2001, the program's impact on increased total per capita expenditures ranged from US$54 to US$237; in 2002, this range was US$20 to US$99, with households at the top of the distribution receiving more than five times the impact than households with lower expenditures.

Thus, simply relying on average treatment impacts may not reveal important areas of concern, such as, perhaps, that households at the lower end of the expenditure distribution experience higher costs (and thus reduced benefits) from participating.

A related departure from perfect randomization is when randomization is a function of some set of observables (climate, population density, and the like) affecting the probabilities that certain areas will be selected. Treatment status is therefore randomly conditioned on a set of observed characteristics. Within each treated area, however, treatment is randomized across individuals or communities. Treatment and comparison observations within each area can therefore be made, and a weighted average can be taken over all areas to give the average effect of the program on the treated samples.

Value of a Baseline Study

Conducting baseline surveys in a randomized setting conveys several advantages. First, baseline surveys make it possible to examine interactions between initial conditions and the impact of the program. In many cases, this comparison will be of considerable importance for assessing external validity. Baseline data are also useful when conducting policy experiments, because treated areas might have had access to similar programs or initiatives before implementation of the new initiative. Comparing participants' uptake of activities, such as credit before and after the randomized intervention, can also be useful in evaluating responses to the experiment.

Other values of a baseline study include the opportunity to check that the randomization was conducted appropriately. Governments participating in randomized schemes may feel the need, for example, to compensate control areas for not receiving the program by introducing other schemes at the same time. Data collected on program interventions in control areas before and during the course of the survey will help in accounting for these additional sources of spillovers. Collecting baseline data also offers an opportunity to test and refine data collection procedures.

Baseline surveys can be costly, however, and should be conducted carefully. One issue with conducting a baseline is that it may lead to bias in program impacts by altering the counterfactual. The decision whether to conduct a baseline survey boils down to comparing the cost of the intervention, the cost of data collection, and the impact that variables for which data can be collected in a baseline survey may have on the final outcome (box 3.7).

Difficulties with Randomization

Because they minimize selection bias in program impacts, randomized evaluations can be very attractive in developing countries. Unfortunately, contextual factors in such settings are rife with situations that can confound randomized implementation and hence the quality of program effects. Detailed data collection on these confounding factors and use of a combination of methods, in addition to examining the ATEs, can therefore help in accounting for resulting individual heterogeneity in treatment impacts (box 3.8).

BOX 3.7   **Case Study: Effects of Conducting a Baseline**

Giné, Karlan, and Zinman (2008), in a study of a rural hospitalization insurance program offered by the Green Bank in the Philippines, examined the impact of conducting a randomly allocated baseline on a subset of individuals to whom the program was ultimately offered. The baseline (which surveyed a random sample of 80 percent of the roughly 2,000 individual liability borrowers of the Green Bank) elicited indicators such as income, health status, and risky behavior. To avoid revealing information about the upcoming insurance program, the baseline did not cover questions about purchases of insurance, and no connection was discussed between the survey and the bank. However, after the insurance initiative was introduced, take-up was found to be significantly higher (about 3.4 percentage points) among those surveyed than those who were not.

The study therefore points to the benefits of capturing characteristics of surveyed individuals in the baseline that might reveal potential behavioral patterns in subsequent decision making, including their influence in decision making over such issues before program implementation. Randomized variation in the timing of program implementation after the baseline might also be used to test how these effects persist over time.

BOX 3.8   **Case Study: Persistence of Unobserved Heterogeneity in a Randomized Program**

Behrman and Hoddinott (2005) examined nutritional effects on children from PROGRESA, which also involved the distribution of food supplements to children. Although the program was randomized across localities, a shortage in one nutritional supplement provided to preschool children led local administrators to exercise discretion in how they allocated this supplement, favoring children with poorer nutritional status. As a result, when average outcomes between treatment and control groups were compared, the effect of the program diminished. Behrman and Hoddinott examined a sample of about 320 children in project and control households (for a total sample of about 640). Introducing child-specific fixed-effects regressions revealed a positive program impact on health outcomes for children; height of recipient children increased by about 1.2 percent. Behrman and Hoddinott predicted that this effect alone could potentially increase lifetime earnings for these children by about 3 percent. The fixed-effects estimates controlled for unobserved heterogeneity that were also correlated with access to the nutritional supplement.

Even in the context of industrial countries, Moffitt (2003) discusses how randomized field trials of cash welfare programs in the United States have had limited external validity in terms of being able to shed light on how similar policies might play out at the national level. Although nonexperimental studies also face similar issues with external validity, Moffitt argues for a comprehensive approach comparing experimental with nonexperimental studies of policies and programs; such comparisons may reveal potential mechanisms affecting participation, outcomes, and other participant behavior, thereby helping evaluators understand potential implications of such programs when applied to different contexts.

In the nonexperimental studies discussed in the following chapters, this book attempts to account for the selection bias issue in different ways. Basically, nonexperimental studies try to replicate a natural experiment or randomization as much as possible. Unlike randomization, where selection bias can be corrected for directly (although problems exist in this area also), in nonexperimental evaluations a different approach is needed, usually involving assumptions about the form of the bias.

One approach is to make the case for assuming unconfoundedness—or of conditional exogeneity of program placement, which is a weaker version of unconfoundedness. The propensity score matching technique and double-difference methods fall under this category. The instrumental variable approach does not need to make this assumption. It attempts to find instruments that are correlated with the participation decision but not correlated with the outcome variable conditional on participation. Finally, other methods, such as regression discontinuity design (also an instrumental variable method), exploit features of program design to assess impact.

Questions

1. The following equation represents an outcome equation in case of pure randomization:

$$Y = \alpha + \beta T + \varepsilon,$$

where Y is household's monthly income, T is a microfinance intervention ($T = 1$ if household gets the intervention and $T = 0$ if household does not get the intervention), and ε is the error term. Under pure randomization designed and implemented properly, the impact of microfinance program on household income is given by

(a) $\alpha + \beta$
(b) β
(c) $\alpha + \beta - \varepsilon$
(d) $\alpha - \varepsilon$

2. The following equations represent the same outcome equations as in question 1 but in this case for partial randomization; where treatment and control units are chosen randomly but conditional on some observed characteristics X:

$$Y^T = \alpha^T + \beta^T X + \varepsilon^T \tag{1}$$

$$Y^C = \alpha^C + \beta^C X + \varepsilon^C, \tag{2}$$

where equation 1 is for those receiving the intervention and equation 2 is for those not receiving intervention. Under the common-impact model, the impact of microfinance program on household income is given by

(a) $\alpha^T + \alpha^C$

(b) $\beta^T + \beta^C$

(c) $\alpha^T - \alpha^C$

(d) $\beta^T - \beta^C$

3. Which of the following statement(s) is (are) true about randomization technique?
   A. The ATE requires only external validity.
   B. The TOT requires both internal and external validity.
   C. The ATE requires both internal and external validity.

   (a) A and B

   (b) B and C

   (c) C only

4. In oversubscription randomization, intervention is given only to a subset of eligible participants because
   A. this approach ensures that a valid control group is present.
   B. it is a common knowledge that not everybody takes the intervention even when it is offered.
   C. programs usually do not have enough resources to provide intervention to all eligible participants.

   (a) All of the above

   (b) A and B

   (c) B and C

   (d) C only

5. What are the major concerns of randomization?
   A. Ethical issues
   B. External validity
   C. Compliance and spillover

   (a) All of the above

   (b) A and B

   (c) B and C

   (d) C only

6. Which of the following statement(s) is (are) true?
   A. Conducting a baseline survey is very useful for randomized setting.
   B. In a nonrandomized setting, the propensity score matching technique can be an attractive option.
   C. Randomization is not very useful for panel surveys.

   (a) All of the above

   (b) A and B

   (c) B and C

   (d) C only

Notes

1. As mentioned in Heckman and Vytlacil (2000), this characterization of *Y* is identified under different approaches. It is known, for example, as the *Neyman-Fisher-Cox-Rubin model* of potential outcomes; it is also referred to as the *switching regression model of Quandt* (Quandt 1972) and the *Roy model of income distribution* (Roy 1951).
2. Specifically, the Hawthorne effect relates to beneficiaries feeling differently because they know they are treated; this simple realization may change their choices and behavior. Factors other than the actual workings of the program may therefore change participant outcomes.

References

Abadie, Alberto, Joshua D. Angrist, and Guido W. Imbens. 2002. "Instrumental Variables Estimates of the Effect of Subsidized Training on the Quantiles of Trainee Earnings." *Econometrica* 70 (1): 91–117.

Angrist, Joshua, Eric Bettinger, Erik Bloom, Elizabeth King, and Michael Kremer. 2002. "Vouchers for Private Schooling in Colombia: Evidence from a Randomized Natural Experiment." *American Economic Review* 92 (5): 1535–58.

Banerjee, Abhijit, Shawn Cole, Esther Duflo, and Leigh Linden. 2007. "Remedying Education: Evidence from Two Randomized Experiments in India." *Quarterly Journal of Economics* 122 (3): 1235–64.

Behrman, Jere, and John Hoddinott. 2005. "Programme Evaluation with Unobserved Heterogeneity and Selective Implementation: The Mexican 'PROGRESA' Impact on Child Nutrition." *Oxford Bulletin of Economics and Statistics* 67 (4): 547–69.

Behrman, Jere, Susan Parker, and Petra Todd. 2009. "Long-Term Impacts of the *Oportunidades* Conditional Cash-Transfer Program on Rural Youth in Mexico." In *Poverty, Inequality, and Policy in Latin America*, ed. Stephan Klasen and Felicitas Nowak-Lehmann, 219–70. Cambridge, MA: MIT Press.

Björklund, Anders, and Robert Moffitt. 1987. "The Estimation of Wage Gains and Welfare Gains in Self-Selection Models." *Review of Economics and Statistics* 69 (1): 42–49.

Dammert, Ana. 2007. "Heterogeneous Impacts of Conditional Cash Transfers: Evidence from Nicaragua." Working Paper, McMaster University, Hamilton, ON, Canada.

de Janvry, Alain, Frederico Finan, Elisabeth Sadoulet, and Renos Vakis. 2006. "Can Conditional Cash Transfer Programs Serve as Safety Nets in Keeping Children at School and from Working When Exposed to Shocks?" *Journal of Development Economics* 79 (2): 349–73.

Djebbari, Habiba, and Jeffrey Smith. 2008. "Heterogeneous Impacts in PROGRESA." IZA Discussion Paper 3362, Institute for the Study of Labor, Bonn, Germany.

Duflo, Esther, Rachel Glennerster, and Michael Kremer. 2008. "Using Randomization in Development Economics Research: A Toolkit." In *Handbook of Development Economics*, vol. 4, ed. T. Paul Schultz and John Strauss, 3895–962. Amsterdam: North-Holland.

Gertler, Paul. 2004. "Do Conditional Cash Transfers Improve Child Health? Evidence from PROGRESA's Control Randomized Experiment." *American Economic Review, Papers and Proceedings* 94 (2): 336–41.

Giné, Xavier, Dean Karlan, and Jonathan Zinman. 2008. "The Risk of Asking: Measurement Effects from a Baseline Survey in an Insurance Takeup Experiment." Working Paper, Yale University, New Haven, CT.

Heckman, James J., and Edward J. Vytlacil. 2000. "Local Instrumental Variables." NBER Technical Working Paper 252, National Bureau of Economic Research, Cambridge, MA.

———. 2005. "Structural Equations, Treatment Effects, and Econometric Policy Evaluation." *Econometrica* 73 (3): 669–738.

Hoddinott, John, and Emmanuel Skoufias. 2004. "The Impact of PROGRESA on Food Consumption." *Economic Development and Cultural Change* 53 (1): 37–61.

Imbens, Guido, and Joshua Angrist. 1994. "Identification and Estimation of Local Average Treatment Effects." *Econometrica* 62 (2): 467–76.

Kish, Leslie. 1987. *Statistical Design for Research.* New York: Wiley.

Miguel, Edward, and Michael Kremer. 2004. "Worms: Identifying Impacts on Education and Health in the Presence of Treatment Externalities." *Econometrica* 72 (1): 159–217.

Moffitt, Robert. 2003. "The Role of Randomized Field Trials in Social Science Research: A Perspective from Evaluations of Reforms from Social Welfare Programs." NBER Technical Working Paper 295, National Bureau of Economic Research, Cambridge, MA.

Quandt, Richard. 1972. "Methods for Estimating Switching Regressions." *Journal of the American Statistical Association* 67 (338): 306–10.

Ravallion, Martin. 2008. "Evaluating Anti-Poverty Programs." In *Handbook of Development Economics,* vol. 4, ed. T. Paul Schultz and John Strauss, 3787–846. Amsterdam: North-Holland.

Roy, Andrew D. 1951. "Some Thoughts on the Distribution of Earnings." *Oxford Economic Papers* 3 (2): 135–46.

Schultz, T. Paul. 2004. "School Subsidies for the Poor: Evaluating the Mexican PROGRESA Poverty Program." *Journal of Development Economics* 74 (1): 199–250.

Skoufias, Emmanuel, and Vincenzo di Maro. 2007. "Conditional Cash Transfers, Adult Work Incentives, and Poverty." Policy Research Working Paper 3973, World Bank, Washington, DC.

Todd, Petra, and Kenneth Wolpin. 2006. "Assessing the Impact of a School Subsidy Program in Mexico: Using a Social Experiment to Validate a Dynamic Behavioral Model of Child Schooling and Fertility." *American Economic Review* 96 (5): 1384–417.

4. Propensity Score Matching

Summary

Propensity score matching (PSM) constructs a statistical comparison group that is based on a model of the probability of participating in the treatment, using observed characteristics. Participants are then matched on the basis of this probability, or *propensity score*, to nonparticipants. The average treatment effect of the program is then calculated as the mean difference in outcomes across these two groups. The validity of PSM depends on two conditions: (a) conditional independence (namely, that unobserved factors do not affect participation) and (b) sizable common support or overlap in propensity scores across the participant and nonparticipant samples.

Different approaches are used to match participants and nonparticipants on the basis of the propensity score. They include nearest-neighbor (NN) matching, caliper and radius matching, stratification and interval matching, and kernel matching and local linear matching (LLM). Regression-based methods on the sample of participants and nonparticipants, using the propensity score as weights, can lead to more efficient estimates.

On its own, PSM is a useful approach when only observed characteristics are believed to affect program participation. Whether this belief is actually the case depends on the unique features of the program itself, in terms of targeting as well as individual takeup of the program. Assuming selection on observed characteristics is sufficiently strong to determine program participation, baseline data on a wide range of preprogram characteristics will allow the probability of participation based on observed characteristics to be specified more precisely. Some tests can be conducted to assess the degree of selection bias or participation on unobserved characteristics.

Learning Objectives

After completing this chapter, the reader will be able to discuss

- Calculation of the propensity score and underlying assumptions needed to apply PSM
- Different methods for matching participants and nonparticipants in the area of common support
- Drawbacks of PSM and methods to assess the degree of selection bias on unobserved characteristics
- Use of PSM in regression-based methods

PSM and Its Practical Uses

Given concerns with the implementation of randomized evaluations, the approach is still a perfect impact evaluation method in theory. Thus, when a treatment cannot be randomized, the next best thing to do is to try to mimic randomization—that is, try to have an observational analogue of a randomized experiment. With matching methods, one tries to develop a counterfactual or control group that is as similar to the treatment group as possible in terms of *observed* characteristics. The idea is to find, from a large group of nonparticipants, individuals who are *observationally similar* to participants in terms of characteristics not affected by the program (these can include preprogram characteristics, for example, because those clearly are not affected by subsequent program participation). Each participant is matched with an observationally similar nonparticipant, and then the average difference in outcomes across the two groups is compared to get the program treatment effect. If one assumes that differences in participation are based solely on differences in observed characteristics, and if enough nonparticipants are available to match with participants, the corresponding treatment effect can be measured even if treatment is not random.

The problem is to credibly identify groups that look alike. Identification is a problem because even if households are matched along a vector, X, of different characteristics, one would rarely find two households that are exactly similar to each other in terms of many characteristics. Because many possible characteristics exist, a common way of matching households is propensity score matching. In PSM, each participant is matched to a nonparticipant on the basis of a single propensity score, reflecting the probability of participating conditional on their different observed characteristics X (see Rosenbaum and Rubin 1983). PSM therefore avoids the "curse of dimensionality" associated with trying to match participants and nonparticipants on every possible characteristic when X is very large.

What Does PSM Do?

PSM constructs a statistical comparison group by modeling the probability of participating in the program on the basis of observed characteristics unaffected by the program. Participants are then matched on the basis of this probability, or propensity score, to nonparticipants, using different methods outlined later in the chapter. The average treatment effect of the program is then calculated as the mean difference in outcomes across these two groups. On its own, PSM is useful when only observed characteristics are believed to affect program participation. This assumption hinges on the rules governing the targeting of the program, as well as any factors driving self-selection of individuals or households into the program. Ideally, if available, pre-program baseline data on participants and nonparticipants can be used to calculate the propensity score and to match the two groups on the basis of the propensity score.

Selection on observed characteristics can also help in designing multiwave experiments. Hahn, Hirano, and Karlan (2008) show that available data on covariates for individuals targeted by an experiment, say in the first stage of a two-stage intervention, can be used to choose a treatment assignment rule for the second stage—conditioned on observed characteristics. This equates to choosing the propensity score in the second stage and allows more efficient estimation of causal effects.

PSM Method in Theory

The PSM approach tries to capture the effects of different observed covariates X on participation in a single propensity score or index. Then, outcomes of participating and nonparticipating households with similar propensity scores are compared to obtain the program effect. Households for which no match is found are dropped because no basis exists for comparison.

PSM constructs a statistical comparison group that is based on a model of the probability of participating in the treatment T conditional on observed characteristics X, or the propensity score: $P(X) = \Pr(T = 1|X)$. Rosenbaum and Rubin (1983) show that, under certain assumptions, matching on $P(X)$ is as good as matching on X. The necessary assumptions for identification of the program effect are (a) conditional independence and (b) presence of a common support. These assumptions are detailed in the following sections.

Also, as discussed in chapters 2 and 3, the treatment effect of the program using these methods can either be represented as the average treatment effect (ATE) or the treatment effect on the treated (TOT). Typically, researchers and evaluators can ensure only internal as opposed to external validity of the sample, so only the TOT can be estimated. Weaker assumptions of conditional independence as well as common support apply to estimating the TOT and are also discussed in this chapter.

Assumption of Conditional Independence

Conditional independence states that given a set of observable covariates X that are not affected by treatment, potential outcomes Y are independent of treatment assignment T. If Y_i^T represent outcomes for participants and Y_i^C outcomes for nonparticipants, conditional independence implies

$$(Y_i^T, Y_i^C) \perp T_i \,|\, X_i. \tag{4.1}$$

This assumption is also called *unconfoundedness* (Rosenbaum and Rubin 1983), and it implies that uptake of the program is based entirely on observed characteristics. To estimate the TOT as opposed to the ATE, a weaker assumption is needed:

$$Y_i^C \perp T_i \,|\, X_i. \tag{4.2}$$

Conditional independence is a strong assumption and is not a directly testable criterion; it depends on specific features of the program itself. If unobserved characteristics determine program participation, conditional independence will be violated, and PSM is not an appropriate method.[1] Chapters 5 to 9 discuss approaches when unobserved selection is present. Having a rich set of preprogram data will help support the conditional independence assumption by allowing one to control for as many observed characteristics as might be affecting program participation (assuming unobserved selection is limited). Alternatives when selection on unobserved characteristics exists, and thus conditional independence is violated, are discussed in the following chapters, including the instrumental variable and double-difference methods.

Assumption of Common Support

A second assumption is the *common support* or *overlap condition*: $0 < P(T_i = 1|X_i) < 1$. This condition ensures that treatment observations have comparison observations "nearby" in the propensity score distribution (Heckman, LaLonde, and Smith 1999). Specifically, the effectiveness of PSM also depends on having a large and roughly equal number of participant and nonparticipant observations so that a substantial region of common support can be found. For estimating the TOT, this assumption can be relaxed to $P(T_i = 1|X_i) < 1$.

Treatment units will therefore have to be similar to nontreatment units in terms of observed characteristics unaffected by participation; thus, some nontreatment units may have to be dropped to ensure comparability. However, sometimes a nonrandom subset of the treatment sample may have to be dropped if similar comparison units do not exist (Ravallion 2008). This situation is more problematic because it creates a possible sampling bias in the treatment effect. Examining the characteristics of dropped units may be useful in interpreting potential bias in the estimated treatment effects.

Heckman, Ichimura, and Todd (1997) encourage dropping treatment observations with weak common support. Only in the area of common support can inferences be made about causality, as reflected in figure 4.1. Figure 4.2 reflects a scenario where the common support is weak.

The TOT Using PSM

If conditional independence holds, and if there is a sizable overlap in $P(X)$ across participants and nonparticipants, the PSM estimator for the TOT can be specified as the mean difference in Y over the common support, weighting the comparison units by the propensity score distribution of participants. A typical cross-section estimator can be specified as follows:

$$\text{TOT}_{\text{PSM}} = E_{P(X)\,|\,T=1}\{E[Y^T \mid T = 1, P(X)] - E[Y^C \mid T = 0, P(X)]\}. \tag{4.3}$$

Figure 4.1 Example of Common Support

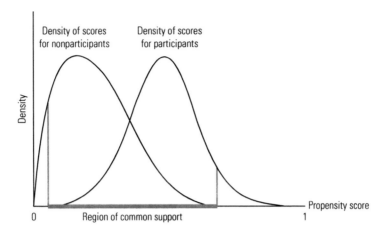

Source: Authors' representation.

Figure 4.2 Example of Poor Balancing and Weak Common Support

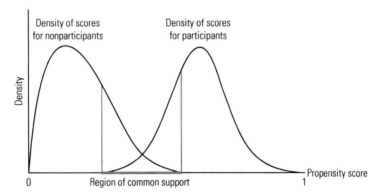

Source: Authors' representation.

More explicitly, with cross-section data and within the common support, the treatment effect can be written as follows (see Heckman, Ichimura, and Todd 1997; Smith and Todd 2005):

$$\Rightarrow \text{TOT}_{\text{PSM}} = \frac{1}{N_T} \left[\sum_{i \in T} Y_i^T - \sum_{j \in C} \omega(i, j) Y_j^C \right] \quad (4.4)$$

where N_T is the number of participants i and $\omega(i, j)$ is the weight used to aggregate outcomes for the matched nonparticipants j.[2]

57

Application of the PSM Method

To calculate the program treatment effect, one must first calculate the propensity score $P(X)$ on the basis all observed covariates X that jointly affect participation and the outcome of interest. The aim of matching is to find the closest comparison group from a sample of nonparticipants to the sample of program participants. "Closest" is measured in terms of observable characteristics not affected by program participation.

Step 1: Estimating a Model of Program Participation

First, the samples of participants and nonparticipants should be pooled, and then participation T should be estimated on all the observed covariates X in the data that are likely to determine participation. When one is interested only in comparing outcomes for those participating ($T = 1$) with those not participating ($T = 0$), this estimate can be constructed from a probit or logit model of program participation. Caliendo and Kopeinig (2008) also provide examples of estimations of the participation equation with a nonbinary treatment variable, based on work by Bryson, Dorsett, and Purdon (2002); Imbens (2000); and Lechner (2001). In this situation, one can use a multinomial probit (which is computationally intensive but based on weaker assumptions than the multinomial logit) or a series of binomial models.

After the participation equation is estimated, the predicted values of T from the participation equation can be derived. The predicted outcome represents the estimated probability of participation or propensity score. Every sampled participant and nonparticipant will have an estimated propensity score, $\hat{P}(X|T = 1) = \hat{P}(X)$. Note that the participation equation is not a determinants model, so estimation outputs such as t-statistics and the adjusted R^2 are not very informative and may be misleading. For this stage of PSM, causality is not of as much interest as the correlation of X with T.

As for the relevant covariates X, PSM will be biased if covariates that determine participation are not included in the participation equation for other reasons. These reasons could include, for example, poor-quality data or poor understanding of the local context in which the program is being introduced. As a result, limited guidance exists on how to select X variables using statistical tests, because the observed characteristics that are more likely to determine participation are likely to be data driven and context specific.[3] Heckman, Ichimura, and Todd (1997, 1998) show that the bias in PSM program estimates can be low, given three broad provisions. First, if possible, the same survey instrument or source of data should be used for participants and nonparticipants. Using the same data source helps ensure that the observed characteristics entering the logit or probit model of participation are measured similarly across the two groups and thereby reflect the same concepts. Second, a representative sample survey of eligible nonparticipants as well as participants can greatly improve the precision of the propensity score. Also, the larger the sample of eligible nonparticipants is, the more good matching will be facilitated. If the two samples come from different surveys, then they should be highly comparable surveys (same questionnaire, same interviewers or interviewer training, same survey period, and so on). A related point is that participants and nonparticipants should be facing the same economic incentives that might drive choices such as program participation (see Ravallion 2008; such incentives might include access to similar markets, for example). One could account for this factor by choosing participants and nonparticipants from the same geographic area.

Nevertheless, including too many X variables in the participation equation should also be avoided; overspecification of the model can result in higher standard errors for the estimated propensity score $\hat{P}(X)$ and may also result in perfectly predicting participation for many households ($\hat{P}(X) = 1$). In the latter case, such observations would drop out of the common support (as discussed later). As mentioned previously, determining participation is less of an issue in the participating equation than obtaining a distribution of participation probabilities.

Step 2: Defining the Region of Common Support and Balancing Tests

Next, the region of common support needs to be defined where distributions of the propensity score for treatment and comparison group overlap. As mentioned earlier, some of the nonparticipant observations may have to be dropped because they fall outside the common support. Sampling bias may still occur, however, if the dropped nonparticipant observations are systematically different in terms of observed characteristics from the retained nonparticipant sample; these differences should be monitored carefully to help interpret the treatment effect.

Balancing tests can also be conducted to check whether, within each quantile of the propensity score distribution, the average propensity score and mean of X are the same. For PSM to work, the treatment and comparison groups must be balanced in that similar propensity scores are based on similar observed X. Although a treated group and its matched nontreated comparator might have the same propensity scores, they are not necessarily observationally similar if misspecification exists in the participation equation. The distributions of the treated group and the comparator must be similar, which is what balance implies. Formally, one needs to check if $\hat{P}(X|T=1) = \hat{P}(X|T=0)$.

Step 3: Matching Participants to Nonparticipants

Different matching criteria can be used to assign participants to non-participants on the basis of the propensity score. Doing so entails calculating a weight for each matched participant-nonparticipant set. As discussed below, the choice of a particular matching technique may therefore affect the resulting program estimate through the weights assigned:

- *Nearest-neighbor matching.* One of the most frequently used matching techniques is NN matching, where each treatment unit is matched to the comparison unit with the closest propensity score. One can also choose n nearest neighbors and do matching (usually $n=5$ is used). Matching can be done with or without replacement. Matching with replacement, for example, means that the same non-participant can be used as a match for different participants.

- *Caliper or radius matching.* One problem with NN matching is that the difference in propensity scores for a participant and its closest nonparticipant neighbor may still be very high. This situation results in poor matches and can be avoided by imposing a threshold or "tolerance" on the maximum propensity score distance (*caliper*). This procedure therefore involves matching with replacement, only among propensity scores within a certain range. A higher number of dropped non-participants is likely, however, potentially increasing the chance of sampling bias.

- *Stratification or interval matching.* This procedure partitions the common support into different strata (or intervals) and calculates the program's impact within each interval. Specifically, within each interval, the program effect is the mean difference in outcomes between treated and control observations. A weighted average of these interval impact estimates yields the overall program impact, taking the share of participants in each interval as the weights.

- *Kernel and local linear matching.* One risk with the methods just described is that only a small subset of nonparticipants will ultimately satisfy the criteria to fall within the common support and thus construct the counterfactual outcome. Nonparametric matching estimators such as kernel matching and LLM use a weighted average of all nonparticipants to construct the counterfactual match for each participant. If P_i is the propensity score for participant i and P_j is the propensity score for nonparticipant j, and if the notation in equation 4.4 is followed, the weights for kernel matching are given by

$$\omega(i,j)_{KM} = \frac{K\left(\dfrac{P_j - P_i}{a_n}\right)}{\displaystyle\sum_{k \in C} K\left(\dfrac{P_k - P_i}{a_n}\right)}, \tag{4.5}$$

where $K(\cdot)$ is a kernel function and a_n is a bandwidth parameter. LLM, in contrast, estimates a nonparametric locally weighted (*lowess*) regression of the comparison group outcome in the neighborhood of each treatment observation (Heckman, Ichimura, and Todd 1997). Kernel matching is analogous to regression on a constant term, whereas LLM uses a constant and a slope term, so it is "linear." LLM can include a faster rate of convergence near boundary points (see Fan 1992, 1993). The LLM estimator has the same form as the kernel-matching estimator, except for the weighting function:

$$\omega(i,j)_{LLR} = \frac{K_{ij}\displaystyle\sum_{k \in C} K_{ik}(P_k - P_i)^2 - \left[K_{ij}(P_j - P_i)\right]\displaystyle\sum_{k \in C} K_{ik}(P_k - P_i)}{\displaystyle\sum_{j \in C} K_{ij}\displaystyle\sum_{k \in C} K_{ik}(P_k - P_i)^2 - \left(\displaystyle\sum_{k \in C} K_{ik}(P_k - P_i)\right)^2}. \tag{4.6}$$

- *Difference-in-difference matching.* With data on participant and control observations before and after program intervention, a difference-in-difference (DD) matching estimator can be constructed. The DD approach is discussed in greater detail in chapter 5; importantly, it allows for unobserved characteristics affecting program take-up, assuming that these unobserved traits do not vary over time. To present the DD estimator, revisit the setup for the cross-section PSM estimator given in equation 4.4. With panel data over two time periods $t = \{1,2\}$, the local linear DD estimator for the mean difference in outcomes Y_{it} across participants i and nonparticipants j in the common support is given by

$$\text{TOT}_{\text{PSM}}^{\text{DD}} = \frac{1}{N_T}\left[\sum_{i\in T}(Y_{i2}^T - Y_{i1}^T) - \sum_{j\in C}\omega(i,j)(Y_{j2}^C - Y_{j1}^C)\right]. \qquad (4.7)$$

With only cross-sections over time rather than panel data (see Todd 2007), $\text{TOT}_{\text{PSM}}^{\text{DD}}$ can be written as

$$\text{TOT}_{\text{PSM}}^{\text{DD}} = \frac{1}{N_{T_2}}\left[\sum_{i\in T_2}Y_{i2}^T - \sum_{j\in C_2}\omega(i,j)Y_{j2}^C\right] - \frac{1}{N_{T_1}}\left[\sum_{i\in T_1}Y_{i1}^T - \sum_{j\in C_1}\omega(i,j)Y_{j1}^C\right]. \qquad (4.8)$$

Here, Y_{it}^T and Y_{jt}^C, $t = \{1,2\}$ are the outcomes for different participant and nonparticipant observations in each time period t. The DD approach combines traditional PSM and DD approaches discussed in the next chapter. Observed as well as unobserved characteristics affecting participation can thus be accounted for if unobserved factors affecting participation are assumed to be constant over time. Taking the difference in outcomes over time should also difference out time-invariant unobserved characteristics and thus potential unobserved selection bias. Again, chapter 5 discusses this issue in detail. One can also use a regression-adjusted estimator (described in more detail later in this chapter as well as in chapter 5). This method assumes using a standard linear model for outcomes and for estimating the TOT (such as $Y_i = \alpha + \beta T_i + \gamma X_i + \varepsilon_i$) and applying weights on the basis of the propensity score to the matched comparison group. It can also allow one to control for selection on unobserved characteristics, again assuming these characteristics do not vary over time.

A number of steps, therefore, can be used to match participants to nonparticipants. Comparing results across different matching methods can reveal whether the estimated program effect is robust. Box 4.1 describes some of these methods, from a study on the impact of a pilot farmer-field-school (FFS) program in Peru on farmers' knowledge of pest management practices related to potato cultivation (Godtland and

---

BOX 4.1   **Case Study: Steps in Creating a Matched Sample of Nonparticipants to Evaluate a Farmer-Field-School Program**

A farmer-field-school program was started in 1998 by scientists in collaboration with CARE-Peru. In their study of the program, Godtland and others (2004) applied three different steps for generating a common support of propensity scores to match nonparticipants to the participant sample. These steps, as described here, combined methods that have been formally discussed in the PSM literature and informal rules commonly applied in practice.

First, a propensity score cutoff point was chosen, above which all households were included in the comparison group. No formal rule exists for choosing this cutoff point, and Godtland and others used as a benchmark the average propensity score among participants of 0.6. Second, the comparison group was chosen, using a nearest-neighbor matching method, matching to each participant five nonparticipants with the closest value of the propensity score (within a proposed 0.01 bound). Matches not in this range were removed from the sample. As a third approach, the full sample of nonparticipants (within the common support) was used to construct a weighted match for each participant, applying a nonparametric kernel regression method proposed by Heckman, Ichimura, and Todd (1998).

To evaluate the comparability of the participant and matched nonparticipant samples across these three methods, Godtland and others (2004) conducted balancing tests to see whether the means of the observable variables for each group were significantly different. For the first and second methods, the balancing test was performed by dividing each comparison and treatment group into two strata, ordered by probability propensity scores. Within each stratum, a *t*-test of equality of means across participants and matched nonparticipants was conducted for each variable in the farmer participation equation. Godtland and others found that the null was not rejected for all but a few variables across the first two methods. For the third method, a test for the equality of means was conducted across the samples of participants and their weighted matches. The null was not rejected for all but two variables at the 10 percent level. Overall, their results found no systematic differences in observed characteristics across the participant and nonparticipant samples.

others 2004). Farmers self-selected into the program. The sample of nonparticipants was drawn from villages where the FFS program existed, villages without the FFS program but with other programs run by CARE-Peru, as well as control villages. The control villages were chosen to be similar to the FFS villages across such observable characteristics as climate, distance to district capitals, and infrastructure. Simple comparison of knowledge levels across participants and nonparticipants would yield biased estimates of the program effect, however, because the program was not randomized and farmers were self-selecting into the program potentially on the basis of observed characteristics. Nonparticipants would therefore need to be matched to participants over a set of common characteristics to ensure comparability across the two groups.

Calculating the Average Treatment Impact

As discussed previously, if conditional independence and a sizable overlap in propensity scores between participants and matched nonparticipants can be assumed, the PSM average treatment effect is equal to the mean difference in outcomes over the common support, weighting the comparison units by the propensity score distribution of participants. To understand the potential observed mechanisms driving the estimated program effect, one can examine the treatment impact across different observable characteristics, such as position in the sample distribution of income, age, and so on.

Estimating Standard Errors with PSM: Use of the Bootstrap

Compared to traditional regression methods, the estimated variance of the treatment effect in PSM should include the variance attributable to the derivation of the propensity score, the determination of the common support, and (if matching is done without replacement) the order in which treated individuals are matched (Caliendo and Kopeinig 2008). Failing to account for this additional variation beyond the normal sampling variation will cause the standard errors to be estimated incorrectly (see Heckman, Ichimura, and Todd 1998).

One solution is to use bootstrapping (Efron and Tibshirani 1993; Horowitz 2003), where repeated samples are drawn from the original sample, and properties of the estimates (such as standard error and bias) are reestimated with each sample. Each bootstrap sample estimate includes the first steps of the estimation that derive the propensity score, common support, and so on. Formal justification for bootstrap estimators is limited; however, because the estimators are asymptotically linear, bootstrapping will likely lead to valid standard errors and confidence intervals (Imbens 2004).

Critiquing the PSM Method

The main advantage (and drawback) of PSM relies on the degree to which observed characteristics drive program participation. If selection bias from unobserved characteristics is likely to be negligible, then PSM may provide a good comparison with randomized estimates. To the degree participation variables are incomplete, the PSM results can be suspect. This condition is, as mentioned earlier, not a directly testable criteria; it requires careful examination of the factors driving program participation (through surveys, for example).

Another advantage of PSM is that it does not necessarily require a baseline or panel survey, although in the resulting cross-section, the observed covariates entering the logit model for the propensity score would have to satisfy the conditional independence assumption by reflecting observed characteristics X that are not affected by participation. A preprogram baseline is more helpful in this regard, because it covers observed X variables that are independent of treatment status. As discussed earlier, data on participants and nonparticipants over time can also help in accounting for some unobserved selection bias, by combining traditional PSM approaches with DD assumptions detailed in chapter 5.

PSM is also a semiparametric method, imposing fewer constraints on the functional form of the treatment model, as well as fewer assumptions about the distribution of the error term. Although observations are dropped to achieve the common support, PSM increases the likelihood of sensible comparisons across treated and matched control units, potentially lowering bias in the program impact. This outcome is true, however, only if the common support is large; sufficient data on nonparticipants are essential in ensuring a large enough sample from which to draw matches. Bias may also result from dropping nonparticipant observations that are systematically different from those retained; this problem can also be alleviated by collecting data on a large sample of nonparticipants, with enough variation to allow a representative sample. Otherwise, examining the characteristics of the dropped nonparticipant sample can refine the interpretation of the treatment effect.

Methods to address potential selection bias in PSM program estimates are described in a study conducted by Jalan and Ravallion (2003) in box 4.2. Their study estimates the net income gains of the Trabajar workfare program in Argentina (where participants must engage in work to receive benefits) during the country's economic crisis in 1997. The average income benefit to participants from the program is muddled by the fact that participants need not have been unemployed prior to joining Trabajar. Measurement of forgone income and, hence, construction of a proper counterfactual were therefore important in this study. Neither a randomized methodology nor a baseline survey was available, but Jalan and Ravallion were able to construct the counterfactual using survey data conducted about the same time covering a large sample of nonparticipants.

PSM and Regression-Based Methods

Given that matching produces consistent estimates under weak conditions, a practical advantage of PSM over ordinary least squares (OLS) is that it reduces the number of dimensions on which to match participants and comparison units. Nevertheless, consistent OLS estimates of the ATE can be calculated under the assumption of conditional exogeneity. One approach suggested by Hirano, Imbens, and Ridder (2003) is to estimate a weighted least squares regression of the outcome on treatment T and other observed covariates X unaffected by participation, using the inverse of

---

Case Study: Use of PSM and Testing for Selection Bias

In their study of the Trabajar workfare program in Argentina, Jalan and Ravallion (2003) conducted a postintervention survey of both participants and nonparticipants. The context made it more likely that both groups came from a similar economic environment: 80 percent of Trabajar workers came from the poorest 20 percent of the population, and the study used a sample of about 2,800 Trabajar participants along with nonparticipants from a large national survey.

Kernel density estimation was used to match the sample of participants and nonparticipants over common values of the propensity scores, excluding nonparticipants for whom the estimated density was equal to zero, as well as 2 percent of the nonparticipant sample from the top and bottom of the distribution. Estimates of the average treatment effect based on the nearest neighbor, the nearest five neighbors, and a kernel-weighted matching were constructed, and average gains of about half the maximum monthly Trabajar wage of US$200 were realized.

Jalan and Ravallion (2003) also tested for potential remaining selection bias on unobserved characteristics by applying the Sargan-Wu-Hausman test. Specifically, on the sample of participants and matched nonparticipants, they ran an ordinary least squares regression of income on the propensity score, the residuals from the logit participation equation, as well as a set of additional control variables Z that exclude the instruments used to identify exogenous variation in income gains. In the study, the identifying instruments were provincial dummies, because the allocations from the program varied substantially across equally poor local areas but appeared to be correlated with the province that the areas belonged to. This test was used to detect selection bias in the nearest-neighbor estimates, where one participant was matched to one nonparticipant, which lent itself to a comparable regression-based approach.

If the coefficient on the residuals is significantly different from zero, selection bias may continue to pose a problem in estimating the program's impact. In the analysis, this coefficient was not statistically significant under the null hypothesis of no selection bias, and the coefficient on the propensity score was similar to the average impact in the nearest-neighbor matching estimate.

---

a nonparametric estimate of the propensity score. This approach leads to a fully efficient estimator, and the treatment effect is estimated by $Y_{it} = \alpha + \beta T_{i1} + \gamma X_{it} + \varepsilon_{it}$ with weights of 1 for participants and weights of $\hat{P}(X)/(1 - \hat{P}(X))$ for the control observations. T_{i1} is the treatment indicator, and the preceding specification attempts to account for latent differences across treatment and comparison units that would affect selection into the program as well as resulting outcomes. For an estimate of the ATE for the population, the weights would be $1/\hat{P}(X)$ for the participants and $1/(1 - \hat{P}(X))$ for the control units.

Box 4.3, based on a study conducted by Chen, Mu, and Ravallion (2008) on the effects of the World Bank–financed Southwest China Poverty Reduction Project, describes an application of this approach. It allows the consistency advantages of matching to be combined with the favorable variance properties of regression-based methods.

BOX 4.3   **Case Study: Using Weighted Least Squares Regression in a Study of the Southwest China Poverty Reduction Project**

The Southwest China Poverty Reduction Project (SWP) is a program spanning interventions across a range of agricultural and nonagricultural activities, as well as infrastructure development and social services. Disbursements for the program covered a 10-year period between 1995 and 2005, accompanied by surveys between 1996 and 2000 of about 2,000 households in targeted and non-targeted villages, as well as a follow-up survey of the same households in 2004 to 2005.

Time-varying selection bias might result in the treatment impact across participants and non-participants if initial differences across the two samples were substantially different. In addition to studying treatment effects based on direct propensity score matching, Chen, Mu, and Ravallion (2008) examined treatment effects constructed by OLS regressions weighted by the inverse of propensity score. As part of the analysis, they examined average treatment impacts over time and specifically used a fixed-effects specification for the weighted regression. Among the different outcomes they examined, Chen, Mu, and Ravallion found that the initial gains to project areas for such outcomes as income, consumption, and schooling diminish over the longer term (through 2004–05). For example, the SWP impact on income using the propensity score weighted estimates in the trimmed sample fell from about US$180 in 2000 (*t*-ratio: 2.54) to about US$40 in 2004 to 2005 (*t*-ratio: 0.45). Also, school enrollment of children 6 to 14 years of age improved significantly (by about 7.5 percentage points) in 2000 but fell over time to about 3 percent—although this effect was not significant—by 2004 to 2005. This outcome may have resulted from the lapse in tuition subsidies with overall program disbursements.

The methods described here, however, assume that a matched comparison unit prior to program implementation provides the counterfactual of what would have happened over time to mean outcomes for participants in the absence of treatment. If spillovers exist, the intervention changes outcomes for nonparticipants and creates an additional source of bias. Chen, Mu, and Ravallion (2008) tested for spillovers by examining non-SWP projects in nontargeted villages and found positive spillover effects on the control villages through the displacement of non-SWP spending; however, they found these spillovers were unlikely to bias the treatment effects substantially.

Questions

1. Which of the following statement(s) is (are) true about the propensity score matching technique?

   A. PSM focuses on only observed characteristics of participants and nonparticipants.

   B. PSM focuses on only unobserved characteristics of participants and nonparticipants.

   C. PSM focuses on both observed and unobserved characteristics of participants and nonparticipants.

   (a) A

   (b) B

   (c) C

2. The first-stage program participation equation in PSM is estimated by
   A. a probit model.
   B. a logit model.
   C. an ordinary least square (OLS) model.
     (a) A or B
     (b) B only
     (c) A only
     (d) C

3. Weak common support in PSM is a problem because
   A. it may drop observations from the treatment sample nonrandomly.
   B. it may drop observations from the control sample nonrandomly.
   C. it always drops observations from both treatment and control samples nonrandomly.
     (a) A and B
     (b) B
     (c) A
     (d) C

4. Balancing property in PSM ensures that
   A. allocation of project resources is balanced in different stages of the projects.
   B. sample observations of participants and nonparticipants are balanced in some predefined way.
   C. means of control variables are the same for participants and nonparticipants whose propensity scores are close.
     (a) A and B
     (b) B
     (c) A
     (d) C

5. An advantage of PSM is
   A. PSM does not need to be concerned about unobserved characteristics that may influence program participation.
   B. PSM does not assume a functional relationship between the outcome and control variables.
   C. PSM can be applied without having data on control observations.
     (a) A and B
     (b) B only
     (c) B and C
     (d) C only

Notes

1. If unobserved variables indeed affect both participation and outcomes, this situation yields what is called a "hidden bias" (Rosenbaum 2002). Although the conditional independence

assumption, or unconfoundedness, cannot be verified, the sensitivity of the estimated results of the PSM method can be checked with respect to deviations from this identifying assumption. In other words, even if the extent of selection or hidden bias cannot be estimated, the degree to which the PSM results are sensitive to this assumption of unconfoundedness can be tested. Box 4.2 addresses this issue.

2. As described further in the chapter, various weighting schemes are available to calculate the weighted outcomes of the matched comparators.

3. See Dehejia (2005) for some suggestions on selection of covariates.

References

Bryson, Alex, Richard Dorsett, and Susan Purdon. 2002. "The Use of Propensity Score Matching in the Evaluation of Active Labour Market Policies." Working Paper 4, Department for Work and Pensions, London.

Caliendo, Marco, and Sabine Kopeinig. 2008. "Some Practical Guidance for the Implementation of Propensity Score Matching." *Journal of Economic Surveys* 22 (1): 31–72.

Chen, Shaohua, Ren Mu, and Martin Ravallion. 2008. "Are There Lasting Impacts of Aid to Poor Areas? Evidence for Rural China." Policy Research Working Paper 4084, World Bank, Washington, DC.

Dehejia, Rajeev. 2005. "Practical Propensity Score Matching: A Reply to Smith and Todd." *Journal of Econometrics* 125 (1–2): 355–64.

Efron, Bradley, and Robert J. Tibshirani. 1993. *An Introduction to the Bootstrap.* Boca Raton, FL: Chapman & Hall.

Fan, Jianqing. 1992. "Design-Adaptive Nonparametric Regression." *Journal of the American Statistical Association* 87 (420): 998–1004.

———. 1993. "Local Linear Regression Smoothers and Their Minimax Efficiencies." *Annals of Statistics* 21 (1): 196–216.

Godtland, Erin, Elisabeth Sadoulet, Alain de Janvry, Rinku Murgai, and Oscar Ortiz. 2004. "The Impact of Farmer-Field-Schools on Knowledge and Productivity: A Study of Potato Farmers in the Peruvian Andes." *Economic Development and Cultural Change* 52 (1): 129–58.

Hahn, Jinyong, Keisuke Hirano, and Dean Karlan. 2008. "Adaptive Experimental Design Using the Propensity Score." Working Paper 969, Economic Growth Center, Yale University, New Haven, CT.

Heckman, James J., Hidehiko Ichimura, and Petra Todd. 1997. "Matching as an Econometric Evaluation Estimator: Evidence from Evaluating a Job Training Programme." *Review of Economic Studies* 64 (4): 605–54.

———. 1998. "Matching as an Econometric Evaluation Estimator." *Review of Economic Studies* 65 (2): 261–94.

Heckman, James J., Robert LaLonde, and Jeffrey Smith. 1999. "The Economics and Econometrics of Active Labor Market Programs." In *Handbook of Labor Economics,* vol. 3, ed. Orley Ashenfelter and David Card, 1865–2097. Amsterdam: North-Holland.

Hirano, Keisuke, Guido W. Imbens, and Geert Ridder. 2003. "Efficient Estimation of Average Treatment Effects Using the Estimated Propensity Score." *Econometrica* 71 (4): 1161–89.

Horowitz, Joel. 2003. "The Bootstrap in Econometrics." *Statistical Science* 18 (2): 211–18.

Imbens, Guido. 2000. "The Role of the Propensity Score in Estimating Dose-Response Functions." *Biometrika* 87 (3): 706–10.

———. 2004. "Nonparametric Estimation of Average Treatment Effects under Exogeneity: A Review." *Review of Economics and Statistics* 86 (1): 4–29.

Jalan, Jyotsna, and Martin Ravallion. 2003. "Estimating the Benefit Incidence of an Antipoverty Program by Propensity-Score Matching." *Journal of Business and Economic Statistics* 21 (1): 19–30.

Lechner, Michael. 2001. "Identification and Estimation of Causal Effects of Multiple Treatments under the Conditional Independence Assumption." In *Econometric Evaluation of Labor Market Policies*, ed. Michael Lechner and Friedhelm Pfeiffer, 43–58. Heidelberg and New York: Physica-Verlag.

Ravallion, Martin. 2008. "Evaluating Anti-Poverty Programs." In *Handbook of Development Economics*, vol. 4, ed. T. Paul Schultz and John Strauss, 3787–846. Amsterdam: North-Holland.

Rosenbaum, Paul R. 2002. *Observational Studies.* New York and Berlin: Springer-Verlag.

Rosenbaum, Paul R., and Donald B. Rubin. 1983. "The Central Role of the Propensity Score in Observational Studies for Causal Effects." *Biometrika* 70 (1): 41–55.

Smith, Jeffrey, and Petra Todd. 2005. "Does Matching Overcome LaLonde's Critique of Nonexperimental Estimators?" *Journal of Econometrics* 125 (1–2): 305–53.

Todd, Petra. 2007. "Evaluating Social Programs with Endogenous Program Placement and Selection of the Treated." In *Handbook of Development Economics*, vol. 4, ed. T. Paul Schultz and John Strauss, 3847–94. Amsterdam: North-Holland.

5. Double Difference

Summary

Double-difference (DD) methods, compared with propensity score matching (PSM), assume that unobserved heterogeneity in participation is present—but that such factors are time invariant. With data on project and control observations before and after the program intervention, therefore, this fixed component can be differenced out.

Some variants of the DD approach have been introduced to account for potential sources of selection bias. Combining PSM with DD methods can help resolve this problem, by matching units in the common support. Controlling for initial area conditions can also resolve nonrandom program placement that might bias the program effect. Where a baseline might not be available, using a triple-difference method with an entirely separate control experiment after program intervention (that is, a separate set of untreated observations) offers an alternate calculation of the program's impact.

Learning Objectives

After completing this chapter, the reader will be able to discuss

- How to construct the double-difference estimate
- How to address potential violations of the assumption of time-invariant heterogeneity
- How to account for nonrandom program placement
- What to do when a baseline is not available

Addressing Selection Bias from a Different Perspective: Using Differences as Counterfactual

The two methods discussed in the earlier chapters—randomized evaluation and PSM—focus on various single-difference estimators that often require only an appropriate cross-sectional survey. This chapter now discusses the double-difference estimation technique, which typically uses panel data. Note, however, that DD can be used on repeated cross-section data as well, as long as the composition of participant and control groups is fairly stable over time.

In a panel setting, DD estimation resolves the problem of missing data by measuring outcomes and covariates for both participants and nonparticipants in pre- and postintervention periods. DD essentially compares treatment and comparison groups in terms of outcome changes over time relative to the outcomes observed for a preintervention baseline. That is, given a two-period setting where $t = 0$ before the program and $t = 1$ after program implementation, letting Y_t^T and Y_t^C be the respective outcomes for a program beneficiary and nontreated units in time t, the DD method will estimate the average program impact as follows:

$$DD = E(Y_1^T - Y_0^T \,|\, T_1 = 1) - E(Y_1^C - Y_0^C \,|\, T_1 = 0) \cdot \qquad (5.1)$$

In equation 5.1, $T_1 = 1$ denotes treatment or the presence of the program at $t = 1$, whereas $T_1 = 0$ denotes untreated areas. The following section returns to this equation. Unlike PSM alone, the DD estimator allows for *unobserved heterogeneity* (the unobserved difference in mean counterfactual outcomes between treated and untreated units) that may lead to selection bias. For example, one may want to account for factors unobserved by the researcher, such as differences in innate ability or personality across treated and control subjects or the effects of nonrandom program placement at the policy-making level. DD assumes this unobserved heterogeneity is time invariant, so the bias cancels out through differencing. In other words, the outcome changes for nonparticipants reveal the counterfactual outcome changes as shown in equation 5.1.

DD Method: Theory and Application

The DD estimator relies on a comparison of participants and nonparticipants before and after the intervention. For example, after an initial baseline survey of both nonparticipants and (subsequent) participants, a follow-up survey can be conducted of both groups after the intervention. From this information, the difference is calculated between the observed mean outcomes for the treatment and control groups before and after program intervention.

When baseline data are available, one can thus estimate impacts by assuming that unobserved heterogeneity is time invariant and uncorrelated with the treatment over time. This assumption is weaker than conditional exogeneity (described in chapters 2 and 3) and renders the outcome changes for a comparable group of nonparticipants (that is, $E(Y_1^C - Y_0^C \,|\, T_1 = 0)$) as the appropriate counterfactual, namely, equal to $E(Y_1^C - Y_0^C \,|\, T_1 = 1)$.[1] Nevertheless, justifiable concerns exist with this assumption that are brought up later in this chapter.

The DD estimate can also be calculated within a regression framework; the regression can be weighted to account for potential biases in DD (discussed in later sections in this chapter). In particular, the estimating equation would be specified as follows:

$$Y_{it} = \alpha + \beta T_{i1} t + \rho T_{i1} + \gamma t + \varepsilon_{it} \cdot \qquad (5.2)$$

In equation 5.2, the coefficient β on the interaction between the postprogram treatment variable (T_{il}) and time $(t = 1...T)$ gives the average DD effect of the program. Thus, using the notation from equation 5.1, $\beta = $ DD. In addition to this interaction term, the variables T_{il} and t are included separately to pick up any separate mean effects of time as well as the effect of being targeted versus not being targeted. Again, as long as data on four different groups are available to compare, panel data are not necessary to implement the DD approach (for example, the t subscript, normally associated with time, can be reinterpreted as a particular geographic area, $k = 1...K$).

To understand the intuition better behind equation 5.2, one can write it out in detail in expectations form (suppressing the subscript i for the moment):

$$E(Y_1^T - Y_0^T \mid T_1 = 1) = (\alpha + DD + \rho + \gamma) - (\alpha + \rho) \tag{5.3a}$$

$$E(Y_1^C - Y_0^C \mid T_1 = 0) = (\alpha + \gamma) - \alpha. \tag{5.3b}$$

Following equation 5.1, subtracting 5.3b from 5.3a gives DD. Note again that DD is unbiased only if the potential source of selection bias is *additive* and *time invariant*. Using the same approach, if a simple pre- versus postestimation impact on the participant sample is calculated (a reflexive design), the calculated program impact would be DD + γ, and the corresponding bias would be γ.[2] As discussed in chapter 2, without a control group, justifying that other factors were not responsible in affecting participant outcomes is difficult. One might also try comparing just the postprogram difference in outcomes across treatment and control units; however, in this case, the estimated impact of the policy would be DD + ρ, and the bias would be ρ. Systematic, unmeasured differences that could be correlated with treatment cannot be separated easily.

Remember that for the above DD estimator to be interpreted correctly, the following must hold:

1. The model in equation (outcome) is correctly specified. For example, the additive structure imposed is correct.
2. The error term is uncorrelated with the other variables in the equation:

$$Cov(\varepsilon_{it}, T_{il}) = 0$$

$$Cov(\varepsilon_{it}, t) = 0$$

$$Cov(\varepsilon_{it}, T_{il}t) = 0.$$

The last of these assumptions, also known as the *parallel-trend* assumption, is the most critical. It means that unobserved characteristics affecting program participation do not vary over time with treatment status.

Panel Fixed-Effects Model

The preceding two-period model can be generalized with multiple time periods, which may be called the *panel fixed-effects model.* This possibility is particularly important for a model that controls not only for the unobserved time-invariant heterogeneity but also for heterogeneity in observed characteristics over a multiple-period setting. More specifically, Y_{it} can be regressed on T_{it}, a range of time-varying covariates X_{it}, and unobserved time-invariant individual heterogeneity η_i that may be correlated with both the treatment and other unobserved characteristics ε_{it}. Consider the following revision of equation 5.2:

$$Y_{it} = \phi T_{it} + \delta X_{it} + \eta_i + \varepsilon_{it}. \tag{5.4}$$

Differencing both the right- and left-hand side of equation 5.4 over time, one would obtain the following differenced equation:

$$(Y_{it} - Y_{it-1}) = \phi(T_{it} - T_{it-1}) + \delta(X_{it} - X_{it-1}) + (\eta_i - \eta_i) + (\varepsilon_{it} - \varepsilon_{it-1}) \tag{5.5a}$$

$$\Rightarrow \Delta Y_{it} = \phi \Delta T_{it} + \delta \Delta X_{it} + \Delta \varepsilon_{it} \tag{5.5b}$$

In this case, because the source of endogeneity (that is, the unobserved individual characteristics η_i) is dropped from differencing, ordinary least squares (OLS) can be applied to equation 5.5b to estimate the unbiased effect of the program (ϕ). With two time periods, ϕ is equivalent to the DD estimate in equation 5.2, controlling for the same covariates X_{it}; the standard errors, however, may need to be corrected for serial correlation (Bertrand, Duflo, and Mullainathan 2004). With more than two time periods, the estimate of the program impact will diverge from DD.

Implementing DD

To apply a DD approach using panel data, baseline data need to be collected on program and control areas before program implementation. As described in chapter 2, quantitative as well as qualitative information on these areas will be helpful in determining who is likely to participate. Follow-up surveys after program intervention also should be conducted on the same units.[3] Calculating the average difference in outcomes separately for participants and nonparticipants over the periods and then taking an additional difference between the average changes in outcomes for these two groups will give the DD impact. An example is shown in figure 5.1: $DD = (Y_4 - Y_0) - (Y_3 - Y_1)$.

The lowermost line in figure 5.1 also depicts the true counterfactual outcomes, which are never observed (see chapter 2). Under the DD approach, unobserved characteristics that create a gap between measured control outcomes and true counterfactual outcomes are assumed to be time invariant, such that the gap between the two trends is

Figure 5.1 An Example of DD

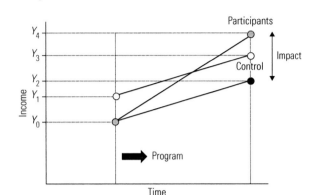

Source: Authors' representation.

the same over the period. This assumption implies that $(Y_3 - Y_2) = (Y_1 - Y_0)$. Using this equality in the preceding DD equation, one gets DD = $(Y_4 - Y_2)$.

One application of DD estimation comes from Thomas and others (2004). They examine a program in Indonesia that randomized the distribution of iron supplements to individuals in primarily agricultural households, with half the respondents receiving treatment and controls receiving a placebo. A baseline was also conducted before the intervention. Using DD estimation, the study found that men who were iron deficient before the intervention experienced improved health outcomes, with more muted effects for women. The baseline was also useful in addressing concerns about bias in compliance with the intervention by comparing changes in outcomes among subjects assigned to the treatment group relative to changes among subjects assigned to the control group.

As another example, Khandker, Bakht, and Koolwal (2009) examine the impact of two rural road-paving projects in Bangladesh, using a quasi-experimental household panel data set surveying project and control villages before and after program implementation. Both project and control areas shared similar socioeconomic and community-level characteristics before program implementation; control areas were also targets for future rounds of the road improvement program. Each project had its own survey, covered in two rounds—the first in the mid-1990s before the projects began and the second about five years later after program completion. DD estimation was used to determine the program's impacts across a range of outcomes, including household per capita consumption (a measure of household welfare), prices, employment outcomes for men and women, and children's school enrollment. Using an additional fixed-effects approach that accounted for initial conditions, the study found that households had benefited in a variety of ways from road investment.

Although DD typically exploits a baseline and resulting panel data, repeated cross-section data over time can also be used. Box 5.1 describes the use of different data sources in a study of a conditional cash-transfer program in Pakistan.

Advantages and Disadvantages of Using DD

The advantage of DD is that it relaxes the assumption of conditional exogeneity or selection only on observed characteristics. It also provides a tractable, intuitive way to account for selection on unobserved characteristics. The main drawback, however, rests precisely with this assumption: the notion of time-invariant selection bias is implausible for many targeted programs in developing countries. The case studies discussed here and in earlier chapters, for example, reveal that such programs often have wide-ranging approaches to poverty alleviation that span multiple sectors. Given that such programs are also targeted in areas that are very poor and have low initial growth, one might expect over several years that the behavior and choices of targeted areas would respond dynamically (in both observed and unobserved ways) to the program. Training programs, which are also widely examined in the evaluation literature, provide

---

BOX 5.1   Case Study: DD with Panel Data and Repeated Cross-Sections

Aside from panel data, repeated cross-section data on a particular area may be pooled to generate a larger sample size and to examine how characteristics of the sample are broadly changing over time. Chaudhury and Parajuli (2006) examined the effects of the Female School Stipend Program in the Punjab province of Pakistan on public school enrollment, using school-level panel data from 2003 (before the program) and 2005 (after the program), as well as repeated cross-section data at the child level between 2001–02 and 2004–05.

Under the program, girls received a PRs 200 stipend conditional on being enrolled in grades 6 through 8 in a girls' public secondary school within targeted districts and maintaining average class attendance of at least 80 percent. The program was specifically targeted toward low-literacy districts and was not randomly assigned. As part of their analysis, Chaudhury and Parajuli (2006) used both panel and repeated cross-section data to calculate separate difference-in-difference program impacts on girls' enrollment, assuming time-invariant unobserved heterogeneity.

The panel data were drawn from the provincial school censuses across 15 districts receiving the stipend program (covering about 1,780 schools) and 19 control districts (spanning about 3,150 schools) where the program was not available. Using these data, the researchers found the program increased girls' enrollment by about 23 percent. The child-level cross-section data over time were drawn from household surveys and were considered to be potentially more objective relative to the school administrative data. The study found, for 10- to 14-year-old girls, that the average effect of the program ranged from 10 to 13 percentage points. Compared with the panel data regressions, the corresponding regressions with the pooled cross-section data included interaction terms of the stipend program dummy as well as a postprogram time dummy with whether the child was female.

---

another example. Suppose evaluating the impact of a training program on earnings is of interest. Enrollment may be more likely if a temporary (perhaps shock-induced) slump in earnings occurs just before introduction of the program (this phenomenon is also known as *Ashenfelter's Dip*). Thus, the treated group might have experienced faster growth in earnings even without participation. In this case, a DD method is likely to overestimate the program's effect.[4] Figure 5.2 reflects this potential bias when the difference between nonparticipant and counterfactual outcomes changes over time; time-varying, unobserved heterogeneity could lead to an upward or downward bias.

In practice, ex ante, time-varying unobserved heterogeneity could be accounted for with proper program design, including ensuring that project and control areas share similar preprogram characteristics. If comparison areas are not similar to potential participants in terms of observed and unobserved characteristics, then changes in the outcome over time may be a function of this difference. This factor would also bias the DD. For example, in the context of a school enrollment program, if control areas were selected that were initially much farther away from local schools than targeted areas, DD would overestimate the program's impact on participating localities. Similarly, differences in agroclimatic conditions and initial infrastructural development across treated and control areas may also be correlated with program placement and resulting changes in outcomes over time. Using data from a poverty-alleviation program in China, Jalan and Ravallion (1998) show that a large bias exists in the DD estimate of the project's impact because changes over time are a function of initial conditions that also influence program placement. Controlling for the area characteristics that initially attracted the development projects can correct for this bias; by doing so, Jalan and Ravallion found significant longer-term impacts whereas none had been evident in the standard DD estimator. The next section discusses this issue in more detail.

Figure 5.2   Time-Varying Unobserved Heterogeneity

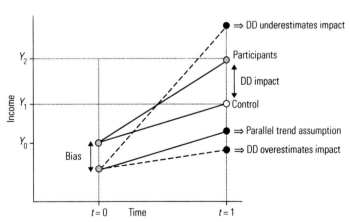

Source: Authors' representation.

As discussed in chapter 4, applying PSM could help match treatment units with observationally similar control units before estimating the DD impact. Specifically, one would run PSM on the base year and then conduct a DD on the units that remain in the common support. Studies show that weighting the control observations according to their propensity score yields a fully efficient estimator (Hirano, Imbens, and Ridder 2003; also see chapter 4 for a discussion). Because effective PSM depends on a rich baseline, however, during initial data collection careful attention should be given to characteristics that determine participation.

Even if comparability of control and project areas could be ensured before the program, however, the DD approach might falter if macroeconomic changes during the program affected the two groups differently. Suppose some unknown characteristics make treated and nontreated groups react differently to a common macroeconomic shock. In this case, a simple DD might overestimate or underestimate the true effects of a program depending on how the treated and nontreated groups react to the common shock. Bell, Blundell, and van Reenen (1999) suggest a differential time-trend-adjusted DD for such a case. This alternative will be discussed later in terms of the triple-difference method. Another approach might be through instrumental variables, which are discussed in chapter 6. If enough data are available on other exogenous or behavior-independent factors affecting participants and nonparticipants over time, those factors can be exploited to identify impacts when unobserved heterogeneity is not constant. An instrumental variables panel fixed-effects approach could be implemented, for example; chapter 6 provides more detail.

Alternative DD Models

The double-difference approach described in the previous section yields consistent estimates of project impacts if unobserved community and individual heterogeneity are time invariant. However, one can conceive of several cases where unobserved characteristics of a population may indeed change over time—stemming, for example, from changes in preferences or norms over a longer time series. A few variants of the DD method have therefore been proposed to control for factors affecting these changes in unobservables.

Do Initial Conditions Matter?

One case in which unobserved heterogeneity may not remain constant over time is where public investments depend on initial (preprogram) local area conditions. Not controlling for initial area conditions when assessing the impact of an antipoverty program may lead to significant omitted variable bias—if local conditions were also responsible for the improvement of household outcomes or program targeting was correlated with such area characteristics. Approaches to controlling for initial area conditions in a DD approach, using data over multiple years as well as data covering only two time periods, are discussed in box 5.2.

> **BOX 5.2**   **Case Study: Accounting for Initial Conditions with a DD Estimator—Applications for Survey Data of Varying Lengths**
>
> **Long-Term Data with Multiple Rounds**
>
> Jalan and Ravallion (1998) examined the impact of a development program in a poor area on growth in household consumption by using panel data from targeted and nontargeted areas across four contiguous provinces in southwest China. Using data on about 6,650 households between 1985 and 1990 (supplemented by additional field visits in 1994–95), they employed a generalized method-of-moments time-series estimation model for household consumption growth, including initial area conditions on the right-hand side and using second and higher lags of consumption as instruments for lagged consumption to obtain consistent estimates of a dynamic growth model with panel data.
>
> Their results show that program effects are indeed influenced by initial household and community wealth; dropping initial area conditions (such as initial wealth and fertilizer use) caused the national program effect to lose significance completely, with provincial program effects changing sign and becoming slightly negative. In particular, after correcting for the area characteristics that initially attracted the development projects, Jalan and Ravallion (1998) found significant longer-term impacts than those obtained using simple fixed-effects methods. Thus, failing to control for factors underlying potential differences in local and regional growth trajectories can lead to a substantial underestimation of the welfare gains from the program.
>
> **Data with Two Time Periods**
>
> With fewer time periods (for example, with two years) a simpler OLS-first difference model can be applied on the data, incorporating a range of initial area characteristics across project and control areas prior to program implementation. In their study on rural roads (discussed later in this chapter), Khandker, Bakht, and Koolwal (2009) used two rounds of data—namely, baseline and postprogram data on treated and control areas—to compare DD results based on a household fixed-effects approach with OLS-first difference estimations on the same outcomes and covariates. These OLS-first difference estimates control for a number of preproject characteristics of villages where households were located. These initial area characteristics included local agroclimatic factors; the number of banks, schools, and hospitals serving the village; the distance from the village to the nearest paved road; the average short-term interest rate in the village; and the number of active microfinance institutions in the village.
>
> Although the project estimates are similar across both specifications for a number of outcomes, the study found that the beneficial household impact of the program was also strengthened for many outcomes when initial area conditions were controlled for. Because the project's effect did not disappear for most outcomes after initial area conditions were controlled for, the study provides one indication that program targeting was not entirely predisposed toward certain areas with particular initial development characteristics.

PSM with DD

As mentioned earlier, provided that rich data on control and treatment areas exist, PSM can be combined with DD methods to better match control and project units on preprogram characteristics. Specifically, recalling the discussion in chapter 4, one notes that the propensity score can be used to match participant and control units in the base (preprogram) year, and the treatment impact is calculated across participant and matched control units within the common support. For two time periods $t = \{1,2\}$, the DD estimate for each treatment area i will be calculated as $DD_i = (Y_{i2}^T - Y_{i1}^T) - \sum_{j \in C} \omega(i,j)(Y_{j2}^C - Y_{j1}^C)$, where $\omega(i,j)$ is the weight (using a PSM approach) given to the jth control area matched to treatment area i. Different types of matching approaches discussed in chapter 4 can be applied.

In terms of a regression framework (also discussed in chapter 4), Hirano, Imbens, and Ridder (2003) show that a weighted least squares regression, by weighting the control observations according to their propensity score, yields a fully efficient estimator:

$$\Delta Y_{it} = \alpha + \beta T_i + \gamma \Delta X_{it} + \varepsilon_{it}, \beta = DD. \tag{5.6}$$

The weights in the regression in equation 5.6 are equal to 1 for treated units and to $\hat{P}(X)/(1 - \hat{P}(X))$ for comparison units. See box 5.3 for a case study.

Triple-Difference Method

What if baseline data are not available? Such might be the case during an economic crisis, for example, where a program or safety net has to be set up quickly. In this context, a triple-difference method can be used. In addition to a "first experiment" comparing certain project and control groups, this method exploits the use of an entirely separate control experiment after program intervention. That is, this separate control group reflects a set of nonparticipants in treated and nontreated areas that are not part of the

---

BOX 5.3   **Case Study: PSM with DD**

In a study on rural road rehabilitation in Vietnam, van de Walle and Mu (2008) controlled for time-invariant unobserved heterogeneity and potential time-varying selection bias attributable to differences in initial observable characteristics by combining DD and PSM using data from 94 project and 95 control communes over three periods: a baseline survey in 1997, followed by surveys in 2001 and 2003.

Highlighting the importance of comparing short-term versus long-term impacts, the study found that most outcomes were realized at different stages over the period. Primary school completion, for example, reflected sustained growth between 1997 and 2003, increasing by 15 to 25 percent. Other outcomes, such as the expansion of markets and availability of non-food-related goods, took a longer time to emerge (markets, for example, developed in about 10 percent more project than control communes after seven years) than did short-run effects such as the number of secondary schools and availability of food-related goods. Moreover, van de Walle and Mu found that market impacts were greater if the commune initially was poorly developed.

first control group. These new control units may be different from the first control group in socioeconomic characteristics if evaluators want to examine the project's impact on participants relative to another socioeconomic group. Another difference from the first experiment would then be taken from the change in the additional control sample to examine the impact of the project, accounting for other factors changing over time (see, for example, Gruber 1994). This method would therefore require data on multiple years after program intervention, even though baseline data were missing.

Box 5.4 discusses an example of a triple-difference approach from Argentina, where Ravallion and others (2005) examine program impacts on income for "stayers" versus "leavers" in the Trabajar workfare program in Argentina (see chapter 4 for a discussion of the program). Given that the program was set up shortly after the 1997 financial crisis, baseline data were not available. Ravallion and others therefore

---

BOX 5.4   **Case Study: Triple-Difference Method—Trabajar Program in Argentina**

Lacking baseline data for the Trabajar program, and to avoid making the assumption that stayers and leavers had similar opportunities before joining the program, Ravallion and others (2005) proposed a triple-difference estimator, using an entirely separate control group that never participated in the program (referred to as *nonparticipants* here). The triple-difference estimator is first calculated by taking the DD between matched stayers and nonparticipants and then the DD for matched leavers and nonparticipants. Finally, the DD of these two sets of groups is calculated across matched stayers and leavers.

Specifically, letting $D_{it} = 1$ and $D_{it} = 0$ correspond to participants and matched nonparticipants, respectively, in round t, $t = \{1,2\}$, the study first calculated the DD estimates $A = \left[(\bar{Y}_2^T - \bar{Y}_1^T) - (\bar{Y}_2^C - \bar{Y}_1^C) | D_{i2} = 1 \right]$ (corresponding to the stayers in period 2, matched with nonparticipants from the separate urban survey) and $B = \left[(\bar{Y}_2^T - \bar{Y}_1^T) - (\bar{Y}_2^C - \bar{Y}_1^C) | D_{i2} = 0 \right]$ (corresponding to the leavers in period 2, matched with nonparticipants). The triple-difference estimator was then calculated as $A - B$.

Ravallion and others (2005) used a sample of 419 stayers matched with 400 leavers (originally taken from a random sample of 1,500 Trabajar workers), surveyed in May and June 1999, October and November 1999, and May and June 2000. Nonparticipants were drawn from a separate urban household survey conducted around the same time, covering a range of socioeconomic characteristics; this survey was conducted twice a year and covered about 27,000 households.

Interpreting the triple-difference estimate as a measure of the average gains to participants, however, requires that (a) there was no selection bias in dropping out from the program and (b) there were no current income gains to nonparticipants. Ravallion and others (2005) used a third round of the survey to test these conditions jointly, comparing the triple-difference estimate for those who dropped out and for those who stayed in the program. Using this test, they were not able to reject the conditions required for using the triple-difference measure as an estimate of the gains to current participants. They also found evidence of an Ashenfelter's Dip, where people were able to recover an increasing share of the Trabajar wage after dropping out of the program as time went on.

examine the difference in incomes for participants leaving the program and those still participating, after differencing out aggregate economywide changes by using an entirely separate, matched group of nonparticipants. Without the matched group of nonparticipants, a simple DD between stayers and leavers will be unbiased only if counterfactual earnings opportunities outside of the program were the same for each group. However, as Ravallion and others (2005) point out, individuals who choose to remain in the program may intuitively be less likely to have better earnings opportunities outside the program than those who dropped out early. As a result, a DD estimate comparing just these two groups will underestimate the program's impact. Only in circumstances such as an exogenous program contraction, for example, can a simple DD between stayers and leavers work well.

Adjusting for Differential Time Trends

As mentioned earlier, suppose one wants to evaluate a program such as employment training introduced during a macroeconomic crisis. With data available for treated and nontreated groups before and after the program, one could use a DD approach to estimate the program's effect on earnings, for example. However, such events are likely to create conditions where the treated and nontreated groups would respond differently to the shock. Bell, Blundell, and van Reenen (1999) have constructed a DD method that accounts for these differential time-trend effects. Apart from the data on treated and nontreated groups before and after treatment, another time interval is needed (say, $t - 1$ to t) for the same treated and nontreated groups. The recent past cycle is likely the most appropriate time interval for such comparison. More formally, the time-trend-adjusted DD is defined as follows:

$$DD = [E(Y_1^T - Y_0^T \mid T_1 = 1) - E(Y_1^C - Y_0^C \mid T_1 = 0)]$$
$$- [E(Y_t^T - Y_{t-1}^T \mid T_1 = 1) - E(Y_t^C - Y_{t-1}^C \mid T_1 = 0)]. \qquad (5.7)$$

Questions

1. Which of the following statement(s) is (are) true about the double-difference method?
   A. DD is very suitable for analyzing panel data.
   B. Like PSM, DD can never control for unobserved characteristics that may affect outcome variables.
   C. DD compares changes in outcome variable between pre- and postintervention periods for participants and nonparticipants.
   (a) A and B
   (b) B and C
   (c) A and C
   (d) C only

2. The following table gives mean income during the pre- and postintervention period for a microfinance intervention in the rural Lao People's Democratic Republic:

	Mean income (KN thousand)	
	Participants	Nonparticipants
Preintervention period	80	90
Postintervention period	125	120

Impact of microfinance intervention on participants' income using DD is
   (a) KN 45,000
   (b) KN 30,000
   (c) KN 15,000

3. The following equation is a DD representation of an outcome equation for panel data:

$$Y = \alpha + \beta T + \gamma t + \delta Tt + \varepsilon,$$

where Y is household's monthly income, T is a microfinance intervention ($T = 1$ if household gets the intervention, and $T = 0$ if household does not get the intervention); t is the round of survey ($t = 0$ for baseline, and $t = 1$ for follow-up); and ε is the error term. If DD is used, the impact of microfinance program on household income is given by
   (a) β
   (b) γ
   (c) δ
   (d) $\beta + \delta$

4. Which of the following can improve on the basic functional form of DD specified in question 3, if treatment is not exogenous?
   A. Run an instrumental variable model.
   B. Extend it by adding control (X) variables that may affect outcomes.
   C. Run a fixed-effects model to implement it.
   (a) A and B
   (b) B and C
   (c) A and C
   (d) C only
   (e) A, B, and C

5. Which of the following is (are) the limitation(s) of the double-difference method?
   A. DD cannot be applied to cross-sectional data.
   B. DD may give biased estimates if characteristics of project and control areas are significantly different.
   C. DD cannot control for unobserved characteristics that may affect outcomes if they vary between pre- and postintervention periods.

(a) A and B

(b) B and C

(c) A and C

(d) C only

Notes

1. Refer to chapter 2 for an introductory discussion of the role of the counterfactual in specifying the treatment effect of a program.

2. Note that when the counterfactual means are time invariant ($E[Y_1^C - Y_0^C \mid T_1 = 1] = 0$), the DD estimate in equation 5.1 becomes a reflexive comparison where only outcomes for the treatment units are monitored. Chapter 2 also discusses reflexive comparisons in more detail. This approach, however, is limited in practice because it is unlikely that the mean outcomes for the counterfactual do not change.

3. Although some large-scale studies are not able to revisit the same households or individuals after program intervention, they can survey the same villages or communities and thus are able to calculate DD program impacts at the local or community level. Concurrent surveys at the beneficiary and community levels are important in maintaining this flexibility, particularly because surveys before and after program intervention can span several years, making panel data collection more difficult.

4. A similar argument against the DD method applies in the case of evaluating a program using repeated cross-sectional survey data. That is, if individuals self-select into a program according to some unknown rule and repeated cross-section data are used, the assumption of time-invariant heterogeneity may fail if the composition of the group changes and the intervention affects the composition of treated versus nontreated groups.

References

Bell, Brian, Richard Blundell, and John van Reenen. 1999. "Getting the Unemployed Back to Work: An Evaluation of the New Deal Proposals." *International Tax and Public Finance* 6 (3): 339–60.

Bertrand, Marianne, Esther Duflo, and Sendhil Mullainathan. 2004. "How Much Should We Trust Differences-in-Differences Estimates?" *Quarterly Journal of Economics* 119 (1): 249–75.

Chaudhury, Nazmul, and Dilip Parajuli. 2006. "Conditional Cash Transfers and Female Schooling: The Impact of the Female School Stipend Program on Public School Enrollments in Punjab, Pakistan." Policy Research Working Paper 4102, World Bank, Washington, DC.

Gruber, Jonathan, 1994. "The Incidence of Mandated Maternity Benefits." *American Economic Review* 84 (3): 622–41.

Hirano, Keisuke, Guido W. Imbens, and Geert Ridder. 2003. "Efficient Estimation of Average Treatment Effects Using the Estimated Propensity Score." *Econometrica* 71 (4): 1161–89.

Jalan, Jyotsna, and Martin Ravallion. 1998. "Are There Dynamic Gains from a Poor-Area Development Program?" *Journal of Public Economics* 67 (1):65–85.

Khandker, Shahidur R., Zaid Bakht, and Gayatri B. Koolwal. 2009. "The Poverty Impacts of Rural Roads: Evidence from Bangladesh." *Economic Development and Cultural Change* 57 (4): 685–722.

Ravallion, Martin, Emanuela Galasso, Teodoro Lazo, and Ernesto Philipp. 2005. "What Can Ex-Participants Reveal about a Program's Impact?" *Journal of Human Resources* 40 (1): 208–30.

Thomas, Duncan, Elizabeth Frankenberg, Jed Friedman, Jean-Pierre Habicht, Mohammed Hakimi, Jaswadi, Nathan Jones, Christopher McKelvey, Gretel Pelto, Bondan Sikoki, Teresa Seeman, James P. Smith, Cecep Sumantri, Wayan Suriastini, and Siswanto Wilopo. 2004. "Iron Deficiency and the Well-Being of Older Adults: Preliminary Results from a Randomized Nutrition Intervention." University of California–Los Angeles, Los Angeles, California.

van de Walle, Dominique, and Ren Mu. 2008. "Rural Roads and Poor Area Development in Vietnam." Policy Research Working Paper 4340, World Bank, Washington, DC.

6. Instrumental Variable Estimation

Summary

Instrumental variable (IV) methods allow for endogeneity in individual participation, program placement, or both. With panel data, IV methods can allow for time-varying selection bias. Measurement error that results in attenuation bias can also be resolved through this procedure. The IV approach involves finding a variable (or instrument) that is highly correlated with program placement or participation but that is not correlated with unobserved characteristics affecting outcomes. Instruments can be constructed from program design (for example, if the program of interest was randomized or if exogenous rules were used in determining eligibility for the program).

Instruments should be selected carefully. Weak instruments can potentially worsen the bias even more than when estimated by ordinary least squares (OLS) if those instruments are correlated with unobserved characteristics or omitted variables affecting the outcome. Testing for weak instruments can help avoid this problem. Another problem can arise if the instrument still correlates with unobserved anticipated gains from the program that affect participation; local average treatment effects (LATEs) based on the instruments can help address this issue.

Learning Objectives

After completing this chapter, the reader will be able to discuss

- How instrumental variables can resolve selection bias in participation, program placement, or both
- How the IV approach differs in assumptions from propensity score matching (PSM) and double-difference (DD) methods
- What sources are available for finding good instruments
- How to test for weak instruments
- What the difference is between standard IV methods and the LATE

Introduction

This handbook now turns to methods that relax the exogeneity assumption of OLS or PSM and that are also robust to time-varying selection bias, unlike DD. Remember that for DD methods one cannot control for selection bias that changes over time (chapter 5). By relaxing the exogeneity assumption, the IV method makes different identifying assumptions from the previous methods—although assumptions underlying IV may not apply in all contexts.

Recall the setup discussed in chapter 2 of an estimating equation that compares outcomes of treated and nontreated groups:

$$Y_i = \alpha X_i + \beta T_i + \varepsilon_i \qquad (6.1)$$

If treatment assignment T is random in equation 6.1, selection bias is not a problem at the level of randomization (see chapter 3). However, treatment assignment may not be random because of two broad factors. First, *endogeneity* may exist in program targeting or placement—that is, programs are placed deliberately in areas that have specific characteristics (such as earnings opportunities or social norms) that may or may not be observed and that are also correlated with outcomes Y. Second, *unobserved individual heterogeneity* stemming from individual beneficiaries' self-selection into the program also confounds an experimental setup. As discussed in chapter 2, selection bias may result from both of these factors because unobserved characteristics in the error term will contain variables that also correlate with the treatment dummy T. That is, $\mathrm{cov}(T, \varepsilon) \neq 0$ implies violation of one of the key assumptions of OLS in obtaining unbiased estimates: independence of regressors from the disturbance term ε. The correlation between T and ε naturally biases the other estimates in the equation, including the estimate of the program effect β.

Equation 6.1, as well as the corresponding concerns about endogeneity, can be generalized to a panel setting. In this case, unobserved characteristics over time may be correlated with the program as well as other with observed covariates. To an extent, this issue was discussed in chapter 5. DD methods resolved the issue by assuming that unobserved characteristics of targeted and nontargeted units were time invariant and then by differencing out the heterogeneity. When panel data are available, IV methods permit a more nuanced view of unobserved heterogeneity, allowing for these factors to change over time (such as unobserved entrepreneurial talent of targeted subjects, ability to maintain social ties and networks, and so on, all of which may vary with the duration of the program).

The IV aims to clean up the correlation between T and ε. That is, the variation in T that is uncorrelated with ε needs to be isolated. To do so, one needs to find an instrumental variable, denoted Z, that satisfies the following conditions:

1. Correlated with T: $\mathrm{cov}(Z,T) \neq 0$
2. Uncorrelated with ε: $\mathrm{cov}(Z,\varepsilon) = 0$

Thus, instrument Z affects selection into the program but is not correlated with factors affecting the outcomes (also known as an *exclusion restriction*).

A related issue is that measurement error in observed participation may underestimate or overestimate the program's impact. As discussed in chapter 3, an IV can be introduced to resolve this attenuation bias by calculating an intention-to-treat (ITT) estimate of the program. This estimate would account for actual participation being different from intended participation because of targeting and eligibility rules.

Khandker (2006) provides an example of how concerns regarding exogeneity and attenuation bias can be addressed. In this study, the impact of microfinance expansion on consumption expenditure and poverty is estimated using panel data from Bangladesh, spanning household surveys for 1991–92 and 1998–99.[1] The study intended to test the sensitivity of findings in Pitt and Khandker (1998) using the 1991–92 data set. Households were sampled in villages with and without a program; both eligible and ineligible households were sampled in both types of villages, and both program participants and nonparticipants were sampled among the eligible households in villages with microfinance programs. The two central underlying conditions for identifying the program's impact were (a) the program's eligibility restriction (any household with a landholding of less than half an acre was eligible to participate in microfinance programs) and (b) its gender-targeted program design (men could join only groups with other men, and women could join only groups with other women). A gender-based restriction is easily enforceable and thus observable, whereas a land-based identification restriction, for various reasons, may not be (see Morduch 1998). Thus, if the land-based restriction is not observable, using the gender-based program design to identify the program effect by gender of participation is far more efficient.

A village-level fixed-effect DD method might be used to resolve unobserved heterogeneity in this example, given the existence of panel data. However, the assumption of time-invariant unobserved heterogeneity might be violated. For example, unobserved household income, which may condition credit demand, may increase temporarily from the program so that with a larger cushion against risk, households may be willing to assume more loans. Similarly, unobserved local market conditions that influence a household's demand for credit may change over time, exerting a more favorable effect on credit demand. Also, the unmeasured determinants of credit at both the household and the village levels may vary over time, and if credit is measured with errors (which is likely), the error is amplified when differencing over time, especially with only two time periods. This measurement error will impart attenuation bias to the credit impact coefficients, biasing the impact estimates toward zero. A standard correction for both types of bias (one attributable to measurement error and one to time-varying heterogeneity in credit demand) is IV estimation. This approach is discussed further later in the chapter.

Two-Stage Least Squares Approach to IVs

To isolate the part of the treatment variable that is independent of other unobserved characteristics affecting the outcome, one first regresses the treatment on the instrument

Z, the other covariates in equation 6.1, and a disturbance, u_i. This process is known as the *first-stage regression*:

$$T_i = \gamma Z_i + \phi X_i + u_i. \tag{6.2}$$

The predicted treatment from this regression, $\hat{T}$, therefore reflects the part of the treatment affected only by Z and thus embodies only exogenous variation in the treatment. $\hat{T}$ is then substituted for treatment in equation 6.1 to create the following reduced-form outcome regression:

$$Y_i = \alpha X_i + \beta(\hat{\gamma} Z_i + \hat{\phi} X_i + u_i) + \varepsilon_i. \tag{6.3}$$

The IV (also known as *two-stage least squares*, or 2SLS) estimate of the program impact is then $\hat{\beta}_{IV}$. Specifically, looking at $Y_i = \beta T_i + \varepsilon_i$, a simplified version of equation 6.1, and knowing that by assumption $\text{cov}(Z, \varepsilon) = 0$, one can also write the treatment effect under IV (β) as $\text{cov}(Y, Z)/\text{cov}(T, Z)$:

$$\text{cov}(Y_i, Z_i) = \text{cov}[(\beta T_i + \varepsilon_i), Z_i] = \beta \text{cov}(T_i, Z_i) \tag{6.4}$$

$$\Rightarrow \frac{\text{cov}(Y_i, Z_i)}{\text{cov}(T_i, Z_i)} = \beta. \tag{6.5}$$

This derivation becomes important when examining the effects of instrument quality on the estimated program impact under IV (see the next section 6.3).

Through instrumenting, therefore, T is cleaned of its correlation with the error term. If the assumptions $\text{cov}(T, Z) \neq 0$ and $\text{cov}(Z, \varepsilon) = 0$ hold, then IV consistently identifies the mean impact of the program attributable to the instrument. Specifically, it can be shown that $\hat{\beta}_{IV} = \beta + \text{cov}(Z, \varepsilon)/\text{cov}(Z, T)$. This idea is also discussed further in the next section.

Although detailed information on program implementation and participation can directly reveal the presence of selection bias, endogeneity of treatment can also be assessed using the Wu-Hausman test, which in the following example uses a regression-based method:

1. First, regress T on Z and the other exogenous covariates X, and obtain the residuals $\hat{u}_i$. These residuals reflect all unobserved heterogeneity affecting treatment not captured by the instruments and exogenous variables in the model.
2. Regress Y on X, Z, and $\hat{u}_i$. If the coefficient on $\hat{u}_i$ is statistically different from zero, unobserved characteristics jointly affecting the treatment T and outcomes Y are significant, and the null that T is exogenous is rejected.

The IV model has some variations. For example, one could rewrite the instrument equation as a nonlinear binary response model (such as a probit or logit) and use the predicted propensity score as the IV for program placement. Also, if panel data exist,

IV can be combined with a panel fixed-effects approach as follows (see Semykina and Wooldridge 2005):

$$Y_{it} = \delta Q_{it} + \eta_i + v_{it}, t = 1,\ldots,T, \tag{6.6}$$

In equation 6.6, η_i is the unobserved fixed effect (discussed in chapter 5) that may be correlated with participation in the program, v_{it} represents a time-varying idiosyncratic error, and Q_{it} is a vector of covariates that includes exogenous variables X as well as the program T. In this specification, therefore, correlation between η_i and the treatment variable in Q_{it} is accounted for through the fixed-effects or differencing approach, and instruments Z_{it} are introduced to allow for correlation between some of the regressors in Q_{it} (such as T) and v_{it}. The idea here would be to find instruments correlated with program uptake (but not outcomes) over time. The remaining assumptions and interpretation of the estimate are similar.

Concerns with IVs

Concerns with IVs include weak instruments and correlation with unobserved characteristics.

Implications of Weak Instruments on Estimates

A drawback of the IV approach is the potential difficulty in finding a good instrument. When the instrument is correlated with the unobserved characteristics affecting the outcome (that is, $cov(Z, \varepsilon) \neq 0$), the estimates of the program effect will be biased. Furthermore, if the instrument only weakly correlates with the treatment variable T, the standard error of the IV estimate is likely to increase because the predicted impact on the outcome will be measured less precisely. Consistency of the IV estimate (that is, asymptotic bias) is also likely to be large when Z and T are weakly correlated, even if the correlation between Z and ε is low. This problem can violate the assumption underlying IV estimation as seen here. As mentioned in the previous section, asymptotically, $\beta_{IV} = \beta + cov(Z, \varepsilon)/cov(Z, T)$; thus, the lower $cov(Z, T)$, the greater the asymptotic bias of $\hat{\beta}$ away from the true β.

Testing for Weak Instruments

One cannot test for whether a specific instrument satisfies the exclusion restriction; as mentioned earlier, justifications can be made only through direct evidence of how the program and participation evolved. With multiple instruments, however, quantitative tests (also known as *tests of overidentifying restrictions*) exist. They involve the following steps:

1. Estimate the structural equation by 2SLS, and obtain the residuals $\hat{\varepsilon}_i$.
2. Regress $\hat{\varepsilon}_i$ (which embody all heterogeneity not explained by the instruments Z and other exogenous variables X) on X and Z. Obtain the R^2.

3. Use the null hypothesis that all the instrumental variables are uncorrelated with the residuals, $nR^2 \sim \chi_q^2$, where q is the number of instrumental variables from outside the model minus the total number of endogenous explanatory variables. If nR^2 is statistically greater than the critical value at a certain significance level (say, 5 percent) in the χ_q^2 distribution, then the null hypothesis is rejected, and one can conclude that at least one of the instrumental variables is not exogenous.

Local Average Treatment Effects

As mentioned earlier, the IV estimate of the program effect is ultimately an intent-to-treat impact, where the measured effect of the program will apply to only a subset of participants. Imperfect targeting is one case where only intent-to-treat impacts can be measured; the researcher then has to search for an exogenous indicator of participation that can account for unobserved heterogeneity. A good instrument in this case would satisfy the exclusion restriction and be well correlated with participation. However, the instrument would very unlikely be perfectly correlated with participation, so only a subset of participants would be picked up by the instrument and resulting IV effect. The same holds where an instrument is needed to correct for errors in measuring participation; similar ITT impacts relating to a subset of participants would result. The resulting IV program effect would therefore apply only to the subset of participants whose behavior would be affected by the instrument.

One difficulty arises with the standard IV estimate if individuals know more about their expected gains from the program than the evaluator or researcher does. That is, individuals are anticipating gains from the program that the evaluator or researcher cannot observe. Consequently, unobserved selection occurs in participation, because those individuals that end up benefiting more from the program, given their characteristics X, may also be more likely to participate. Because the instrument Z affects participation, unobserved characteristics driving participation will also correlate with Z, and the IV estimate will be biased.

Heckman (1997), for example, brings up a study by Angrist (1990) that examines the effect of military service on earnings. As an instrument for joining the military, Angrist uses the 1969 U.S. military draft lottery, which randomly assigned priority numbers to individuals with different dates of birth. A higher number meant the person was less likely to be drafted. However, even if a person received a high number, if he nevertheless enrolled in military service, one could assume that his unobserved anticipated gains from military service were also likely to be higher. Thus, the instrument causes systematic changes in participation rates that relate to unobserved anticipated gains from the program. This change creates bias in comparing participants and nonparticipants.

Imbens and Angrist (1994) address this problem by introducing the local average treatment effect. In the special case where heterogeneity exists in individuals' response to the program, IV methods consistently estimate the average effect of the program only for those whose participation changes because of changes in instrument Z. Specifically, the LATE estimates the treatment effect only for those who decide to participate because of a change in Z (see, for example, Imbens and Angrist 1994). In the context of schooling, for example, if outcome Y is a test score, T is an indicator for whether a student is in a Catholic high school, and instrument Z is an indicator for whether the student is Catholic, then the LATE is the mean effect on test scores for students who choose to go to a Catholic high school because they are Catholic (see Wooldridge 2001). The LATE avoids the problem of unobserved forecasting of program gains by limiting the analysis to individuals whose behavior is changed by local changes in Z in a way unrelated to potential outcomes. In the previous military service example, for instance, those with high anticipated gains from participating are unlikely to be among the shifters. Note that, as a result, the LATE does not measure the treatment effect for individuals whose behavior is not changed by the instrument.

One of the underlying assumptions for the LATE is monotonicity, or that an increase in Z from $Z = z$ to $Z = z'$ leads some to participate but no one to drop out of the program. Participation T in this case depends on certain values of the instruments Z (say, $Z = z$ versus $Z = z'$), such that $P(T = 1|Z = z)$ is the probability of participating when $Z = z$, and $P(T = 1|Z = z')$ is the probability of participating when $Z = z'$.[2] Note that, recalling chapter 4, $P(T = 1|Z = z)$ and $P(T = 1|Z = z')$ can also be interpreted as the propensity scores for participation based on instruments Z—that is, $P(z)$ and $P(z')$, respectively.

The LATE, $\beta_{IV, LATE}$, can then be written as

$$\beta_{IV, LATE} = \frac{E(Y|P(Z) = P(z)) - E(Y|P(Z) = P(z'))}{P(z) - P(z')}. \tag{6.7}$$

The denominator in equation 6.7 is the difference in the probability of participating in the program (probability of $T = 1$) under the different values of the instrument, $Z = z$ and $Z = z'$.

Using equation 6.7, one can estimate the LATE using linear IV methods. In the first stage, program participation T is estimated as a function of the instruments Z to obtain the propensity score, $\hat{P}(Z) = \hat{P}(T = 1|Z)$. Second, a linear regression can be estimated of the outcome $Y_i = [T_i \cdot Y_i(1) + (1 - T_i) \cdot Y_i(0)]$ on $\hat{P}(Z)$. The interpretation of the estimated program effect $\hat{\beta}_{IV}$ is the average change in outcomes Y from a change in the estimated propensity score of participating $\hat{P}(Z)$, holding other observed covariates X fixed.

Recent Approaches: Marginal Treatment Effect

The marginal treatment effect (MTE), introduced in chapter 3, is the limit form of the LATE and has been discussed recently (see Heckman and Vytlacil 2005; Todd 2007) as a method for estimating treatment effects when conditional exogeneity does not hold. As mentioned earlier, the MTE is the average gain in outcomes for participants near the threshold or at the margin of participating, given a set of observed characteristics and conditioning on a set of unobserved characteristics in the participation equation. Following Heckman and Vytlacil (2000), the MTE can be written as

$$\text{MTE} = E(Y_i(1) - Y_i(0)|X_i = x, U_i = u). \tag{6.8}$$

In equation 6.8, $Y_i(1)$ is the outcome for those under treatment, $Y_i(0)$ is the outcome for those not receiving treatment, $X_i = x$ are observed characteristics for individual i, and $U_i = u$, $U_i \in (0,1)$ are unobserved characteristics for individual i that also determine participation. Looking at the effect of U_i on participation T_i (recall from earlier chapters that $T_i = 1$ for participants and $T_i = 0$ for nonparticipants), Heckman and Vytlacil (2000) assume that T_i is generated by a latent variable T_i^*:[3]

$$T_i^* = \mu_T(Z_i) - U_i$$
$$T_i = 1 \text{ if } T_i^* > 0, \ T_i = 0 \text{ if } T_i^* \leq 0, \tag{6.9}$$

where Z_i are observed instruments affecting participation and $\mu_T(Z_i)$ is a function determining potential outcomes Y from Z that are conditional on participation. Individuals with unobserved characteristics u close to zero, therefore, are the most likely to participate in the program (T_i closer to 1), and individuals with u close to one are the least likely to participate. The MTE for individuals with $U_i = u$ close to zero therefore reflects the average treatment effect (ATE) for individuals most inclined to participate, and the MTE for individuals with $U_i = u$ close to one represents the ATE for individuals least likely to participate.

Why is the MTE helpful in understanding treatment effects? Also, if both the MTE and the LATE examine the varying impact of unobserved characteristics on participation, what is the difference between them? Both the MTE and the LATE allow for individuals to anticipate gains in Y on the basis of unobserved characteristics. However, just as the LATE is a finer version of the treatment effect on the treated (TOT) (Heckman 1997), the MTE is the limit form of the LATE and defines the treatment effect much more precisely as the LATE for an infinitesimal change in Z (Blundell and Dias 2008; Heckman and Vytlacil 2000).

A useful property of the MTE (see Heckman and Vytlacil 2000, 2005) is that the ATE, TOT, and LATE can all be obtained by integrating under different regions of the MTE. The ATE, which, as discussed in chapter 3, is the average effect for the entire population (that is, the effect of the program for a person randomly drawn from the population), can be obtained by integrating the MTE over the entire support ($u = 0$ to $u = 1$).

The TOT, which is the average treatment effect for those who choose to participate, can be obtained by integrating MTE from $u = 0$ to $u = P(z)$. As described earlier, $P(z)$

is the propensity score, or probability, of participating when the instrument $Z = z$. Thus, the TOT is the treatment effect for individuals whose unobserved characteristics make them most likely to participate in the program.

Finally, if one assumes (as previously) that the instrument Z can take values $Z = z'$ and $Z = z$, and one also assumes that $P(z') < P(z)$, then LATE integrates MTE from $u = P(z')$ to $u = P(z)$. This outcome occurs because, when $P(z') < P(z)$, some individuals who would not have participated when $Z = z'$ will participate when $Z = z$, but no individual who was participating at $Z = z'$ will drop out of the program when $Z = z$.

How, then, to estimate the MTE? Heckman and Vytlacil (2000) propose a two-stage local instrumental variable estimator:

$$\beta_{\text{LIV, MTE}} = \lim_{P(z') \to P(z)} \frac{E(Y|P(Z) = P(z)) - E(Y|P(Z) = P(z'))}{P(z) - P(z')}. \qquad (6.10)$$

The approach is similar to the estimation of the LATE previously discussed. In the first stage, program participation is still estimated as a function of the instruments Z to obtain the propensity score $\hat{P}(Z)$. In the second stage, however, a nonparametric local linear regression can be estimated of the outcome $Y_i = [T_i \cdot Y_i(1) + (1 - T_i) \cdot Y_i(0)]$ on $\hat{P}(Z)$. Evaluating this function at different values of the propensity score yields the MTE function. Local IV is differevnt from the IV approach used to estimate the LATE, in the sense that local IV estimates the average change in Y around a local neighborhood of $P(Z)$, whereas the LATE is estimated globally over the support (this difference can be seen as well by comparing equations 6.7 and 6.10).

Approaches to estimating the MTE are new and evolving. Moffitt (2008) also proposes a nonparametric method for estimating the MTE. Instead of a two-step procedure where participation is first instrumented and then the average change Y is calculated on the basis of predicted participation, Moffitt estimates the outcome and participation equations jointly through nonlinear least squares. This method relaxes some of the assumptions embedded in the IV and latent linear index models. Very few applications of MTE exist thus far, however, particularly in developing countries.

Sources of IVs

Understanding the factors underlying program targeting and take-up can help in finding appropriate instruments. For example, collecting detailed information on how the program was targeted and implemented can reveal sources of exogenous variation in the program's evolution. This information can be collected for both the baseline and the follow-up quantitative surveys together with qualitative information (stemming from interviews with program officials, for example).

Randomization as a Source of IVs

As discussed in chapter 3, randomization may not perfectly identify participants. Even when randomization takes place at an aggregate (say, regional) level, selection bias may persist in individual take-up. Randomization also does not ensure that targeted subjects will all participate. Nevertheless, if program targeting under this scheme is highly correlated with participation, randomized assignment (which by definition satisfies the exclusion restriction) can still act as an IV. Box 3.2 in chapter 3 describes the use of randomization, even when intention to treat is different from actual take-up of the program.

Nonexperimental Instruments Used in Prior Evaluations: Case Studies

Within a nonrandomized setting, common sources of instruments have included geographic variation, correlation of the program with other policies, and exogenous shocks affecting program placement. Box 6.1 describes how, in the context of the Food for Education program in Bangladesh, geography can be used as a source of instruments. Box 6.2 presents a study from Ghana of improved child health on schooling outcomes. It uses different approaches to address the endogeneity of estimates, including an IV reflecting geographic distance to medical facilities.

Instruments might also be determined from program design, such as eligibility rules or the nature of treatment. Boxes 6.3 and 6.4 discuss examples from Bangladesh and Pakistan, and chapter 7 on discontinuity designs discusses this concept further.

BOX 6.1   **Case Study: Using Geography of Program Placement as an Instrument in Bangladesh**

In a study on the Food for Education program in Bangladesh, Ravallion and Wodon (2000) examined the claim that child labor displaces schooling and so perpetuates poverty in the longer term. The Food for Education program, in which 2.2 million children were participating in 1995 and 1996, involved targeted subsidies to households to enroll their children in school and was used in the study as the source of a change in the price of schooling in the study's model of schooling and child labor. To address the endogeneity of program placement at the individual level, Ravallion and Wodon used prior program placement at the village level as the IV.

To counter the concern that village placement correlated with geographic factors that might also affect outcomes, Ravallion and Wodon (2000) used administrative assignment rules to construct exogeneity tests that supported their identification strategy. Using a sample of about 2,400 boys and 2,300 girls from the rural sample of the 1995–96 Bangladesh Household Expenditure Survey, the study indicated that the subsidy increased schooling (at the mean of the sample, an extra 100 kilograms of rice increased the probability of going to school by 0.17 for a boy and by 0.16 for a girl) by far more than it reduced child labor. Substitution effects appear to have helped protect current incomes from the higher school attendance induced by the subsidy.

BOX 6.2   **Case Study: Different Approaches and IVs in Examining the Effects of Child Health on Schooling in Ghana**

Glewwe and Jacoby (1995) examined the effects of child health and nutrition on education outcomes in Ghana, including age of enrollment and years of completed schooling. They used cross-sectional data on about 1,760 children 6 to 15 years of age, from 1988 to 1989. In the process, they showed what the options and challenges are for using cross-sections to identify effects.

Given the cross-section data, unobserved characteristics of parents (such as preferences) may correlate across both child health and education. One of the approaches in the study by Glewwe and Jacoby (1995) was to seek instruments that affect child health characteristics (such as height-for-age anthropometric outcomes) but are not correlated with unobserved family characteristics affecting child education. They proposed as instruments for child health (a) distance to the closest medical facility and (b) maternal height. Both justifiably correlate with child health, but Glewwe and Jacoby also point out that mother's height could affect her labor productivity and, hence, household income and the resulting time she has to spend on her children's education. Distance to nearby medical facilities could also correlate with other community characteristics, such as presence of schools. Both of these caveats weaken the assumption that $cov(Z, \varepsilon) = 0$. From the IV estimates, as well as alternate estimates specifying fixed effects for families, Glewwe and Jacoby found strong negative effects of child health on delayed enrollment but no statistically significant effect on completed years of schooling.

BOX 6.3   **Case Study: A Cross-Section and Panel Data Analysis Using Eligibility Rules for Microfinance Participation in Bangladesh**

Pitt and Khandker (1998) studied the impact of microfinance programs in Bangladesh to assess the impact of participation by men versus women on per capita expenditure, schooling enrollment of children, and other household outcomes. They used a quasi-experimental data set from 1991 to 1992 of about 1,800 households across a random sample of 29 thanas (about 1,540 households from 24 thanas targeted by credit initiatives, and the remainder from 5 nontargeted thanas). Of the targeted households, about 60 percent were participating in microcredit programs.

As the source of identification, Pitt and Khandker (1998) relied on exogenous eligibility conditions based on household landholding (specifically, an eligibility cutoff of one-half acre of land owned) as a way of identifying program effects. The fact that men could participate only in men's groups and women only in women's groups added another constraint on which impacts could be identified. Village fixed effects (for example, to account for why some villages have just men-only groups and other villages have just female-only groups) were also included in the estimations. Pitt and Khandker found that when women are the program participants, program credit has a larger impact on household outcomes, including an increase in annual household expenditure of Tk 18, compared with Tk 11 for men.

Some of the conditions, however, are restrictive and might not be reliable (for example, the nonenforceability of the landholding criterion for program participation). An impact assessment can be carried out using a follow-up survey to test the sensitivity of the findings. As discussed at the beginning of this chapter, Khandker (2006) used the 1998–99 follow-up survey to the 1991–92

(Box continues on the following page.)

BOX 6.3   Case Study: A Cross-Section and Panel Data Analysis Using Eligibility Rules for Microfinance Participation in Bangladesh (continued)

survey to assess the sensitivity of the earlier findings on the poverty effects of microfinance in rural Bangladesh. The panel data analysis helps to estimate the effects on poverty using an alternative estimation technique and also helps to estimate the impacts of past and current borrowing, assuming that gains from borrowing, such as consumption gains, vary over time. The instrument is whether the household qualifies to participate in the program on the basis of the landholding criteria. The instrumented decision to participate is then interacted with household-level exogenous variables and village fixed effects.

Khandker's (2006) follow-up study found that the average returns to cumulative borrowing for female members of microfinance programs are as much as 21 percent in 1998–99, up from 18 percent in 1991–92. However, the impact on poverty reduction among program participants was lower in 1998–99 (2 percentage points) than in 1991–92 (5 percentage points). This result is due to diminishing returns to additional borrowing, so that despite the increase in the stock of borrowing by female members, the resulting increases in consumption were not large enough to reduce poverty as expected.

BOX 6.4   Case Study: Using Policy Design as Instruments to Study Private Schooling in Pakistan

As another example, Andrabi, Das, and Khwaja (2006) examined the effect of private schooling expansion in Pakistan during the 1990s on primary school enrollment. The growth in private schools exhibited variation that the study exploited to determine causal impacts. Specifically, using data from a sample of about 18,000 villages in rural Punjab province (spanning data from national censuses of private schools, village-level socioeconomic characteristics from 1981 and 2001, and administrative data on the location and date of public schools), Andrabi, Das, and Khwaja found that private schools were much more likely to set up in villages where public girls' secondary schools (GSS) had already been established.

To obtain an identifying instrument for private school expansion, Andrabi, Das, and Khwaja (2006) therefore exploited official eligibility rules for placement of GSS across villages. Specifically, villages with larger population were given preference for construction of GSS, as long as no other GSS were located within a 10-kilometer radius. The study also exploited an administrative unit called a *Patwar Circle* (PC), which was four or five contiguous villages roughly spanning a 10-kilometer radius. From historical records, Andrabi, Das, and Khwaja determined that PCs were primarily defined for revenue purposes. The IV estimate would be unbiased if (a) private school placement did not follow the same discontinuous relationship with local population and (b) unobserved characteristics of PCs with the highest population rank were also not correlated with private school expansion as well as educational market outcomes. If the latter were not true, for example, then $cov(Z, \varepsilon) \neq 0$.

Andrabi, Das, and Khwaja (2006) found that a public girls' secondary school increased the likelihood of a private school in the village by 35 percent. However, they found little or no relationship between the placement of these private schools and preexisting coeducational primary

> **BOX 6.4**   **Case Study: Using Policy Design as Instruments to Study Private Schooling in Pakistan (continued)**
>
> schools or secondary schools for boys. Robustness checks using propensity score matching on the baseline data compared the change in private schools and GSS for matching villages; the existence of GSS raised the probability that private schools would be introduced by 11 to 14 percent. Regarding the program effect on outcomes, using data from about 7,000 villages, they found that preexisting public GSS roughly doubled the supply of local skilled women. However, with few earning opportunities for women, overall wages for women fell by about 18 percent, as did teaching costs for private schools.

Questions

1. Which of the following statement(s) is (are) true about the instrumental variable method?
   A. IV is used for cross-sectional data only.
   B. IV can control for unobserved characteristics that may affect outcomes and vary over time.
   C. Finding the right instrument(s) is critical to unbiased IV implementation.
   (a) A and B
   (b) B and C
   (c) A and C
   (d) C only

2. IV controls for biases (endogeneity) that arise from which of the following situations?
   A. Nonrandom program placement
   B. Nonrandom participation of households
   C. Nonrandom movement of nonparticipants between project and control areas
   (a) A and B
   (b) B and C
   (c) A and C
   (d) C only

3. A good instrument in IV implementation has following properties:
   A. It affects program participation directly.
   B. It does not affect outcome variables directly but only through program participation.
   C. It affects control (X) variables directly.
   (a) A and B
   (b) B and C
   (c) A and C
   (d) C only

4. Which of the following names a test that determines whether an IV model or OLS is better?
   A. *t*-test
   B. *Z*-test
   C. Endogeneity test
      (a) A and B
      (b) B and C
      (c) A and C
      (d) C only

5. Which method provides local average treatment effect under certain conditions?
   A. PSM
   B. IV
   C. PSM and DD
      (a) A and B
      (b) B and C
      (c) A and C
      (d) B only

Notes

1. These data sets are also used in the Stata exercises in part 2 of the handbook.
2. As discussed earlier, T is the treatment variable equal to 1 for participants and equal to 0 for non-participants. Outcomes Y and participation T are also functions of other observed covariates X, which have been suppressed for simplicity in equation 6.7.
3. This equation is also known as a linear latent index model (see Heckman and Hotz 1989; Heckman and Robb 1985; Imbens and Angrist 1994).

References

Andrabi, Tahir, Jishnu Das, and Asim Ijaz Khwaja. 2006. "Students Today, Teachers Tomorrow? Identifying Constraints on the Provision of Education." Harvard University, Cambridge, MA.

Angrist, Joshua. 1990. "Lifetime Earnings and the Vietnam Era Draft Lottery: Evidence from Social Security Administration Records." *American Economic Review* 80 (3): 313–35.

Blundell, Richard, and Monica Costa Dias. 2008. "Alternative Approaches to Evaluation in Empirical Microeconomics." CeMMAP Working Paper 26/08, Centre for Microdata Methods and Practice, Institute for Fiscal Studies, London.

Glewwe, Paul, and Hanan G. Jacoby. 1995. "An Economic Analysis of Delayed Primary School Enrollment in a Low Income Country: The Role of Early Childhood Nutrition." *Review of Economic Statistics* 77 (1): 156–69.

Heckman, James J. 1997. "Instrumental Variables: A Study of Implicit Behavioral Assumptions Used in Making Program Evaluations." *Journal of Human Resources* 32 (3): 441–62.

Heckman, James J., and V. Joseph Hotz. 1989. "Choosing among Alternative Nonexperimental Methods for Estimating the Impact of Social Programs: The Case of Manpower Training." *Journal of the American Statistical Association* 84 (408): 862–74.

Heckman, James J., and Richard Robb. 1985. "Alternative Methods for Estimating the Impact of Interventions." In *Longitudinal Analysis of Labor Market Data*, ed. James Heckman and Burton Singer, 156–245. New York: Cambridge University Press.

Heckman, James J., and Edward J. Vytlacil. 2000. "Causal Parameters, Structural Equations, Treatment Effects, and Randomized Evaluations of Social Programs." University of Chicago, Chicago, IL.

———. 2005. "Structural Equations, Treatment Effects, and Econometric Policy Evaluation." *Econometrica* 73 (3): 669–738.

Imbens, Guido, and Joshua Angrist. 1994. "Identification and Estimation of Local Average Treatment Effects." *Econometrica* 62 (2): 467–76.

Khandker, Shahidur R. 2006. "Microfinance and Poverty: Evidence Using Panel Data from Bangladesh." *World Bank Economic Review* 19 (2): 263–86.

Moffitt, Robert. 2008. "Estimating Marginal Treatment Effects in Heterogeneous Populations." Economic Working Paper Archive 539, Johns Hopkins University, Baltimore, MD. http://www.econ.jhu.edu/people/moffitt/welfls0_v4b.pdf.

Morduch, Jonathan. 1998. "Does Microfinance Really Help the Poor? New Evidence on Flagship Programs in Bangladesh." Princeton University, Princeton, NJ.

Pitt, Mark, and Shahidur Khandker. 1998. "The Impact of Group-Based Credit Programs on Poor Households in Bangladesh: Does the Gender of Participants Matter?" *Journal of Political Economy* 106 (5): 958–98.

Ravallion, Martin, and Quentin Wodon. 2000. "Does Child Labour Displace Schooling? Evidence on Behavioural Responses to an Enrollment Subsidy." *Economic Journal* 110 (462): 158–75.

Semykina, Anastasia, and Jeffrey M. Wooldridge. 2005. "Estimating Panel Data Models in the Presence of Endogeneity and Selection: Theory and Application." Working Paper, Michigan State University, East Lansing, MI.

Todd, Petra. 2007. "Evaluating Social Programs with Endogenous Program Placement and Selection of the Treated." In *Handbook of Development Economics*, vol. 4, ed. T. Paul Schultz and John Strauss, 3847–94. Amsterdam: North-Holland.

Wooldridge, Jeffrey. 2001. *Econometric Analysis of Cross Section and Panel Data*. Cambridge, MA: MIT Press.

7. Regression Discontinuity and Pipeline Methods

Summary

In a nonexperimental setting, program eligibility rules can sometimes be used as instruments for exogenously identifying participants and nonparticipants. To establish comparability, one can use participants and nonparticipants within a certain neighborhood of the eligibility threshold as the relevant sample for estimating the treatment impact. Known as *regression discontinuity* (RD), this method allows observed as well as unobserved heterogeneity to be accounted for. Although the cutoff or eligibility threshold can be defined nonparametrically, the cutoff has in practice traditionally been defined through an instrument.

Concerns with the RD approach include the possibility that eligibility rules will not be adhered to consistently, as well as the potential for eligibility rules to change over time. Robustness checks can be conducted to examine the validity of the discontinuity design, including sudden changes in other control variables at the cutoff point. Examining the pattern in the variable determining eligibility can also be useful—whether, for example, the average outcome exhibits jumps at values of the variable other than the eligibility cutoff—as well as any discontinuities in the conditional density of this variable.

Pipeline comparisons exploit variation in the timing of program implementation, using as a comparison group eligible participants who have not yet received the program. One additional empirical strategy considered by program evaluators is to exploit data on program expansion along a given route (for example, an infrastructure project such as water, transport, or communication networks) to compare outcomes for eligible participants at different sides of the project boundary as the program is phased in. This method involves a combination of pipeline and RD approaches that could yield interesting comparisons over time.

Learning Objectives

After completing this chapter, the reader will be able to discuss

- RD as a method that accounts for potential selection or participation on observed and unobserved characteristics
- Robustness checks to ensure that the discontinuity design and eligibility cutoffs are valid

- The identification strategy of pipeline comparisons
- Ways to combine the RD approach and pipeline method

Introduction

Discontinuities and delays in program implementation, based on eligibility criteria or other exogenous factors, can be very useful in nonexperimental program evaluation. People above and below the threshold, assuming they are similar in observed characteristics, can be distinguished in terms of outcomes. However, the samples across which to compare would have to be sufficiently close to the eligibility cutoff to ensure comparability. Furthermore, unobserved heterogeneity may be a factor if people within the eligible targeting range exhibit variation in actual take-up of the program, leading to selection bias. In that case, eligible and noneligible samples close to the eligibility cutoff would be taken to compare the average program effect.

Discontinuity approaches are therefore similar to instrumental variable (IV) methods because they introduce an exogenous variable that is highly correlated with participation, albeit not akin to participation. For example, Grameen Bank's microcredit is targeted to households with landholdings of less than half an acre; pension programs are targeted to populations above a certain age; and scholarships are targeted to students with high scores on standardized tests. By looking at a narrow band of units that are below and above the cutoff point and comparing their outcomes, one can judge the program's impact because the households just below and above the threshold are likely to be very similar to each other.

Regression Discontinuity in Theory

To model the effect of a particular program on individual outcomes y_i through an RD approach, one needs a variable S_i that determines program eligibility (such as age, asset holdings, or the like) with an eligibility cutoff of s^*. The estimating equation is $y_i = \beta S_i + \varepsilon_i$, where individuals with $s_i \leq s^*$, for example, receive the program, and individuals with $s_i > s^*$ are not eligible to participate. Individuals in a narrow band above and below s^* need to be "comparable" in that they would be expected to achieve similar outcomes prior to program intervention. Figure 7.1 gives an example of this property, where individuals below s^* are considered poor, and those above the threshold are considered nonpoor.

If one assumes that limits exist on either side of the threshold s^*, the impact estimator for an arbitrarily small $\varepsilon > 0$ around the threshold would be the following:

$$E[y_i|s^* - \varepsilon] - E[y_i|s^* + \varepsilon] = E[\beta S_i|s^* - \varepsilon] - E[\beta S_i s^* + \varepsilon]. \tag{7.1}$$

Taking the limit of both sides of equation 7.1 as $\varepsilon \to 0$ would identify β as the ratio of the difference in outcomes of individuals just above and below the threshold, weighted by the difference in their realizations of S_i:

Figure 7.1 Outcomes before Program Intervention

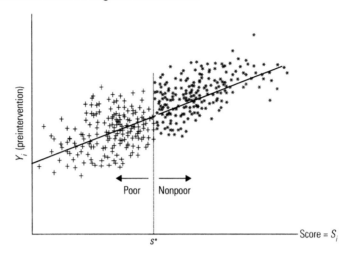

Source: Authors' representation.

$$\lim_{\varepsilon \to 0} E[y_i | s^* - \varepsilon] - \lim_{\varepsilon \to 0} E[y_i | s^* + \varepsilon] = y^- - y^+ = \beta(S^- - S^+)$$

$$\Rightarrow \beta = \frac{y^- - y^+}{S^- - S^+}$$

(7.2)

According to the setup in figure 7.1, outcomes after program intervention as measured by the discontinuity model are reflected in figure 7.2.

Because in practice the determination or enforcement of eligibility may not be "sharp" (as in a randomized experiment), s can be replaced with a probability of participating $P(S) = E(T|S)$, where $T = 1$ if treatment is received and $T = 0$ otherwise (see Hahn, Todd, and van der Klaauw 2001; Ravallion 2008). In this case, the discontinuity is stochastic or "fuzzy," and instead of measuring differences in outcomes above and below s^*, the impact estimator would measure the difference around a neighborhood of s^*. This result might occur when eligibility rules are not strictly adhered to or when certain geographic areas are targeted but boundaries are not well defined and mobility is common. If the eligibility threshold is exogenously determined by the program and highly correlated with treatment, one might also use s^* as an IV for participation.

Steps in Applying the RD Approach

Standard nonparametric regression can be used to estimate the treatment effect in either the sharp or the fuzzy regression discontinuity setup. For a sharp discontinuity design, the treatment effect can be estimated by a simple comparison of the mean

Figure 7.2   Outcomes after Program Intervention

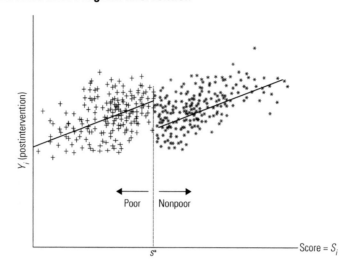

Source: Authors' representation.

outcomes of individuals to the left and the right of the threshold. Specifically, local linear regressions on the outcome y, given a set of covariates x, should be run for people on both sides of the threshold, to estimate the difference $y^- - y^+$:

$$y^- - y^+ = \lim_{s_i \uparrow s*} E(y_i|s_i = s*) - \lim_{s_i \downarrow s*} E(y_i|s_i = s*). \tag{7.3}$$

As an example, y^- and y^+ can be specified through kernel estimates:

$$y^- = \frac{\sum_{i=1}^{n} y_i^* \alpha_i^* K(u_i)}{\sum_{i=1}^{n} \alpha_i^* K(u_i)}$$

$$y^+ = \frac{\sum_{i=1}^{n} y_i^* (1-\alpha_i)^* K(u_i)}{\sum_{i=1}^{n} (1-\alpha_i)^* K(u_i)} \, . \tag{7.4}$$

For a fuzzy discontinuity design, a two-step process is needed. Local linear regression can be applied on the outcome for people on both sides of the threshold to determine the magnitude of the difference (or discontinuity) for the outcome. Similarly, local linear regression can be applied to the treatment indicator to arrive at a difference or discontinuity for the treatment indicator. The ratio of the outcome discontinuity to the treatment discontinuity is the treatment effect for a fuzzy discontinuity design.

Although impacts in a neighborhood of the cutoff point are nonparametrically identified for discontinuity designs, the applied literature has more often used an alternative parametric method in which the discontinuity in the eligibility criterion is used as an IV for program placement. Box 7.1 gives an example of this method, using data from a pension program in South Africa.

Graphing the predicted treatment effect also provides a useful contrast across eligible and noneligible populations, as well as for those in a narrow band around the threshold. Plotting the density of the variable determining eligibility around the threshold can also help show whether the RD design is valid (that is, that members of the noneligible sample do not ultimately become participants, which could happen, for example, if they were aware of the threshold and adjusted their reported value of the eligibility variable to qualify). Plotting the average values of the covariates around the threshold also can provide an indication of specification problems, with either a sharp discontinuity or a fuzzy discontinuity approach.

Variations of RD

Numerous variations of RD designs are possible, including combinations with randomized tie-breaking experiments around the threshold to create stronger inferences. Depending on the nature of the eligibility rule (that is, whether it is a function of a variable changing over time or from a one-time intervention), panel or cross-section data can be used in RD analysis.

BOX 7.1 **Case Study: Exploiting Eligibility Rules in Discontinuity Design in South Africa**

In a study from South Africa, Duflo (2003) examined what the impact of newly expanded old-age pensions to the black population in the early 1990s was on child height and weight and whether the gender of the recipient had a systematic effect on these impacts. The expanded pension program was initially means tested, became universal in the 1990s, and by 1993 was operational in all areas.

The study used the fact that men were eligible for pensions at age 65, whereas women were eligible at age 60, to compare the stature of children in households with members slightly above and below the pension age. Using a sample of children from 9,000 randomly selected households of different areas and races, Duflo (2003) regressed anthropometric outcomes on a number of covariates, including dummies for whether a man, a woman, or both in the household were receiving a pension. The eligible age requirements for men and women were therefore used as instruments for whether they received pensions. Duflo ultimately found that pensions received by women had a significant positive effect on the anthropometric status of girls (raising weight for height by 1.19 standard deviations and height for age by 1.19 standard deviations) but no significant effect for boys. Pensions received by men had no such effects.

A tie-breaker randomization, for example, involves a situation where an overlap occurs between treatment and control groups across the variable determining eligibility for the program. In this situation, treatment would be randomly assigned to observations in the area of overlap. Figure 7.3 describes this situation.

Another variant is where more than one cutoff point can be exploited to compare treatment effects. The corresponding regression to estimate the program impact, therefore, would include two treatment groups—one corresponding to each discontinuity. Figure 7.4 describes this context.

Advantages and Disadvantages of the RD Approach

The advantages of the RD method are (a) that it yields an unbiased estimate of treatment effect at the discontinuity, (b) that it can many times take advantage of a known rule for assigning the benefit that is common in the designs of social policy, and (c) that a group of eligible households or individuals need not be excluded from treatment. However, the concerns with RD are (a) that it produces local average treatment effects that are not always generalizable; (b) that the effect is estimated at the discontinuity, so, generally, fewer observations exist than in a randomized experiment with the same sample size; and (c) that the specification can be sensitive to functional form, including nonlinear relationships and interactions.

One concern with the RD method is behavioral (Ravallion 2008). Program officials may not always know precisely the eligibility criteria; hence, behavioral responses to the program intervention may be confused with actual targeting rules. Data collected prior

Figure 7.3 Using a Tie-Breaking Experiment

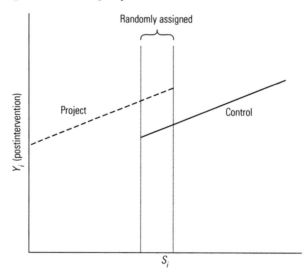

Source: Authors' representation.

Figure 7.4   Multiple Cutoff Points

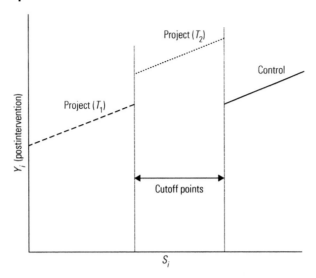

Source: Authors' representation.

to program intervention, in the form of a baseline, for example, may help to clarify program design and corresponding uptake.

Another concern is that the exercise focuses only on individuals or units closely situated around the threshold s^*. Whether this group is materially interesting for the evaluator needs to be addressed; if program officials are interested, for example, in identifying the effects of a program around a geographic border and in determining whether the program should be expanded across borders, the limited sample may not be as great a concern. A similar example can be constructed about a poverty alleviation program concerned with households whose status hovers near the poverty line.

If the eligibility rules are not adhered to or change over time, the validity of the discontinuity approach also needs to be examined more carefully. Robustness checks can be conducted to examine the validity of the discontinuity design, including sudden changes in other control variables at the cutoff point. Examining the pattern in the variable determining eligibility can also be useful—whether, for example, the average outcome exhibits jumps at values of the variable other than the eligibility cutoff, as well as any discontinuities in the conditional density of this variable. If the control data exhibit nonlinearities—for example, a steeper slope than the treatment data—then a squared term for the selection variable can be added in the outcome regression equation. Nonlinearities in the functional form can also be addressed by interacting the selection variable with the cutoff point or, perhaps, by using shorter, denser regression lines to capture narrower comparisons.

Pipeline Comparisons

Pipeline comparisons exploit variation in the timing of program implementation, using as a comparison group eligible nontargeted observations that have not yet received the program. Among randomized interventions, PROGRESA (now Oportunidades) provides one example: one-third of the eligible sample among targeted localities could not participate during the first 18 months of the program (box 7.2). Nonexperimental pipeline comparisons, one of which is described in box 7.3, are also used. Although best efforts might be made to phase in the program randomly, selective treatment among applications or behavioral responses by applicants awaiting treatment may, in practice, bias program estimates. A fixed-effects or difference estimator, as suggested in chapter 5, might be one way to account for such unobserved heterogeneity, and as discussed next, observed heterogeneity can also be accounted for through methods such as propensity score matching before making the pipeline comparison (Galasso and Ravallion 2004).

Pipeline comparisons can be used with discontinuity designs if a treatment is allocated on the basis of some exogenous characteristic and potential participants (perhaps for a related program) are awaiting the intervention. Such an approach might be used in the context of a program awaiting budget expansion, for example, where individuals awaiting treatment can be used as a comparison group. In this situation, the same RD approach would be used, but with an added (dynamic) subset of nonparticipants. Another example might be where a local investment, such as a road, is the source of additional market improvements, so that individuals around the road boundary would benefit from the future interventions; variation in potential exposure as a function of distance from the road could be exploited as a source of identification (Ravallion 2008).

BOX 7.2   **Case Study: Returning to PROGRESA (Oportunidades)**

As mentioned in chapter 3, Mexico's PROGRESA (now Oportunidades) involved a randomized phase-in of health and schooling cash transfers across localities. One-third of the randomly targeted eligible communities were delayed entry into the program by 18 months, and the remaining two-thirds received the program at inception. RD approaches have been used in comparing targeted and nontargeted households. Buddelmeyer and Skoufias (2004) used the cutoffs in PROGRESA's eligibility rules to measure impacts and compare the results to those obtained by exploiting the program's randomized design. The authors found that the discontinuity design gave good approximations for almost all outcome indicators.

One additional empirical strategy considered by program evaluators was to exploit data on program expansion along a given route (for example, an infrastructure project such as water, transport, or communication networks) and to compare outcomes for eligible participants at different sides of the project boundary as the program is phased in. This method would involve a combination of pipeline and regression discontinuity approaches that could yield interesting comparisons over time.

| BOX 7.3 | Case Study: Nonexperimental Pipeline Evaluation in Argentina |

Galasso and Ravallion (2004) evaluated a large social protection program in Argentina, Jefes y Jefas, which was created by the government in response to the 2001 financial crisis. The program was a public safety net that provided income to families with dependents for whom their main source of earnings (for example, employment of the household head) was lost in the crisis. Several questions arose during the course of the program, however, about whether eligibility rules had been adhered to or whether the work requirements specified by the program had been enforced. Galasso and Ravallion therefore used a nonexperimental approach to assess the impacts of the program.

Specifically, the program design was exploited to construct a counterfactual group. The program was scaling up rapidly, and comparison units were therefore constructed from a subset of applicants who were not yet receiving the program. Participants were matched to comparison observations on the basis of propensity score matching methods. Panel data collected by the central government before and after the crisis were also used to help remove fixed unobserved heterogeneity, by constructing a matched double-difference estimator.

Galasso and Ravallion (2004) ultimately did find that the program's eligibility criteria were not enforced, with about one-third of those receiving the program not satisfying the eligibility criteria. Furthermore, about 80 percent of adults who were eligible were not receiving the program. Nevertheless, using the matched double-difference approach to remove selection bias stemming from observed and unobserved heterogeneity, the study did find some positive benefits from the program accruing to participants—including an attenuation in the drop in income they would have incurred without participation.

Questions

1. As a source of identification of program effects, the regression discontinuity approach can exploit which of the following?
   A. Errors in program targeting
   B. Program eligibility rules
   C. Exogenous shocks affecting outcomes
   (a) A and B
   (b) B and C
   (c) A and C
   (d) B only

2. In its approach to addressing selection bias, regression discontinuity is similar to which of the following?
   A. Difference-in-difference models
   B. Instrumental variable methods
   C. Pipeline methods
   D. Propensity score matching

    (a) A and B

    (b) B and C

    (c) A and D

    (d) B only

    (e) D only

3. Which of the following is an example of a "sharp" discontinuity?

    A. An enforced age cutoff of 15 years

    B. Changing administrative borders between counties

    C. An election

    D. Regional differences in weather patterns

        (a) A and B

        (b) B and C

        (c) A only

        (d) C and D

        (e) A and D

4. Concerns with RD include which of the following?

    A. Unobserved characteristics affecting selection are assumed to be fixed over time.

    B. The treatment impact may not be generalizable.

    C. RD has strong parametric functional form assumptions.

    D. Program enforcement may affect it.

        (a) A and B

        (b) B and C

        (c) B and D

        (d) C and D

        (e) A and D

        (f) D only

5. As a source of identification of program effects, pipeline approaches can exploit which of the following?

    A. Timing of program entry

    B. Socioeconomic characteristics of participants in other regions

    C. Errors in program implementation

        (a) A and B

        (b) B and C

        (c) A and C

        (d) B only

References

Buddelmeyer, Hielke, and Emmanuel Skoufias. 2004. "An Evaluation of the Performance of Regression Discontinuity Design on PROGRESA." Policy Research Working Paper 3386, World Bank, Washington, DC.

Duflo, Esther. 2003. "Grandmothers and Granddaughters: Old Age Pension and Intrahousehold Allocation in South Africa." *World Bank Economic Review* 17 (1): 1–26.

Galasso, Emanuela, and Martin Ravallion. 2004. "Social Protection in a Crisis: Argentina's Plan *Jefes y Jefas.*" *World Bank Economic Review* 18 (3): 367–400.

Hahn, Jinyong, Petra Todd, and Wilbert van der Klaauw. 2001. "Identification of Treatment Effects by Regression Discontinuity Design." *Econometrica* 69 (1): 201–9.

Ravallion, Martin. 2008. "Evaluating Anti-poverty Programs." In *Handbook of Development Economics*, vol. 4, ed. T. Paul Schultz and John Strauss, 3787–846. Amsterdam: North-Holland.

8. Measuring Distributional Program Effects

Summary

In addition to examining the mean impacts of program interventions, policy makers might also find it useful to understand how programs have affected households or individuals across the distribution of outcomes. For example, the impact on poorer households as compared with wealthier households is particularly interesting in the context of programs that aim to alleviate poverty.

A number of approaches exist for characterizing distributional impacts of a program. This chapter explores different econometric methods for evaluating the distributional impacts of policy interventions, including linear and nonlinear (quantile regression) approaches. Whether or not the program is randomized also needs to be considered. Collecting detailed data at the time of the survey on household and individual characteristics is also very important for accurately distinguishing how different groups have benefited from the program.

Learning Objectives

After completing this chapter, the reader will be able to discuss

- Different empirical methods for examining how programs and policies affect individuals at different points in the distribution of outcomes (such as per capita expenditure or income)
- Ways to account for potential selection bias when examining distributional impacts of programs
- Data considerations for examining distributional impacts

The Need to Examine Distributional Impacts of Programs

The average or mean effect of a program or policy, based on the assumption of a common effect across all targeted households or individuals, is a concise way to evaluate its performance. Following Heckman, Smith, and Clements (1997), one can justify assessing a program by its mean impact if researchers and policy makers believe that (a) total output increases total welfare and (b) detrimental effects of the program or policy on certain parts of the population are not important or are offset by transfers—either through an overarching social welfare function or from family members or social networks.

Policy makers often consider it important, however, to understand how gains from a development project might vary by individual or household characteristics (such as age, household income, or household expenditure status) even if the average effect of the program is not significant. Indeed, even if the mean program effect were significant, whether the program had a significant beneficial or detrimental effect might vary across the distribution of targeted households. Studies on "elite capture" of program benefits by better-educated or wealthier households, for example, have raised important questions about the performance of development programs targeting areas with high inequality (see Araujo and others 2008; Gugerty and Kremer 2008; Mansuri and Rao 2004; Platteau 2004). Furthermore, groups that appear to benefit in the short term from a policy intervention may not sustain these benefits in the long run, and vice versa (King and Behrman 2009; van de Walle 2009). The literature on incidence analysis of public spending also distinguishes first-round program effects (identifying who benefits from a program and how public spending affects welfare) from second-round behavioral effects of participants (how beneficiaries actually vary in their responses to the program, such as reallocating their time or spending). See Bourguignon and Pereira da Silva (2003) for a number of studies on this topic. In addition to comparing program effects across households, examining intrahousehold responses to programs is very important in understanding the efficiency and side effects of program targeting (Jacoby 2002). This chapter explores different econometric methods for evaluating the microlevel distributional impacts of policy interventions.

Examining Heterogeneous Program Impacts: Linear Regression Framework

Depending on the policy makers' interest, there are a number of ways to present the distributional impacts of a program. In the context of a poverty alleviation program, the impact might be as direct as the proportion of targeted individuals who fell out of poverty. Policy makers may also be interested in tracking regional disparities in growth or poverty and inequality within a country over time.[1]

One might also want to examine how the program impact varies across different individuals or households. In a linear regression–based framework, heterogeneous program impacts can be represented by varying the intercept α, the coefficient β, or both on the program or treatment variable T_i, across individuals $i = 1,\ldots,n$:

$$Y_i = \alpha_i + \beta_i T_i + \gamma X_i + \varepsilon_i. \tag{8.1}$$

For example, one could divide the sample of households and individuals into different demographic groups (for example, by men and women or by different age cohorts) and run the same regression of T on Y separately on each group. Interacting the treatment with different household socioeconomic characteristics X (such as gender or landowning) is another way to capture differences in program effects, although adding too many interaction terms in the same regression can lead to issues with multicollinearity.

One may also want to understand the incidence of gains from a program in a more descriptive setting. With data before and after an intervention, graphs can help highlight the distributional impacts of the program across treated and control samples, varying outcomes Y for the two samples against a given covariate X_k. Nonparametric locally weighted regressions of Y on X_k can be graphed alongside scatterplots to give a smoother trend of patterns as well.[2]

Using data from the Bangladesh Institute of Development Studies, figure 8.1 gives an example of trends (reflected by locally weighted regressions) of log household per capita expenditure against adult male schooling across project and control areas in rural Bangladesh stemming from the Rural Development Program road intervention.[3] As can be seen in figure 8.1, log household per capita expenditure rises with adult male schooling for households in project and control areas, but from this simple graph, project households with higher education among men appear to have been experiencing greater increases in household per capita expenditure from the road intervention. However, particularly when the program is not randomized, these graphs are useful more as a descriptive preview of the data rather than as a reflection of real program effects. As mentioned previously, the locally weighted regressions are based on a simple weighted regression of the y-axis variable Y on the x-axis variable X_k; other covariates are not accounted for, nor is the identification strategy (difference-in-difference, propensity score matching) to address potential

Figure 8.1   Locally Weighted Regressions, Rural Development Program Road Project, Bangladesh

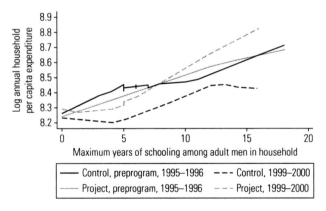

Source: Bangladesh Institute of Development Studies.

Note: Locally weighted regression (lowess) curves are presented on the basis of underlying data. The lowess curve has a bandwidth of 0.8.

selection bias. As a side note, the substantial drop in household per capita expenditure among control areas over the period could be attributable to heavy flooding in Bangladesh in 1998 and 1999.

A related assessment can be made even without data before the intervention. Jalan and Ravallion (2003), for example, use different approaches to examine the poverty impact of Argentina's Trabajar workfare program (discussed in chapter 4). As mentioned earlier, this program was not randomized, nor was there a baseline. Among these approaches, Jalan and Ravallion present a poverty incidence curve of the share of participating households below the poverty line against income per capita (in fact, they examine different possible poverty lines). They then compare this curve with a simulated counterfactual poverty incidence curve of estimated poverty rates after reducing postintervention incomes for participants by the estimated income gains from the program.

A study by Galasso and Umapathi (2009) on the SEECALINE (Surveillance et Éducation d'Écoles et des Communautés en matière d'Alimentation et de Nutrition Élargie, or Expanded School and Community Food and Nutrition Surveillance and Education) program in Madagascar, described in box 8.1, provides an example of how these different approaches can be used to study the distributional impacts of a project. The SEECALINE program was aimed at improving nutritional outcomes for children under three years of age as well as women who were pregnant or still breastfeeding. Local nongovernmental organizations were responsible for implementing the program in targeted areas, which involved distribution and monitoring of guidelines on improving hygiene, food habits, and child care. Using nationally representative baseline and follow-up data across targeted and nontargeted areas, Galasso and Umapathi examine the average impacts of the program, as well as distributional impacts across household- and community-level socioeconomic characteristics.

Quantile Regression Approaches

Another way to present a program's distributional impacts is by examining the program effects for households or individuals across the range of Y, which might include household per capita income or expenditure. One could assess, for example, whether poorer or better-off households experienced larger gains from a particular intervention. Simply investigating changes in the mean program effect, even across different socioeconomic or demographic groups, may not be sufficient when the entire shape of the distribution changes significantly (Buchinsky 1998).

In this scenario, quantile regression is another approach to estimate program effects for a given quantile τ in the distribution of the outcome Y, conditional on observed covariates X. Following the model proposed by Koenker and Bassett (1978), assume that Y_i is a sample of observations on the outcome and that X_i is a $K \times 1$ vector (comprising the project or treatment T, as well as other covariates). The quantile regression model can be expressed as

> ### BOX 8.1   Case Study: Average and Distributional Impacts of the SEECALINE Program in Madagascar
>
> In the study by Galasso and Umapathi (2009), the National Institute of Statistics conducted a baseline survey of about 14,000 households in Madagascar in mid-1997 and mid-1998; one-third of the 420 communities surveyed were selected for program targeting. Targeting was not random, however. Communities that were poorer and had higher malnutrition rates were more likely to be selected. A follow-up nationally representative anthropometric survey was then administered in 2004 to households in the same communities as those in the baseline sample.
>
> Galasso and Umapathi (2009) first examine the average impact of the program, using the baseline and follow-up surveys to construct a propensity score weighted difference-in-difference estimate of the program's impact (following Hirano, Imbens, and Ridder 2003; see chapter 4). Selection bias is therefore assumed to be time invariant, conditional on preprogram community characteristics that affected program placement. The average effect of the program was found to be positive across all nutritional outcomes in treated areas, as compared with control areas, where some of these outcomes (moderate undernutrition, for example) maintained a negative trend over the period.
>
> Looking next at the heterogeneity in program impacts across the sample, Galasso and Umapathi (2009) estimated the same treatment regression for different socioeconomic groups in the sample. Looking first at program effects by mother's schooling level, they found improvements in children's nutritional and anthropometric outcomes to be three times as high in program areas for mothers with secondary school education than for mothers with no schooling or only primary school education. However, they found that less educated mothers were still more likely to have responded to the program in terms of improved sanitation, meal preparation, and breastfeeding practices. Graphs of the distribution of children's anthropometric outcomes across the two surveys, by mother's years of schooling, are also presented for treatment and nontreatment samples.
>
> Nutritional benefits of the program were then estimated on subsamples distinguished by village characteristics. They include subsamples defined by whether the village is in a rural or urban area; by village poverty status; by access to water, roads, and electricity; and by the presence of institutions such as secondary schools and hospitals. Better-off villages exhibited larger program gains in terms of improved anthropometric outcomes and most sanitation and child care practices. The study then estimates interaction effects of the program with mother's education and the same village characteristics, finding that children's health outcomes improved most for educated mothers in the least endowed communities, whereas in better-endowed areas, program benefits accrued across education subgroups.

$$Y_i = \beta_\tau X_i + \varepsilon_{\tau i}, \; Q_\tau(Y_i \mid X_i) = \beta_\tau X_i, \tau \in (0,1), \tag{8.2}$$

where $Q_\tau(Y_i \mid X_i)$ denotes the quantile τ of the outcome Y (say, log per capita expenditure), conditional on the vector of covariates (X). Specifically, the quantile's coefficients can be interpreted as the partial derivative of the conditional quantile of Y with respect to one of the regressors, such as program T.

Quantile Treatment Effects Using Randomized Program Interventions

As with the average treatment effect discussed in chapter 2, a counterfactual problem is encountered in measuring distributional impacts of a program: one does not know where person or household i in the treatment distribution would appear in the non-treatment or control distribution. If the program is randomized, however, the *quantile treatment effect* (QTE) of a program can be calculated (see Heckman, Smith, and Clements 1997). The QTE is the difference in the outcome y across treatment (T) and control (C) households that, within their respective groups, fall in the quantile τ of Y:

$$QTE = Y^T(\tau) - Y^C(\tau). \tag{8.3}$$

QTE reflects how the distribution of outcomes changes if the program is assigned randomly. For example, for $\tau = 0.25$, QTE is the difference in the 25th percentile of Y between the treatment and control groups. However, QTE does not identify the distribution of treatment effects, nor does it identify the impact for individuals at specific quantiles (see Bitler, Gelbach, and Hoynes 2008). This problem is also related to not knowing the counterfactual. The QTE can be derived from the marginal distributions $F_T(Y) \equiv \Pr\left[Y_i^T \leq y\right]$ and $F_C(Y) \equiv \Pr\left[Y_i^C \leq y\right]$, both of which are known;[4] however, the quantiles of the treatment effect $Y_i^T - Y_i^C$ cannot be written as a function of just the marginal distributions. Assumptions are needed about the joint distribution of Y_i^T and Y_i^C. For example, if one knew that a household's position in the distribution of per capita expenditure would be the same regardless of whether the household was in a treated or control group, the QTE would give the treatment effect for a household in quantile τ in the distribution; however, this assumption is a strong one (Bitler, Gelbach, and Hoynes 2008; see also box 8.2).

Quantile Regression Approaches Using Nonexperimental Data

As with average treatment effects, calculating distributional impacts from a non-randomized intervention requires additional assumptions about the counterfactual and selection bias. One approach has been to apply the double-difference methods discussed in chapter 5 to quantile regression. With two-period data on treated and nontreated groups before and after introduction of the program, one can construct a quantile difference-in-difference (QDD) estimate. Specifically, in the QDD approach, the counterfactual distribution is computed by first calculating the change in Y over time at the qth quantile of the control group and then adding this change to the qth quantile of Y (observed before the program) to the treatment group (see Athey and Imbens 2006):

$$QDD_{Y(\tau)} = Y_0^T(\tau) + (Y_1^C(\tau) - Y_0^C(\tau)) \,. \tag{8.4}$$

BOX 8.2   **Case Study: The Canadian Self-Sufficiency Project**

Using quantile treatment effects, Bitler, Gelbach, and Hoynes (2008) examined distributional impacts of the randomly assigned Self-Sufficiency Project (SSP) in Canada, which between 1992 and 1995 offered subsidies to single-parent participants and welfare applicants who were able to find full-time work at or above the minimum wage. Individuals in the control group were eligible to participate in only the existing welfare program, known as Income Assistance (or IA). The study used monthly administrative data on IA and SSP participation from provincial records spanning up to four years before random assignment and nearly eight years after. There were a total of 2,858 SSP participants and 2,827 individuals in the control group.

Bitler, Gelbach, and Hoynes (2008) focused on the impact of SSP on participants' earnings, income, and transfers. Although the study found that the average benefits of the program on employment and earnings were large and statistically significant (control recipients, for example, were found to have worked in 27 percent of the months in the first four years after random assignment, compared with 35 percent among SSP participants), the distributional impacts varied. Using graphs, Bitler, Gelbach, and Hoynes first plotted quantiles of the distributions of these variables across project and control areas and then derived quantile treatment effects for each quantile by calculating the vertical difference between the project and control lines. Bootstrapped confidence intervals for the QTEs are also presented in the graphs.

When examining QTEs, they that found the impact on earnings for participants was zero for the bottom half of the earnings distribution; for the upper third of the distribution, impacts were much higher. The same pattern held for impacts on the income distribution. The positive effects on transfers, however, were focused at the lower end of the transfer distribution. Furthermore, after the subsidy was phased out, Bitler, Gelbach, and Hoynes found that the impacts of SSP on the distributions of earnings, income, and transfers fell to zero. They found that these substantial differences across mean and distributional impacts are useful for policy makers in understanding responses to a welfare program, both short term and long term.

One of the underlying assumptions of QDD is that the counterfactual distribution of Y for the treated group is equal to $(Y_1^C(\tau) - Y_0^C(\tau))$ for $\tau \in (0,1)$. This assumption relies on potentially questionable assumptions about the distribution of Y, however, including that the underlying distribution of unobserved characteristics potentially affecting participation is the same for all subgroups. Under the assumptions of QDD, the standard difference-in-difference (DD) model is a special case of QDD.[5]

- Box 8.3 describes a study by Emran, Robano, and Smith (2009), who compare DD with QDD program estimates of the Targeting the Ultra-Poor Program (TUP) in Bangladesh. The Bangladesh Rural Advancement Committee (BRAC) initiated TUP in 2002 to cover 100,000 households in extreme poverty from 15 of the poorest districts in Bangladesh. TUP targets women in the households, providing health, education, and training, as well as asset transfers and enterprise training, to help them eventually participate in BRAC's standard microcredit program.

> ### BOX 8.3   Case Study: Targeting the Ultra-Poor Program in Bangladesh
>
> Emran, Robano, and Smith (2009) examined the first phase of the Targeting the Ultra-Poor Program, which was conducted across three districts between 2002 and 2006. Potentially eligible (that is, the poorest) households were identified on the basis of a participatory village wealth ranking. Participant households were selected from this pool on the basis of ownership of less than a 10th of an acre of land, lack of any productive assets, women's ability to work outside the home, and other household characteristics related to labor supply. A two-year panel of 5,000 households was constructed among participants and comparison groups identified by the Bangladesh Rural Advancement Committee in this phase; however, examination of the data revealed that households considered ineligible on some criteria were participating, and some households satisfying all the eligibility criteria were ultimately not selected for the program. Emran, Robano, and Smith therefore examined program effects for two sets of treatment-control pairs: (a) households that are eligible and not eligible, according to the stated criteria, and that are correctly included or excluded from the program, respectively, and (b) the BRAC's identification of program and control households.
>
> Emran, Robano, and Smith (2009) calculated DD program effects across participant and control groups, assuming time-invariant unobserved heterogeneity for each of the two treatment-control pairs. The study presented different specifications of the DD, with and without different time trends across the three districts in the sample, and combined DD with matching on initial characteristics across participant and control groups to account for potential selection on observed factors. Finally, Emran, Robano, and Smith calculated QDD program effects across these different specifications as well.
>
> Although the mean impacts they found are positive across a number of outcomes, such as net income, food security, and ownership of livestock and household durables, the distributional impacts show that better-off eligible households gained the most from the program. They found that the treatment effect is much higher for eligible households in the top two deciles of the income distribution than for those in the lower end of the distribution, and regardless of which treatment-control set is examined, the program effect is not statistically significant for households in the lowest decile of income. When selection on observed characteristics was taken into account, the magnitude of the program effect was also diminished, particularly for households at the lower end of the distribution.

Finally, Abrevaya and Dahl (2008) have proposed another approach to applying quantile estimation to panel data. One problem in applying traditional quantile regression to panel data is that differencing the dependent and independent variables will not in general be equal to the difference in the conditional quantiles. Abrevaya and Dahl, following Chamberlain's (1982, 1984) correlated effects model, specify the unobserved fixed effect as a linear function of the other covariates in the model. Thus, both the effects on observed variables as well as impacts correlated with unobserved household characteristics can be estimated over time as a pooled linear quantile regression. The estimates for observed effects could be used to calculate the impact of growth on poverty by quantile.

More specifically, consider the following quantile regression equations for two-period data (variants of equation 8.2) to estimate the distributional effects of growth on per capita income or consumption expenditure y_{it}, $t = \{1,2\}$:

$$Q_\tau(\log y_{i1} | x_{i1}, \mu_i) = \gamma_\tau x_{i1} + \mu_i, \tau \in (0,1) \tag{8.5a}$$

$$Q_\tau(\log y_{i2} | x_{i2}, \mu_i) = \gamma_\tau x_{i2} + \mu_i, \tau \in (0,1). \tag{8.5b}$$

In these equations, X_{it} represents the vector of other observed covariates including treatment T, and μ_i is the unobserved household fixed effect. $Q_\tau(\log y_{i1} | x_{i1}, \mu_i)$ denotes the quantile τ of log per capita income in period 1, conditional on the fixed effect and other covariates in period 1, and $Q_\tau(\log y_{i2} | x_{i2}, \mu_i)$, correspondingly, is the conditional quantile τ of log per capita income in period 2. Unlike the linear DD model, however, one conditional quantile cannot be subtracted from the other to difference out μ_i, because quantiles are not linear operators:

$$Q_\tau(\log y_{i2} - \log y_{i1} | x_{i1}, x_{i2}, \mu_i) \neq Q_\tau(\log y_{i2} | x_{i2}, \mu_i) - Q_\tau(\log y_{i1} | x_{i1}, \mu_i). \tag{8.6}$$

To overcome this obstacle, recent work has aimed at characterizing the relationship between the unobserved fixed effect and the covariates more explicitly. Following Chamberlain (1982, 1984), the fixed effect μ_i may be specified as a linear function of the covariates in periods 1 and 2 as follows:

$$\mu_i = \phi + \lambda_1 x_{i1} + \lambda_2 x_{i2} + \omega_i, \tag{8.7}$$

where ϕ is a scalar and ω_i is an error term uncorrelated with X_{it}, $t = \{1,2\}$. Substituting equation 8.7 into either conditional quantile in equations 8.5a and 8.5b allows estimation of the distributional impacts on per capita expenditure using this adjusted quantile estimation procedure:[6]

$$Q_\tau(\log y_{i1} | x_{i1}, \mu_i) = \phi_\tau^1 + (\gamma_\tau + \lambda_\tau^1) x_{i1} + \lambda_\tau^2 x_{i2}, \tau \in (0,1) \tag{8.8a}$$

$$Q_\tau(\log y_{i2} | x_{i2}, \mu_i) = \phi_\tau^2 + (\gamma_\tau + \lambda_\tau^2) x_{i2} + \lambda_\tau^1 x_{i1}, \tau \in (0,1). \tag{8.8b}$$

Following Abrevaya and Dahl (2008), equations 8.8a and 8.8b use a pooled linear quantile regression, where observations corresponding to the same household are stacked as a pair.

Khandker, Bakht, and Koolwal (2009) use this approach when examining the distributional impacts of two quasi-experimental rural road interventions in Bangladesh. Their study finds positive mean impacts on household per capita expenditure across both programs, comparing project to control areas. The panel quantile estimation results, however, reveal that these road investments have in fact benefited the lowest quantiles of the per capita expenditure distribution; in one of the programs, the gains to poorer households are disproportionately higher than those for households at higher quantiles.

Discussion: Data Collection Issues

Many times, large-scale interventions such as road construction or crisis-induced safety net programs also concern themselves with impacts on the poorest households, even though a broader share of the local population partakes in the initiative. As discussed in this chapter, a number of approaches can be used to examine the distributional impacts of program interventions. Collecting detailed data on community, household, and individual characteristics at the time of the survey is very important for accurately distinguishing how different groups benefit from a program.

One example comes from potential differences across regions within a targeted area. Chapter 5 discussed how differences in preprogram area characteristics within targeted regions, as well as across targeted and control areas, need to be accounted for to avoid bias in the program effect. Heterogeneity across geographic localities targeted by a large-scale program is often a reality, and better-endowed areas (such as those with greater access to natural resources, markets, and other institutions) are more likely to capitalize on program benefits. Policy makers and researchers therefore need to collect detailed information and data on geographic and community-level characteristics to be able to isolate the program effect. Collecting data on geographic characteristics before the program intervention, such as poverty maps in the context of a poverty alleviation program (see Lanjouw 2003), can help both to improve targeting and to allow better understanding program effects later on. New approaches are also being offered by global positioning system (GPS) technology, whereby precise data on the latitude and longitude of household locations can be collected. When collected as part of surveys, household GPS data can help to identify detailed regional and local disparities in program impacts by exploiting household variation in exogenous variables, such as access to natural resources and existing administrative localities, institutions, and infrastructure.

Another issue is whether the program effect itself should be measured as a binary variable, as discussed in chapters 3 and 6. Certain facets of participating should be recorded during the survey process even for treated subjects. For example, in lending networks, the group composition of the networks (by gender, distribution of wealth, or caste or social status) would be important in understanding the mechanisms by which participants are benefiting from the program. Related selection issues arise here as well, and for these additional variables characterizing program participation, additional sources of identification (such as instrumental variables) would need to be explored.

Notes

1. See, for example, Essama-Nssah (1997) for a study in Madagascar examining rural-urban differences in these outcomes between 1962 and 1980 and Ravallion and Chen (2007), who examine trends across rural and urban provinces in China between 1980 and 2001.
2. Specifically, for each distinct value of X_k, the locally weighted regression produces a fitted value of Y by running a regression in a local neighborhood of X_k, giving more weight to points closer to X_k. The size of the neighborhood is called the *bandwidth*, and it represents a trade-off between smoothness and goodness of fit. In Stata, the *lowess* command will create these locally weighted regression curves on the basis of the underlying data.
3. See Khandker, Bakht, and Koolwal (2009) for more detailed description of the data.
4. The quantile τ of the distribution $F_t(Y)$, $t = \{T, C\}$ is defined as $Y^t(\tau) \equiv \inf [Y: F_t(Y) \geq \tau]$, so the treatment effect for quantile τ is just the difference in the quantiles τ of the two marginal distributions.
5. Athey and Imbens (2006) provide further discussion of the underlying assumptions of QDD.
6. Specifically, λ_τ^1 denotes λ_1 for percentile τ, and λ_τ^2 denotes λ_2 for percentile τ. See Khandker, Bakht, and Koolwal (2009) for a more detailed discussion.

References

Abrevaya, Jason, and Christian M. Dahl. 2008. "The Effects of Birth Inputs on Birthweight: Evidence from Quantile Estimation on Panel Data." *Journal of Business and Economic Statistics* 26 (4): 379–97.

Araujo, M. Caridad, Francisco H. G. Ferreira, Peter Lanjouw, and Berk Özler. 2008. "Local Inequality and Project Choice: Theory and Evidence from Ecuador." *Journal of Public Economics* 92 (5–6): 1022–46.

Athey, Susan, and Guido Imbens. 2006. "Identification and Inference in Nonlinear Difference-in-Differences Models." *Econometrica* 74 (2): 431–97.

Bitler, Marianne P., Jonah B. Gelbach, and Hilary W. Hoynes. 2008. "Distributional Impacts of the Self-Sufficiency Project." *Journal of Public Economics* 92 (3–4): 748–65.

Bourguignon, François, and Luiz A. Pereira da Silva, eds. 2003. *The Impact of Economic Policies on Poverty and Income Distribution: Evaluation Techniques and Tools.* Washington, DC: World Bank and Oxford University Press.

Buchinsky, Moshe. 1998. "Recent Advances in Quantile Regression Models: A Practical Guide for Empirical Research." *Journal of Human Resources* 33 (1): 88–126.

Chamberlain, Gary. 1982. "Multivariate Regression Models for Panel Data." *Journal of Econometrics* 18 (1): 5–46.

———. 1984. "Panel Data." In *Handbook of Econometrics, Volume 2*, ed. Zvi Griliches and Michael D. Intriligator, 1247–318. Amsterdam: North-Holland.

Emran, M. Shahe, Virginia Robano, and Stephen C. Smith. 2009. "Assessing the Frontiers of Ultra-Poverty Reduction: Evidence from CFPR/TUP, an Innovative Program in Bangladesh." Working Paper, George Washington University, Washington, DC.

Essama-Nssah, Boniface. 1997. "Impact of Growth and Distribution on Poverty in Madagascar." *Review of Income and Wealth* 43 (2): 239–52.

Galasso, Emanuela, and Nithin Umapathi. 2009. "Improving Nutritional Status through Behavioral Change: Lessons from Madagascar." *Journal of Development Effectiveness* 1 (1): 60–85.

Gugerty, Mary Kay, and Michael Kremer. 2008. "Outside Funding and the Dynamics of Participation in Community Associations." *American Journal of Political Science* 52 (3): 585–602.

Heckman, James J., Jeffrey Smith, and Nancy Clements. 1997. "Making the Most out of Programme Evaluations and Social Experiments: Accounting for Heterogeneity in Programme Impacts." *Review of Economic Studies* 64 (4): 487–535.

Hirano, Keisuke, Guido W. Imbens, and Geert Ridder. 2003. "Efficient Estimation of Average Treatment Effects Using the Estimated Propensity Score." *Econometrica* 71 (4): 1161–89.

Jacoby, Hanan. 2002. "Is There an Intrahousehold 'Flypaper Effect?' Evidence from a School Feeding Programme." *Economic Journal* 112 (476): 196–221.

Jalan, Jyotsna, and Martin Ravallion. 2003. "Estimating the Benefit Incidence for an Antipoverty Program by Propensity-Score Matching." *Journal of Business and Economic Statistics* 21 (1): 19–30.

Khandker, Shahidur R., Zaid Bakht, and Gayatri B. Koolwal. 2009. "The Poverty Impact of Rural Roads: Evidence from Bangladesh." *Economic Development and Cultural Change* 57 (4): 685–722.

King, Elizabeth M., and Jere R. Behrman. 2009. "Timing and Duration of Exposure in Evaluations of Social Programs." *World Bank Research Observer* 24 (1): 55–82.

Koenker, Roger, and Gilbert Bassett. 1978. "Regression Quantiles." *Econometrica* 46 (1) 33–50.

Lanjouw, Peter. 2003. "Estimating Geographically Disaggregated Welfare Levels and Changes." In *The Impact of Economic Policies on Poverty and Income Distribution: Evaluation Techniques and Tools*, ed. François Bourguignon and Luiz A. Pereira da Silva, 85–102. Washington, DC: World Bank and Oxford University Press.

Mansuri, Ghazala, and Vijayendra Rao. 2004. "Community-Based and -Driven Development: A Critical Review." *World Bank Research Observer* 19 (1): 1–39.

Platteau, Jean-Philippe. 2004. "Monitoring Elite Capture in Community-Driven Development." *Development and Change* 35 (2): 223–46.

Ravallion, Martin, and Shaohua Chen. 2007. "China's (Uneven) Progress against Poverty." *Journal of Development Economics* 82 (1): 1–42.

van de Walle, Dominique. 2009. "Impact Evaluation of Rural Road Projects." *Journal of Development Effectiveness* 1 (1): 15–36.

9. Using Economic Models to Evaluate Policies

Summary

Economic models can help in understanding the potential interactions—and interdependence—of a program with other existing policies and individual behavior. Unlike reduced-form estimations, which focus on a one-way, direct relationship between a program intervention and ultimate outcomes for the targeted population, structural estimation approaches explicitly specify interrelationships between endogenous variables (such as household outcomes) and exogenous variables or factors. Structural approaches can help create a schematic for interpreting policy effects from regressions, particularly when multiple factors are at work.

Ex ante evaluations, discussed in chapter 2, also build economic models that predict program impacts amid other factors. Such evaluations can help reduce costs as well by focusing policy makers' attention on areas where impacts are potentially greater. The evaluations can also provide a framework for understanding how the program or policy might operate in a different economic environment if some parameters (such as rates of return on capital or other prices) were changed.

This chapter presents case studies of different modeling approaches for predicting program effects as well as for comparing these predictions with data on outcomes after program implementation.

Learning Objectives

After completing this chapter, the reader will be able to discuss

- Differences between reduced-form and structural estimation frameworks
- Different models for evaluating programs ex ante and empirical strategies to compare these ex ante predictions with ex post program outcomes

Introduction

Thus far, the discussion in this handbook has focused on ex post, data-driven evaluations of programs. Often, however, programs are implemented amid several other policy changes, which can also affect how participants respond. Creating a conceptual model of the economic environment and choices of the population in question can help in understanding the potential interactions—and interdependence—of the program with other factors. At the macroeconomic level, these factors can include other economic or social policy changes (see Essama-Nssah 2005), and at the household or individual level, these factors can include different preferences or other behavioral elements.

This chapter first discusses structural versus reduced-form empirical approaches to estimating the causal effects of policies. It then discusses economic models in macroeconomic contexts, as well as more focused models where households face a single policy treatment, to examine how policy changes unfold within a given economic environment. Because construction of economic models is context specific, the focus is on case studies of different modeling frameworks that have been applied to various programs. When conducted before a program is implemented, economic models can help guide and streamline program design as well as draw policy makers' attention to additional, perhaps unintended, effects from the intervention.

Structural versus Reduced-Form Approaches

The treatment-effect literature discussed in this book centers on a single, direct relationship between a program intervention and ultimate outcomes for the targeted population. Selection bias and the problem of the unobserved counterfactual are the main identification issues addressed through different avenues, experimental or nonexperimental. This one-way effect is an example of a reduced-form estimation approach. A *reduced-form approach*, for example, specifies a household or individual outcome Y_i as a function of a program T_i and other exogenous variables X_i:

$$Y_i = \alpha + \beta T_i + \gamma X_i + \varepsilon_i. \tag{9.1}$$

In equation 9.1, the program and other variables X_i are assumed to be exogenous. The *treatment-effect approach* is a special case of reduced-form estimation, in a context where T_i is appropriated to a subset of the population and Y_i and X_i are also observed for separate comparison groups (see Heckman and Vytlacil 2005). The main relationship of interest is that between the policy intervention and outcome and lies in establishing the internal validity of the program's effect (see chapter 3).

In some cases, however, one may be interested in modeling other factors affecting policies and Y_i in a more comprehensive framework. *Structural models* can help create a schematic for interpreting policy effects from regressions, particularly when multiple factors are at work. These models specify interrelationships among endogenous variables (such as outcomes Y) and exogenous variables or factors.

One example of a structural model is the following simultaneous-equation system (see Wooldridge 2001):

$$Y_{1i} = \alpha_1 + \delta_1 Y_{2i} + \rho_1 Z_{1i} + \varepsilon_{1i} \tag{9.2a}$$

$$Y_{2i} = \alpha_2 + \delta_2 Y_{1i} + \rho_2 Z_{2i} + \varepsilon_{2i} \tag{9.2b}$$

Equations 9.2a and 9.2b are structural equations for the endogenous variables Y_{1i}, Y_{2i}. In equations 9.2a and 9.2b, Z_{2i} and Z_{1i} are vectors of exogenous variables spanning, for example, household and individual characteristics, with $E[Z'\varepsilon] = 0$. The policy T_i itself might be exogenous and therefore included in one of the vectors Z_{ki}, $k = 1, 2$. Imposing exclusion restrictions, such as excluding certain variables from each equation, allows one to solve for the estimates α_k, δ_k, ρ_k, in the model. For example, one could include an exogenous variable in Z_{1i} (such as the policy T_i if one believed it were exogenous) that would not be in Z_{2i} and an exogenous variable in Z_{2i} that would not be in Z_{1i}.

Note that one can solve the structural equations 9.2a and 2b to generate a reduced-form equation. For example, if equation 9.2b is rearranged so that Y_{1i} is on the left-hand side and Y_{2i} is on the right-hand side, one can take the difference of equation 9.2a and equation 9.2b so that Y_{2i} can be written as a function of the exogenous variables Z_{1i} and Z_{2i}:

$$Y_{2i} = \pi_0 + \pi_1 Z_{1i} + \pi_2 Z_{2i} + \upsilon_{2i}. \tag{9.3}$$

In equation 9.3, π_0, π_1, and π_2 are functions of the structural parameters α_k, δ_k, ρ_k, in equations 9.2a and 9.2b, and υ_{2i} is a random error that is a function of ε_1, ε_2, and δ_k. The main distinction between the structural and reduced-form approaches is that if one starts from a reduced-form model such as equation 9.3, one misses potentially important relationships between Y_{1i} and Y_{2i} described in the structural equations.

Heckman's (1974) model of sample selection provides an interesting example in this context. In a very basic version of this model (see Heckman 2001), there are three potential outcome functions, Y_0, Y_1, and Y_2:

$$Y_0 = g_0(X) + U_0 \tag{9.4a}$$

$$Y_1 = g_1(X) + U_1 \tag{9.4b}$$

$$Y_2 = g_2(X) + U_2. \tag{9.4c}$$

In these equations, Y_0, Y_1, and Y_2 are considered latent variables that may not be fully observed (one may either observe them directly or observe choices based on these variables). Outcomes Y are in turn a function of observed (X) and unobserved (U) characteristics, the latter of which explains why observationally similar individuals end up making different choices or decisions.

In the context of a labor supply model, $Y_0 = \ln R$ can be denoted as an individual's log reservation wage, and $Y_1 = \ln W$ as the log market wage. An individual works if the market wage is at least as large as the reservation wage, $Y_1 \geq Y_0$. If Y_2 represents hours of work and if the same individual preferences (and hence parameters) guide Y_2 and Y_0, Y_2 can be written as

$$Y_2 = \frac{\ln W - \ln R}{\gamma}, \gamma > 0. \tag{9.5}$$

Observed hours of work H therefore takes the value $(\ln W - \ln R)/\gamma$ if $\ln W \geq \ln R$ and is missing otherwise. Wages are then observed only if an individual works—that is, $\ln W \geq \ln R$. This formulation is a simple representation of Heckman's model of sample selection, where selective sampling of potential outcomes leads to selection bias.

Empirically, one could estimate this model (Heckman 1979) as follows:

$$Y_1^* = \beta X + \varepsilon_1 \tag{9.6a}$$

$$Y_2^* = \gamma Z + \varepsilon_2. \tag{9.6b}$$

Here, X and Z are vectors of covariates that may include common variables, and the errors ε_1 and ε_2 are jointly bivariate normally distributed with mean zero and variance Σ. The latent variable Y_1^* is of interest, but Y_1^* is observable (that is not missing) only if $Y_2^* > 0$. The econometric specification of this model as a two-stage procedure is well known and straightforward to implement in a limited dependent variable setting (see, for example, Maddala 1986).

Estimating structural parameters in other contexts may not be straightforward, though. One might be interested in more complex relationships across other endogenous variables $Y_{3i}, Y_{4i}, \ldots, Y_{Ki}$ and exogenous variables $Z_{3i}, Z_{4i}, \ldots, Z_{Ki}$. Adding structural equations for these relationships requires additional exclusion restrictions, as well as distributional assumptions to be able to identify the structural parameters.

Ultimately, one might choose to forgo estimating parameters from an economic model in favor of a treatment-effect model if one were interested only in identifying a single direct association between a policy T and resulting outcomes Y for a targeted population, isolated from other potential factors. One advantage of building economic models, however, is that they can shed light on how a particular policy would operate in a different economic environment from the current context—or even before the policy is to be implemented (Heckman 2001). Ex ante program evaluations, discussed in chapter 2 and in more detail later in this chapter, also involve economic modeling to predict program impacts. Note that ex ante evaluations need not be structural.

Modeling the Effects of Policies

Because the effects of policies are very much context specific, coming up with a single approach for modeling policy effects in an economic framework is impossible. However, this chapter presents some basic information to help explain how these models are set up and compared with actual data. Although a number of different modeling approaches exist, here the focus is on models that examine potential price effects from policies and shocks on the utility-maximizing problem for households.

This section draws on Bourguignon and Ferreira (2003), who provide a more detailed, step-by-step approach in modeling household labor supply choices in the face of tax changes. Broadly, household (or individual) preferences are represented as a utility function U, which is typically dependent on their choices over consumption (c) and labor supply (L): $U = U(c, L)$. The household's or individual's problem is to maximize utility subject to a budget constraint: $pc \leq y + wL + \tau$. That is, the budget constraint requires that expenditures pc (where p are market prices for consumption) do not exceed nonlabor income (y), other earnings from work (wL, where w is the market wage rate for labor), and a proposed transfer τ from a program intervention.[1] The solution to this maximization problem is the optimal choices c^* and L^* (that is, the optimal level of consumption and labor supply). These choices, in turn, are a function of the program τ as well as exogenous variables w, y, and p.

Estimating the model and deriving changes in c and L from the program require data on c, L, w, y, p, and τ across households i. That is, from the preceding model, one can construct an econometric specification of L, for example, across households i, as a function of prices and the program intervention:

$$L_i = f(w_i, y_i, p_i; \tau). \tag{9.7}$$

In the modeling approach, one could also make utility U dependent on exogenous household socioeconomic characteristics X as well $U = U(c, L; X)$ so that the optimal labor supply and consumption choices in the econometric specification are also a function of X. Estimating equation 9.4 is not necessarily straightforward, depending on the functional form for U. However, assumptions about the targeting strategy of the program also determine how this equation is to be estimated, as reflected in the case studies in this chapter.

Assessing the Effects of Policies in a Macroeconomic Framework

Modeling the effects of macroeconomic policies such as taxes, trade liberalization, or financial regulation can be very complex, because these policies are likely to be concurrent and to have dynamic effects on household behavior. Economic shocks such as commodity price increases or liquidity constraints stemming from the recent global financial crisis also jointly affect the implementation of these policies and household outcomes; the distributional impacts of these shocks also depend on the extent to which heterogeneity among economic agents is modeled (Essama-Nssah 2005).

A number of studies (for example, Chen and Ravallion 2004; Dixit 1990; Lokshin and Ravallion 2004) have constructed general equilibrium models to examine the effects of macroeconomic policy changes and shocks on the behavior of economic agents (households and firms) across economic sectors. Bourguignon, Bussolo, and Pereira da Silva (2008), as well as Essama-Nssah (2005), provide a useful discussion of different macroeconomic models. Again, the focus here is on a model of the price effects of policies on household utility and firms' profits. Box 9.1 describes a related

---

BOX 9.1 **Case Study: Poverty Impacts of Trade Reform in China**

Chen and Ravallion (2004) examined the effects of China's accession to the World Trade Organization in 2001 and the accompanying relaxation of trade restrictions (lowering of tariffs and export subsidies, for example) on household welfare. Specifically, they modeled the effect on wages and prices facing households and then applied the model to data from China's rural and urban household surveys to measure welfare impacts.

Model

In their model, household utility or preferences U is a function of a consumption q^d (a vector of commodities $j = 1,\ldots,m$ consumed by the household) and labor supply L (which includes outside work and work for the household's own production activities). The household chooses q^d and L subject to its available budget or budget constraint, which is a function of the price of consumption commodities p^d, market wages for labor w, and profits from the household's own enterprises π, which are equal to revenue minus costs. Specifically, $\pi = p^s q^s - p^d z - wL^0$, where p^s is a vector j of supply prices for each commodity, q^s is the vector of quantities supplied, w is the vector of wage rates, L^0 is the vector of labor input into own-production activities for commodity j in the household, and z is a vector of input commodities used in the production of household output. There is no rationing at the household level.

Following Chen and Ravallion's (2004) notation, the household's decision-making process can be written as $\max_{\{q^d, L\}} U(q^d, L)$, subject to the constraint $p^d q^d = wL + \pi$. The constraint reflects consumption equaling total household earnings and income.

Household profits π are obtained from the maximization problem $\max_{\{z, L^0\}}\left[p^s q^s - p^d z - wL^0 \right]$, subject to constraints $q^s_j \leq f_j(z_j, L^0_j), j = 1,\ldots,m; \sum_j z_j \leq z; \sum_j L^0_j \leq L^0$. The constraints here reflect quantity supplied for good j being less than or equal to the production of good j; the total number of inputs z and within-household labor L^0 used in the production for good j are not more than the total number of these respective inputs available to the household.

Chen and Ravallion (2004) then solved these two maximization problems to derive the estimating equation of the effect of price changes related to trade reform on the monetary value of the change in utility for a household i:

$$\frac{dU}{\upsilon_\pi} = \sum_{j=1}^m \left[p^s_j q^s_j \frac{dp^s_j}{p^s_j} - p^d_j(q^d_j + z_j)\frac{dp^d_j}{p^d_j} \right] + \sum_{k=1}^n \left[w_k L^s_k \frac{dw_k}{w_k} \right].$$

Here, υ_π is the marginal utility of income for household i, and $L^s_k = L_k - L^0_k$ is labor supply outside the household in activity k. For simplicity, the i subscript has been suppressed from the variables.

> **BOX 9.1** **Case Study: Poverty Impacts of Trade Reform in China (continued)**
>
> **Estimation**
>
> To calculate empirically the impacts on households on the basis of their model, Chen and Ravallion (2004) used data from China's 1999 Rural Household Surveys and Urban Household Surveys (they assumed that relaxation of trade policies would have begun in the lead-up period to China's accession in 2001) as well as estimates from Ianchovichina and Martin (2004) of price changes over 1995–2001 and 2001–07. Ultimately, on the basis of a sample of about 85,000 households across the two surveys, Chen and Ravallion found only small impacts on household poverty incidence, inequality, and income stemming from looser trade restrictions. Households in urban areas, however, responded more positively in the new environment than did those in rural areas. Chen and Ravallion also discussed in their analysis the potential value of a dynamic model in this setting rather than the static model used in the study.

study from Chen and Ravallion (2004), who construct a general equilibrium analysis to model the household poverty impacts of trade reform in China.

Modeling Household Behavior in the Case of a Single Treatment: Case Studies on School Subsidy Programs

As discussed in chapter 2, ex ante evaluations, which build economic models to predict program impacts before actual implementation, have much to offer in guiding program design as well as subsequent ex post evaluations. They can help reduce costs by focusing policy makers' attention on areas where impacts are potentially greater, as well as provide a framework for understanding how the program or policy might operate in a different economic environment if some parameters (such as rates of return on capital or other prices) were changed.

Counterfactual simulations are an important part of the ex ante evaluation exercise. That is, the researcher has to construct a counterfactual sample that would represent the outcomes and other characteristics of the control group had it received the counterfactual policy. Creating this sample requires a model to describe how the group would respond to such a policy.

An example, also mentioned in chapter 2, comes from Todd and Wolpin (2006a, 2006b), who examine the effects on children's school attendance from schooling subsidies provided by PROGRESA (Programa de Educación, Salud y Alimentación, or Education, Health, and Nutrition Program) in Mexico (now called Oportunidades). In designing the structural models underlying their ex ante predictions, Todd and Wolpin (2006b) develop and estimate a dynamic behavioral model of schooling and fertility that they use to predict the effects of Oportunidades on these outcomes, and they compare these estimates with actual ex post program effects. This model is discussed in more detail in box 9.2. Todd and Wolpin (2006a) specify a simpler household model on the same topic, discussed in box 9.3.

BOX 9.2 **Case Study: Effects of School Subsidies on Children's Attendance under PROGRESA (Oportunidades) in Mexico: Comparing Ex Ante Predictions and Ex Post Estimates—Part 1**

In their model examining the effect of schooling subsidies under Oportunidades on children's school attendance, Todd and Wolpin (2006b) modeled a dynamic household decision-making process where parents make sequential decisions over a finite time horizon on how their children (6–15 years of age) spend their time across schooling and work, as well as parents' fertility. Adult and child wages were considered exogenous, and an important identifying assumption in the model was that children's wages depend on distance to the nearest large city. Parents receive utility from their children, including their schooling and leisure, but household consumption (which also increases utility) goes up with children's earnings. Unobserved characteristics affect preferences, as well as adult and child earnings across households; these variables are also subject to time-varying shocks.

The model is then estimated on initial characteristics of the control group, simulating the introduction of the subsidy as well. The resulting predicted attendance rates for children in the control group were then compared with the ex post attendance rates for participants under the randomized experiment. In this study, Todd and Wolpin (2006b) found the model is better able to predict resulting attendance rates for girls than for boys. They also conducted counterfactual experiments on alternative forms of the subsidy and found another subsidy schedule that, at a similar cost, yielded higher predicted school attainment than the existing schedule.

BOX 9.3 **Case Study: Effects of School Subsidies on Children's Attendance under PROGRESA (Oportunidades) in Mexico: Comparing Ex Ante Predictions and Ex Post Estimates—Part 2**

For the same evaluation problem described in box 9.2, Todd and Wolpin (2006a) specified a simpler household model to examine the effects of school subsidies on children's attendance.

Model

In the model, the household makes a one-period decision about whether to send their children to school or to work. Following their notation, household utility U is a function of consumption (c) and whether or not the child attends school (s). If the child does not go to school, he or she is assumed to work outside for a wage w. The household then solves the problem $\max_{\{s\}} U(c,s)$, given the budget constraint $c = y + w(1 - s)$, where y is household income. The optimal schooling decision s^* is then a function of household income and child wages, $s^* = \phi(y, w)$. If a subsidy υ is introduced

---

Case Study: Effects of School Subsidies on Children's Attendance under PROGRESA (Oportunidades) in Mexico: Comparing Ex Ante Predictions and Ex Post Estimates—Part 2 (continued)

if the household sends its children to school, the budget constraint becomes $c = y + w(1 - s) + \upsilon s$, which can be rewritten as $c = (y + \upsilon) + (w - \upsilon)(1 - s)$. Next, defining $y_n = (y + \upsilon)$ and $w_n = (w - \upsilon)$, the optimal schooling decision from this new scenario is $s^{**} = \phi(y_n, w_n)$. The schooling decision for a family that has income y and expected children's wage w and that receives the subsidy is therefore the same as the schooling choice for a household with income y_n and expected children's wage w_n.

Estimation

As an empirical strategy, therefore, the effect of the subsidy program on attendance can be estimated by matching children from families with income and expected child wage profile (y_n, w_n) to those with profile (y, w) over a region of common support (see chapter 4). Todd and Wolpin (2006a) estimated the matched outcomes nonparametrically, using a kernel regression estimator. Note that no functional form for U needs to be specified to obtain predicted effects from the program. As discussed in box 2.5 in chapter 2, Todd and Wolpin found that the predicted estimates across children 12 to 15 years of age were similar to the ex post experimental estimates in the same age group. For other age groups, the model underestimates attendance compared with actual outcomes for participants.

In another ex ante evaluation of a school subsidy program, Bourguignon, Ferreira, and Leite (2003) use a reduced-form random utility model to forecast the impact of the Bolsa Escola program in Brazil. Bolsa Escola was created in April 2001 to provide subsidies to families with incomes below about US$30, conditional on a few criteria. First, all children 6 to 15 years of age in the household had to be enrolled in school. Second, the rate of attendance had to be at least 85 percent in any given month. Box 9.4 provides more details of the ex ante approach.

Conclusions

This chapter has provided an overview of economic models that can shed light on mechanisms by which programs affect household choices and outcomes. Building economic models can help reduce costs by focusing policy makers' attention on areas where impacts are potentially greater. Economic models can also provide a framework ex ante for understanding how the program or policy might operate in a different economic environment if some parameters (such as rates of return on capital or other prices) were changed. However, estimation of economic models is not necessarily straightforward; careful consideration of assumptions and functional forms of equations in the model affect the estimation strategy.

> **BOX 9.4** **Case Study: Effects of School Subsidies on Children's Attendance under Bolsa Escola in Brazil**
>
> In their ex ante evaluation of the Bolsa Escola program, Bourguignon, Ferreira, and Leite (2003) considered three different scenarios k for children's school or work decisions.
>
> **Model**
> The first scenario ($k = 1$) is if the child is earning in the labor market and not attending school; the second scenario ($k = 2$) is if the child is working and attending school; and the third scenario ($k = 3$) is if the child is only attending school. Following their notation, household utility for child i can be specified as $U_k^i = z_i \beta^k + \alpha^k (Y_i + y_i^k) + \varepsilon_i^k, k = \{1,2,3\}$. Here, z_i represents a vector of child and household characteristics, Y_i is household income less the child's earnings, y_i^k is income earned by the child (depending on the scenario k), and ε_i^k is a random term representing idiosyncratic preferences.
>
> Child earnings y_i^k can be simplified in the household utility function by substituting its realizations under the different scenarios. For $k = 1$, y_i^k is equal to w_i or the observed earnings of the child. For $k = 2$, a share M of the child's time is spent working, so y_i^k is equal to Mw_i. Finally, for $k = 3$, market earnings of the child are zero, but the child is still assumed to engage in some domestic production, denoted as Λw_i, where Λ is not observed. Household utility U can therefore be rewritten as a function similar to a discrete choice labor supply model, $U_k^i = z_i \beta^k + \alpha^k Y_i + \rho^k w_i + \varepsilon_i^k$, where $\rho^1 = \alpha_1$, $\rho^2 = \alpha_2$, M, $\rho^3 = \alpha_3$, Λ.
>
> **Estimation**
> In their empirical strategy, Bourguignon, Ferreira, and Leite (2003) then used this utility specification to construct a multinomial logit model estimating the effects of the program on a schooling choice variable S_i. Specifically, $S_i = 0$ if the child does not go to school (working full time at home or outside in the market), $S_i = 1$ if the child attends school and works outside the home, and $S_i = 2$ if he or she only attends school. Using 1999 national household survey data on children between 10 and 15 years of age and recovering the estimates for $\beta^k, \alpha^k, \varepsilon_i^k$ on the probability of alternative k, $k = \{1,2,3\}$, Bourguignon, Ferreira, and Leite simulated the effect of the subsidy program on the decision over children's school or work by choosing the function with the highest utility across the three different scenarios. The estimated value of M, derived from a comparison of earnings among children who were working and not attending school with children who were attending school, was found to be about 70 percent. The estimated value of Λ was 75 percent. They also found that the share of children involved in both school and work tended to increase, indicating that the program has less effect on work when children are already attending school. Bourguignon, Ferreira, and Leite also found substantial reductions in poverty for children 10 to 15 years of age from the simulated model.

Note

1. Again, although the economic model should be as simple as possible and still retain enough information to describe the relevant factors affecting household or individual behavior, the specification here is a very basic characterization. More detailed specifications of what variables enter

utility and the budget constraint, as well as accompanying assumptions, depend on the context in which households are situated. The case studies in this chapter show how this setup can vary across different economic contexts.

References

Bourguignon, François, Maurizio Bussolo, and Luiz A. Pereira da Silva, eds. 2008. *The Impact of Macroeconomic Policies on Poverty and Income Distribution: Macro-Micro Evaluation Techniques and Tools.* Washington, DC: World Bank and Palgrave Macmillan.

Bourguignon, François, and Francisco H. G. Ferreira. 2003. "Ex Ante Evaluation of Policy Reforms Using Behavioral Models." In *The Impact of Economic Policies on Poverty and Income Distribution: Evaluation Techniques and Tools,* ed. François Bourguignon and Luiz A. Pereira da Silva, 123–41. Washington, DC: World Bank and Oxford University Press.

Bourguignon, François, Francisco H. G. Ferreira, and Philippe Leite. 2003. "Conditional Cash Transfers, Schooling, and Child Labor: Micro-simulating Brazil's Bolsa Escola Program." *World Bank Economic Review* 17 (2): 229–54.

Chen, Shaohua, and Martin Ravallion. 2004. "Welfare Impacts of China's Accession to the World Trade Organization." *World Bank Economic Review* 18 (1): 29–57.

Dixit, Avinash K. 1990. *Optimization in Economic Theory.* Oxford, U.K.: Oxford University Press.

Essama-Nssah, Boniface. 2005. "Simulating the Poverty Impact of Macroeconomic Shocks and Policies." Policy Research Working Paper 3788, World Bank, Washington, DC.

Heckman, James J. 1974. "Shadow Prices, Market Wages, and Labor Supply." *Econometrica* 42 (4): 679–94.

———. 1979. "Sample Selection Bias as a Specification Error." *Econometrica* 47 (1): 153–61.

———. 2001. "Micro Data, Heterogeneity, and the Evaluation of Public Policy: Nobel Lecture." *Journal of Political Economy* 109 (4): 673–748.

Heckman, James J., and Edward J. Vytlacil. 2005. "Structural Equations, Treatment Effects, and Econometric Policy Evaluation." *Econometrica* 73 (3): 669–738.

Ianchovichina, Elena, and Will Martin. 2004. "Impacts of China's Accession to the World Trade Organization." *World Bank Economic Review* 18 (1): 3–27.

Lokshin, Michael, and Martin Ravallion. 2004. "Gainers and Losers from Trade Reform in Morocco." Policy Research Working Paper 3368, World Bank, Washington, DC.

Maddala, G. S. 1986. *Limited-Dependent and Qualitative Variables in Econometrics.* Cambridge, U.K.: Cambridge University Press.

Todd, Petra, and Kenneth Wolpin. 2006a. "Ex Ante Evaluation of Social Programs." PIER Working Paper 06-122, Penn Institute for Economic Research, University of Pennsylvania, Philadelphia.

———. 2006b. "Using a Social Experiment to Validate a Dynamic Behavioral Model of Child Schooling and Fertility: Assessing the Impact of School Subsidy Program in Mexico." *American Economic Review* 96 (5): 1384–417.

Wooldridge, Jeffrey M. 2001. *Econometric Analysis of Cross Section and Panel Data.* Cambridge, MA: MIT Press.

10. Conclusions

Impact evaluation methods examine whether program effects can be *identified*. That is, they seek to understand whether changes in such outcomes as consumption and health can be attributed to the program itself—and not to some other cause. This handbook describes major quantitative methods that are primarily used in ex post impact evaluations of programs and policies. It also discusses how distributional impacts can be measured, as well as ex ante approaches that predict the outcomes of programs and mechanisms by which programs affect targeted areas.

Randomized evaluations seek to identify a program's effect by identifying a group of subjects sharing similar observed characteristics (say, across incomes and earning opportunities) and assigning the treatment randomly to a subset of this group. The nontreated subjects then act as a comparison group to mimic counterfactual outcomes. This method avoids the problem of selection bias from unobserved characteristics.

Randomized evaluations, however, may not always be feasible. In such cases, researchers then turn to so-called nonexperimental methods. The basic problem with a nonexperimental design is that for the most part individuals are not randomly assigned to programs, and as a result selection bias occurs in assessing the program impact. This book discusses a number of approaches that address this problem. Propensity score matching methods, for example, attempt to reduce bias by matching treatment and control households on the basis of observable covariates. Propensity score matching methods therefore assume that selection bias is based only on observed characteristics and cannot account for unobserved heterogeneity in participation.

More can be learned if outcomes are tracked for both participants and nonparticipants over a time period that is deemed sufficient to capture any impacts of the intervention. A popular approach in nonexperimental evaluation is the double-difference (or difference-in-difference) method, although this method can also be used in experimental approaches. This method postulates that if outcomes for both participants and nonparticipants are tracked over a period of time, such tracking would provide a good basis for identifying the program effect. So with double difference, the observed changes over time for nonparticipants provide the counterfactual for participants. Double-difference methods assume that unobserved heterogeneity is present and that it is time invariant—the treatment effect is determined by taking the difference in outcomes across treatment and control units before and after the program intervention.

An instrumental variable method identifies exogenous variation in treatment by using a third variable that affects only the treatment but not unobserved factors correlated with the outcome of interest. Instrumental variable methods relax assumptions about the time-invariant nature of unobserved heterogeneity. These approaches can be applied to cross-section or panel data, and in the latter case they allow selection bias on unobserved characteristics to vary with time. Instruments might be constructed from program design (for example, if the program of interest was randomized, or from exogenous rules in determining who was eligible for the program), as well as from other exogenous shocks that are not correlated with the outcomes of interest.

Regression discontinuity and pipeline methods are extensions of instrumental variable and experimental methods that exploit exogenous program rules (such as eligibility requirements) to compare participants and nonparticipants in a close neighborhood around the rule's cutoff point. Pipeline methods, in particular, construct a comparison group from subjects who are eligible for the program but have not yet received it.

Although experimental methods are, in theory, the ideal approach for impact evaluation, nonexperimental methods are frequently used in practice either because program administrators are not too keen to randomly exclude certain parts of the population from an intervention or because a randomized approach is out of context for a rapid-action project with no time to conduct an experiment. Even with an experimental design, the quality of impact analysis depends ultimately on how it is designed and implemented. Often the problems of compliance, spillovers, and unobserved sample bias hamper clean identification of program effects from randomization. However, nonexperimental methods such as propensity score matching, double difference, and use of instrumental variables have their own strengths and weaknesses and hence are potentially subject to bias for various reasons including faulty design of the evaluation framework.

This handbook also covers methods of examining the distributional impacts of programs, as well as modeling approaches that can highlight mechanisms (such as intermediate market forces) by which programs have an impact. Well-being can be assessed at different levels, for example, among individuals or households, as well as for geographic areas such as villages, provinces, or even entire countries. Impacts can also be differentiated more finely by gender, percentiles of income, or other socioeconomic or demographic characteristics. Factoring in nuances of program effects, either across the distribution of income or through models of market interactions, can help in understanding the mechanisms of the program's effects as well as in reducing costs by focusing policy makers' attention on areas where impacts are potentially greater.

In reality, no single assignment or evaluation method may be perfect, and verifying the findings with alternative methods is wise. Different ex ante and ex post evaluation methods can be combined, as can quantitative and qualitative approaches. The main lesson from the practice of impact evaluation is that an application of particular methods to evaluate a program depends critically on understanding the design and implementation of an intervention, the goals and mechanisms by which program objectives can be achieved, and the detailed characteristics of targeted and nontargeted areas. By conducting good impact assessment over the course of the program and by beginning early in the design and implementation of the project, one can also judge whether certain aspects of the program can be changed to make it better.

PART 2

Stata Exercises

11. Introduction to Stata

Data Sets Used for Stata Exercises

This course works extensively with Stata, using a subset of information from the Bangladesh Household Survey 1991/92–1998/99, conducted jointly by the Bangladesh Institute of Development Studies and the World Bank. The information was collected at individual, household, and community levels. What follows is a description of the data sets and file structure used for these exercises. The data files for these exercises can be downloaded from the World Bank Web site, and as mentioned earlier represent subsets of the actual data for purposes of these exercises only. The Web site is accessible by the following steps:

1. Go to http://econ.worldbank.org
2. In the lower right hand corner, under *Resources* click on: *People and Bios*
3. Click on: *Research Staff (alphabetical list)*
4. Under "K" select: *Shahidur R. Khandker*
5. Click on the link for the book: *Handbook on Impact Evaluation.*

Alternatively, the Web site is accessible at: http://go.worldbank.org/FE8098BI60.

This location has the original full dataset and the subset files which pertain to the exercises.

File Structure

These exercises use and generate many files. There are mainly three types of Stata files. Some contain data sets (identified by the suffix .dta), others contain Stata programs (identified by the suffix .do), and yet others contain a record and output of the work done in Stata (identified by the suffix .log). To keep these files organized, the following directory structure has been created:

```
c:\eval
c:\eval\data
c:\eval\do
c:\eval\log
```

File Descriptions

The data files are located under c:\eval\data. There are three data files:

1. *hh_91.dta.* This file comprises the 1991 household data that contain 826 households (observations). These data have 24 variables on information at the household

(head's education, land ownership, expenditure, and so on) and village (infrastructure, price information of the main consumer goods, and so on) levels.

2. *hh_98.dta.* This file is the 1998 panel version of hh_91.dta. It includes 303 new households, making the total number of households (observations) 1,129. These data contain the same household- and village-level variables as hh_91.dta.

3. *hh_9198.dta.* This is a panel data set restricted to the 826 households interviewed in both years. It is in a time-series format.

A list of variables that are included in the data set appears in figure 11.1.

The .do folder has the program (.do) files specific to different impact evaluation techniques. These files contain all Stata code needed to implement the examples of the corresponding chapter (Microsoft Word file) that walks through the hands-on exercises. A segment of the .do file can be run for a particular example or case, or the whole .do file can be run to execute all examples in the chapters.

The .log folder contains all outputs generated by running the .do files.

Beginning Exercise: Introduction to Stata

Stata is a statistical software package that offers a large number of statistical and econometric estimation procedures. With Stata, one can easily manage data and apply standard statistical and econometric methods such as regression analysis and limited dependent variable analysis to cross-sectional or longitudinal data.

Getting Started

Start a Stata session by double-clicking on the Stata icon on your desktop. The Stata computing environment comprises four main windows. The size and shape of these windows may be changed, and they may be moved around on the screen. Figure 11.2 shows their general look and description.

In addition to these windows, the Stata environment has a menu and a toolbar at the top (to perform Stata operations) and a directory status bar at the bottom (that shows the current directory). You can use the menu and the toolbar to issue different Stata commands (such as opening and saving data files), although most of the time using the Stata Command window to perform those tasks is more convenient. If you are creating a log file (discussed in more detail later), the contents can be displayed on the screen, which is sometimes useful if you want to go back and see earlier results from the current session.

Opening a Data Set

You can open a Stata data set by entering following command in the Stata Command window:

```
use c:\eval\data\hh_98.dta
```

Figure 11.1   Variables in the 1998/99 Data Set

```
Contains data from hh_98.dta
  obs:          1,129
  vars:            24                           1 Apr 2009 12:04
  size:       119,674 (99.9% of memory free)
-------------------------------------------------------------------------------
              storage  display    value
variable name  type    format     label      variable label
-------------------------------------------------------------------------------
nh            double  %7.0f                   HH ID
year          float   %9.0g                   Year of observation
villid        double  %9.0g                   Village ID
thanaid       double  %9.0g                   Thana ID
agehead       float   %3.0f                   Age of HH head: years
sexhead       float   %2.0f                   Gender of HH head: 1=M, 0=F
educhead      float   %2.0f                   Education of HH head: years
famsize       float   %9.2f                   HH size
hhland        float   %9.0g                   HH land: decimals
hhasset       float   %9.0g                   HH total asset: Tk.
expfd         float   %9.0g                   HH per capita food expenditure:
                                                Tk/year
expnfd        float   %9.0g                   HH per capita nonfood
                                                expenditure: Tk/year
exptot        float   %9.0g                   HH per capita total
                                                expenditure: Tk/year
dmmfd         byte    %8.0g                   HH has male microcredit
                                                participant: 1=Y, 0=N
dfmfd         byte    %8.0g                   HH has female microcredit
                                                participant: 1=Y, 0=N
weight        float   %9.0g                   HH sampling weight
vaccess       float   %9.0g                   Village is accessible by road
                                                all year: 1=Y, 0=N
pcirr         float   %9.0g                   Proportion of village land
                                                irrigated
rice          float   %9.3f                   Village price of rice: Tk./kg
wheat         float   %9.3f                   Village price of wheat: Tk./kg
milk          float   %9.3f                   Village price of milk: Tk./liter
potato        float   %9.3f                   Village price of potato: Tk./kg
egg           float   %9.3f                   Village price of egg: Tk./4
                                                counts
oil           float   %9.3f                   Village price of edible oil:
                                                Tk./kg
-------------------------------------------------------------------------------
Sorted by:  nh
```

Source: Bangladesh Institute of Development Studies–World Bank Household Survey 1998/99.

Figure 11.2 The Stata Computing Environment

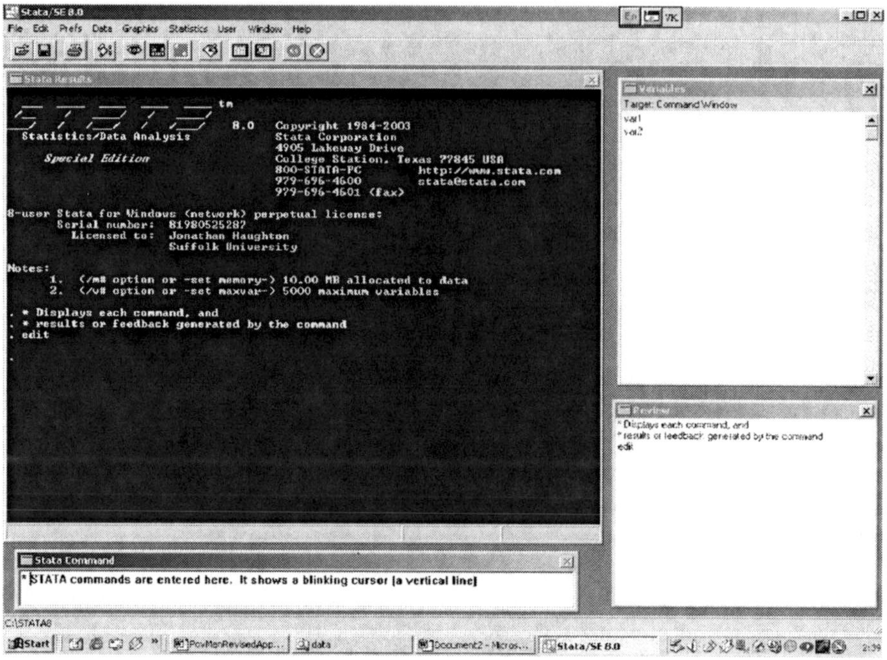

Source: Screenshot of Stata window.

You can also click on File and then Open and then browse to find the file you need. Stata responds by displaying the following in the Stata Results window:

```
. c:\eval\data\hh_98.dta
```

The first line repeats the command you enter, and absence of an error message in a second line implies the command has been executed successfully. From now on, only the Stata Results window will be shown to demonstrate Stata commands. The following points should be noted:

- Stata assumes the file is in Stata format with an extension .dta. Thus, typing "hh_98" is the same as typing "hh_98.dta."
- Only one data set can be open at a time in Stata. In this case, for example, if another data set hh_91.dta is opened, it will replace hh_98.dta with hh_91.dta.
- The preceding command assumes that the file hh_98.dta is not in the current directory. To make c:\eval\data the current directory and then open the file as before, enter the following commands:

```
. cd c:\eval\data
. use hh_98
```

If the memory allocated to Stata (which is by default 1,000 kilobytes, or 1 megabyte) is too little for the data file to be opened, as is typically the case when with large household survey data sets, an error message such as the following will appear:

```
. use hh_98
no room to add more observations
r(901);
```

The third line displays the code associated with the error message. All error messages in Stata have associated codes like this one; further explanations are available in the Stata reference manuals. In this case, more memory must be allocated to Stata. The following commands allocate 30 megabytes to Stata and then try again to open the file:

```
. set memory 30m
[This generates a table with memory information]
. use hh_98
```

Because the file opens successfully, allocated memory is sufficient. If you continue to get an error message, you can use a larger amount of memory, although it may slow down your computer somewhat. Note that the "set memory" command works only if no data set is open (in memory). Otherwise, you will get following error message:

```
. use hh_98
. set memory 10m
no; data in memory would be lost
r(4);
```

You can clear the memory by using one of the two commands: "clear" or "drop _all." The following demonstration shows the first command:

```
. use hh_98
. set memory 10m
no; data in memory would be lost
r(4);
. clear
. set memory 10m
```

Saving a Data Set

If you make changes in an open Stata data file and want to save those changes, you can do so by using the Stata "save" command. For example, the following command saves the hh_98.dta file:

```
. save hh_98, replace
file hh_98.dta saved
```

You can optionally omit the file name here (just "save, replace" is good enough). If you do not use the replace option, Stata does not save the data but issues the following error message:

```
. save hh_98
file hh_98.dta already exists
r(602);
```

The replace option unambiguously tells Stata to overwrite the preexisting original version with the new version. If you do *not* want to lose the original version, you have to specify a different file name in the "save" command.

Exiting Stata

An easy way to exit Stata is to issue the command "exit." However, if you have an unsaved data set open, Stata will issue the following error message:

```
. exit
no; data in memory would be lost
r(4)
```

To remedy this problem, you can save the data file and then issue the "exit" command. If you really want to exit Stata without saving the data file, you can first clear the memory (using the "clear" or "drop _all" command as shown before) and issue the "exit" command. You can also simplify the process by combining two commands:

```
. exit, clear
```

Stata Help

Stata comes with an excellent multivolume set of manuals. However, the on-computer help facility in Stata is extensive and very useful; if you have access to the Web, an even larger set of macros and other useful information are available.

From within Stata, if you know which command or keyword you want the help information about, you can issue the command "help" followed by the command name or keyword. This command works only if you type the full command name or keyword with no abbreviations. For example, the following command will not work:

```
. help mem
help for mem not found
try help contents or search mem
```

However, this command will:

```
. help memory
[output omitted]
```

If you cannot recall the full command name or keyword, or if you are not sure about which command you want, you can use the command "lookup" or "search" followed by the command name or keyword. So the following will work:

```
. search mem
[output omitted]
```

This command will list all commands associated with this keyword and display a brief description of each of those commands. Then you can pick the command that you think is relevant and use help to obtain the specific reference.

The Stata Web site (http://www.stata.com) has excellent help facilities, such as an online tutorial and frequently asked questions (FAQ).

Notes on Stata Commands

Here are some general comments about Stata commands:

- Stata commands are typed in lowercase.
- All names, including commands or variable names, can be abbreviated as long as no ambiguity exists. For example, "describe," "des," and simply "d" do the same job because no confusion exists.
- In addition to typing, some keystrokes can be used to represent a few Stata commands or sequences. The most important of them are the Page-Up and Page-Down keys. To display the previous command in the Stata Command window, you can press the Page-Up key. You can keep doing so until the first command of the session appears. Similarly, the Page-Down key displays the command that follows the currently displayed command in the Stata Command window.
- Clicking once on a command in the Review window will put it into the Stata Command window; double-clicking it will tell Stata to execute the command. This can be useful when commands need to be repeated or edited slightly in the Stata Command window.

Working with Data Files: Looking at the Content

To go through this exercise, open the hh_98.dta file; examples from this data file are used extensively.

Listing the Variables

To see all variables in the data set, use the "describe" command (in full or abbreviated):

```
. describe
```

This command provides information about the data set (name, size, number of observations) and lists all variables (name, storage format, display format, label).

To see just one variable or list of variables, use the describe command followed by the variable name or names:

```
. desc nh villid

                      storage      display      value
variable name           type        format      label      variable label
-------------------------------------------------------------------------
nh                     double       %7.0f                   HH ID
villid                 double       %9.0g                   Village ID
```

As you can see, the describe command shows also the variable type and length, as well as a short description of the variable (if available). The following points should be noted:

- You can abbreviate a list of variables by typing only the first and last variable names, separated by a hyphen (-); the Variables window shows the order in which the variables are stored. For example, to see all variables from "nh" to "famsize," you could type

  ```
  . describe nh-famsize
  ```

- The wild card symbol (*) is helpful to save some typing. For example, to see all variables that start with "exp," you could type

  ```
  . describe exp*
  ```

- You can abbreviate a variable or variable list this way in any Stata command (where it makes sense), not just in the "describe" command.

Listing Data

To see actual data stored in the variables, use the "list" command (abbreviated as "l"). If you type the command "list" by itself, Stata will display values for all variables and all observations, which may not be desirable for any practical purpose (and you may need to use the Ctrl-Break combination to stop data from scrolling endlessly across the screen). Usually you want to see the data for certain variables and for certain observations. This is achieved by typing a "list" command with a variable list and with conditions.

The following command lists all variables of the first three observations:

```
. list in 1/3
```

Here Stata displays all observations starting with observation 1 and ending with observation 3. Stata can also display data as a spreadsheet. To do so, use the two icons in the toolbar called Data Editor and Data Browser (fourth and third from right). Clicking one will cause a new window to pop up where the data will be displayed as a table, with observations as rows and variables as columns. Data Browser will only display the data, whereas you can edit data with Data Editor. The commands "edit" and "browse" will also open the spreadsheet window.

The following command lists household size and head's education for households headed by a female who is younger than 45:

```
. list famsize educhead if (sexhead==0 & agehead<45)
```

The prior statement uses two relational operators (== and <) and one logical operator (&). Relational operators impose a condition on one variable, while logical operators combine two or more relational operators. Table 11.1 shows the relational and logical operators used in Stata.

You can use relational and logical operators in any Stata command (where it makes sense), not just in the "list" command.

Summarizing Data

The very useful command "summarize" (which may be abbreviated "sum") calculates and displays a few summary statistics, including means and standard deviations. If no variable is specified, summary statistics are calculated for all variables in the data set. The following command summarizes the household size and education of the household head:

```
. sum famsize educhead
```

Stata excludes any observation that has a missing value for the variables being summarized from this calculation (missing values are discussed later). If you want to know the median and percentiles of a variable, add the "detail" option (abbreviated "d"):

```
. sum famsize educhead, d
```

A great strength of Stata is that it allows the use of weights. The weight option is useful if the sampling probability of one observation is different from that of another. In most household surveys, the sampling frame is stratified, where the first primary sampling units (often villages) are sampled, and conditional on the selection of primary sampling unit, secondary sampling units (often households) are drawn. Household surveys generally provide weights to correct for sampling design differences and sometimes data collection problems. The implementation in Stata is straightforward:

```
. sum famsize educhead [aw=weight]
```

Table 11.1 Relational and Logical Operators Used in Stata

Relational operators	Logical operators
> (greater than)	~ (not)
< (less than)	| (or)
== (equal)	& (and)
>= (greater than or equal)	
>= (less than or equal)	
!= or ~= (not equal)	

Source: Authors' compilation.

Here, the variable "weight" has the information on the weight to be given to each observation and "aw" is a Stata option to incorporate the weight into the calculation. The use of weights is discussed further in later chapter exercises.

For variables that are strings, the command "summarize" will not be able to give any descriptive statistics except that the number of observations is zero. Also, for variables that are categorical (for example, illiterate = 1, primary education = 2, higher education = 3), interpreting the output of the "summarize" command can be difficult. In both cases, a full tabulation may be more meaningful, which is discussed next.

Often, one wants to see summary statistics by groups of certain variables, not just for the whole data set. Suppose you want to see mean family size and education of household head for participants and nonparticipants. First, sort the data by the group variable (in this case, dfmfd). You can check this sort by issuing the "describe" command after opening each file. The "describe" command, after listing all the variables, indicates whether the data set is sorted by any variables. If no sorting information is listed or the data set is sorted by a variable that is different from the one you want, you can use the "sort" command and then save the data set in this form. The following commands sort the data set by the variable "dfmfd" and show summary statistics of family size and education of household head for participants and nonparticipants:

```
. sort dfmfd
. by dfmfd: sum famsize educhead [aw=weight]
```

A useful alternative to the "summary" command is the "tabstat" command, which allows you to specify the list of statistics you want to display in a single table. It can be conditioned by another variable. The following command shows the mean and standard deviation of the family size and education of household head by the variable "dfmfd":

```
. tabstat famsize educhead, statistics(mean sd) by(dfmfd)
```

Frequency Distributions (Tabulations)

Frequency distributions and cross-tabulations are often needed. The "tabulate" (abbreviated "tab") command is used to do this:

```
. tab dfmfd
```

The following command gives the gender distribution of household heads of participants:

```
. tab sexhead if dfmfd==1
```

In passing, note the use of the == sign here. It indicates that if the regional variable is identically equal to one, then do the tabulation.

The "tabulate" command can also be used to show a two-way distribution. For example, one might want to check whether any gender bias exists in the education of household heads. The following command is used:

```
. tab educhead sexhead
```

To see percentages by row or columns, add options to the "tabulate" command:

```
. tab dfmfd sexhead, col row
```

Distributions of Descriptive Statistics (Table Command)

Another very convenient command is "table," which combines features of the "sum" and "tab" commands. In addition, it displays the results in a more presentable form. The following "table" command shows the mean of family size and of education of household head, by their participation in microfinance programs:

```
. table dfmfd, c(mean famsize mean educhead)
-------------------------------------------
HH has      |
female      |
microcred   |
it          |
participa   |
nt: 1=Y,    |
0=N         | mean(famsize)    mean(educhead)
----------+--------------------------------
        0 |      5.41               3
        1 |      5.21               2
-------------------------------------------
```

The results are as expected. But why is the mean of "educhead" displayed as an integer and not a fraction? This occurs because the "educhead" variable is stored as an integer number, and Stata simply truncated numbers after the decimal. Look at the description of this variable:

```
. d educhead

                storage   display   value
variable name    type     format    label            variable label
-----------------------------------------------------------------------
educhead         float     %2.0f     Education (years) of HH Head
```

Note that "educhead" is a float variable: its format (%2.0f) shows that its digits occupy two places, and it has no digit after the decimal. You can force Stata to reformat the display. Suppose you want it to display two places after the decimal, for a three-digit display. The following command shows that command and the subsequent "table" command:

```
. format educhead %3.2f

. table dfmfd, c(mean famsize mean educhead)
----------------------------------------------
HH has     |
female     |
microcred  |
it         |
participa  |
nt: 1=Y,   |
0=N        | mean(famsize)     mean(educhead)
-----------+----------------------------------
        0  |     5.41               2.95
        1  |     5.21               1.75
----------------------------------------------
```

This display is much better. Formatting changes only the display of the variable, not the internal representation of the variable in the memory. The "table" command can display up to five statistics and variables other than the mean (such as the sum or minimum or maximum). Two-way, three-way, or even higher-dimensional tables can be displayed.

Here is an example of a two-way table that breaks down the education of the household head not just by region but also by sex of household head:

```
. table dfmfd sexhead, c(mean famsize mean educhead)
----------------------
HH has     |
female     |
microcred  |
it         | Gender of
participa  |  HH head:
nt: 1=Y,   |  1=M, 0=F
0=N        |   0    1
-----------+----------
        0  | 4.09 5.53
           | 1.18 3.11
           |
        1  | 4.25 5.31
           | 0.59 1.88
----------------------
```

Missing Values in Stata

In Stata, a missing value is represented by a dot (.). A missing value is considered larger than any number. The "summarize" command ignores the observations with missing values, and the "tabulate" command does the same, unless forced to include missing values.

Counting Observations

The "count" command is used to count the number of observations in the data set:

```
. count
 1129
.
```

The "count" command can be used with conditions. The following command gives the number of households whose head is older than 50:

```
. count if agehead>50
 354
.
```

Using Weights

In most household surveys, observations are selected through a random process and may have different probabilities of selection. Hence, one must use weights that are equal to the inverse of the probability of being sampled. A weight of w_j for the jth observation means, roughly speaking, that the jth observation represents w_j elements in the population from which the sample was drawn. Omitting sampling weights in the analysis usually gives biased estimates, which may be far from the true values.

Various postsampling adjustments to the weights are usually necessary. The household sampling weight that is provided in the hh.dta is the right weight to use when summarizing data that relates to households.

Stata has four types of weights:

- Frequency weights ("fweight"), which indicate how many observations in the population are represented by each observation in the sample, must take integer values.
- Analytic weights ("aweight") are especially appropriate when working with data that contain averages (for example, average income per capita in a household). The weighting variable is proportional to the number of persons over which the average was computed (for example, number of members of a household). Technically, analytic weights are in inverse proportion to the variance of an observation (that is, a higher weight means that the observation was based on more information and so is more reliable in the sense of having less variance).
- Sampling weights ("pweight") are the inverse of the probability of selection because of sample design.
- Importance weights ("iweight") indicate the relative importance of the observation.

The most commonly used are "pweight" and "aweight." Further information on weights may be obtained by typing "help weight."

The following commands show application of weights:

```
. tabstat famsize [aweight=weight], statistics(mean sd) by(dfmfd)
. table dfmfd [aweight=weight], contents(mean famsize sd famsize)
```

	Full sample		Participants		Nonparticipants	
	Mean	Standard deviation	Mean	Standard deviation	Mean	Standard deviation
Household size	_____	_____	_____	_____	_____	_____
Per capita expenditure	_____	_____	_____	_____	_____	_____
Per capita food expenditure	_____	_____	_____	_____	_____	_____
Per capita nonfood expenditure	_____	_____	_____	_____	_____	_____

Are the weighted averages very different from the unweighted ones?

_____

_____

_____

_____

Changing Data Sets

So far, discussion has been limited to Stata commands that display information in the data in different ways without changing the data. In reality, Stata sessions most often involve making changes in the data (for example, creating new variables or changing values of existing variables). The following exercises demonstrate how those changes can be incorporated in Stata.

Generating New Variables

In Stata the command "generate" (abbreviated "gen") creates new variables, while the command "replace" changes the values of an existing variable. The following commands create a new variable called "oldhead" and then set its value to one if the household head is older than 50 years and to zero otherwise:

```
. gen oldhead=1 if agehead>50
(775 missing values generated)
. replace oldhead=0 if agehead<=50
(775 real changes made)
```

What happens here is that, for each observation, the "gen" command checks the condition (whether household head is older than 50) and sets the value of the variable "oldhead" to one for that observation if the condition is true and to missing value otherwise. The "replace" command works in a similar fashion. After the "generate" command, Stata indicates that 775 observations failed to meet the condition, and after the "replace" command Stata indicates that those 775 observations have new values (zero in this case). The following points are worth noting:

- If a "gen" or "replace" command is issued without any conditions, that command applies to all observations in the data file.
- While using the generate command, one should take care to handle missing values properly.
- The right-hand side of the = sign in the "gen" or "replace" commands can be any expression involving variable names, not just a value. Thus, for instance, the command "gen young = (agehead<=32)" would create a variable called "young" that would take on the value of one if the head is 32 years of age or younger (that is, if the bracketed expression is true) and a value of zero otherwise.
- The "replace" command can be used to change the values of any existing variable, independently of the "generate" command.

An extension of the "generate" command is "egen." Like the "gen" command, the "egen" command can create variables to store descriptive statistics, such as the mean, sum, maximum, and minimum. The more powerful feature of the "egen" command is its ability to create statistics involving multiple observations. For example, the following command creates a variable "avgage" containing the average age of household heads for the whole data:

```
. egen avgage=mean(agehead)
```

All observations in the data set get the same value for "avgage." The following command creates the same statistics, but this time for male- and female-headed households separately:

```
. egen avgagemf=mean(agehead), by(sexhead)
```

Labeling Variables

You can attach labels to variables to give them a description. For example, the variable "oldhead" does not have any label now. You can attach a label to this variable by typing

```
. label variable oldhead "HH Head is over 50: 1=Y, 0=N"
```

In the "label" command, variable can be shortened to "var." Now to see the new label, type the following:

```
. des oldhead
```

Labeling Data

Other types of labels can be created. To attach a label to the entire data set, which appears at the top of the "describe" list, try

```
. label data "Bangladesh HH Survey 1998"
```

To see this label, type

```
. des
```

Labeling Values of Variables

Variables that are categorical, like those in "sexhead (1 = male, 0 = female)," can have labels that help one remember what the categories are. For example, using hh_98.dta, tabulating the variable "sexhead" shows only zero and one values:

```
. tab sexhead
```

Gender of HH head: 1=M, 0=F	Freq.	Percent	Cum.
0	104	9.21	9.21
1	1,025	90.79	100.00
Total	1,129	100.00	

To attach labels to the values of a variable, two things must be done. First, define a value label. Then assign this label to the variable. Using the new categories for sexhead, type

```
. label define sexlabel 0 "Female" 1 "Male"
. label values sexhead sexlabel
```

Now, to see the labels, type

```
. tab sexhead
```

If you want to see the actual values of the variable "sexhead," which are still zeros and ones, you can add an option to not display the labels assigned to the values of the variable. For instance, try

```
. tab sexhead, nolabel
```

Keeping and Dropping Variables and Observations

Variables and observations of a data set can be selected by using the "keep" or "drop" commands. Suppose you have a data set with six variables: var1, var2, ..., var6. You would like to keep a file with only three of them (say, var1, var2, and var3). You can use either of the following two commands:

- "keep var1 var2 var3" (or "keep var1-var3" if the variables are in this order)
- "drop var4 var5 var6" (or "drop var4-var6" if the variables are in this order)

Note the use of a hyphen (-) in both commands. It is good practice to use the command that involves fewer variables or less typing (and hence less risk of error). You can also use relational or logical operators. For example, the following command drops those observations where the head of the household is 80 or older:

```
. drop if agehead>=80
```

And this command keeps those observations where household size is six or fewer members:

```
. keep if famsize<=6
```

The preceding two commands drop or keep all variables depending on the conditions. You cannot include a variable list in a "drop" or "keep" command that also uses conditions. For example, the following command will fail:

```
. keep nh famsize if famsize<=6
invalid syntax
r(198)
```

You have to use two commands to do the job:

```
. keep if famsize<=6
. keep nh famsize
```

You can also use the keyword in a "drop" or "keep" command. For example, to drop the first 20 observations:

```
. drop in 1/20
```

Producing Graphs

Stata is quite good at producing basic graphs, although considerable experimentation may be needed to produce beautiful graphs. The following command shows the distribution of the age of the household head in a bar graph (histogram):

```
. histogram agehead
```

In many cases, the easiest way to produce graphs is by using the menus; in this case, click on Graphics and then on Histogram and follow the prompts. An easy way to save a graph is to right-click on it and copy it to paste into a Microsoft Word or Excel document.

Here is a command for a scatterplot of two variables:

```
. twoway (scatter educhead agehead), ytitle(Education of head)
xtitle(Age of head) title(Education by Age)
```

Combining Data Sets

In Stata, only one data file can be worked with at a time—that is, there can be only one data set in memory at a time. However, useful information is often spread across multiple data files that need to be accessed simultaneously. To use such information, Stata has commands that combine those files. Depending on how such information is spread across files, one can *merge* or *append* multiple files.

Merging Data Sets

Merging of data files is done when one needs to use *variables* that are spread over two or more files. As an example of merging, the hh_98.dta will be divided into two data sets in such a way that one contains a variable or variables that the other does not, and then the data sets will be combined (merged) to get the original hh_98.dta back. Open the hh_98.dta file, drop the program participation variables, and save the datafile as hh_98_1.dta.

```
. use hh_98, clear
. drop dmmfd dfmfd
. save hh_98_1.dta,replace
```

You want to give this file a new name (hh_98_1.dta) because you do not want to change the original hh_98.dta permanently. Now open the hh_98.dta again. This time, keep the program participation variables only. Save this file as hh_98_2.dta.

```
. use hh_98, clear
. keep nh dmmfd dfmfd
. save hh_98_2.dta,replace
```

Notice that you kept the household identification ("nh") in addition to the program participation variables. This is necessary because merging requires at least one common identifying variable between the two files that are to be merged. Here "nh" is that common variable between the two files. Now you have two data sets—one has household's program participation variables (hh_98_2.dta), and the other does not have those variables (hh_98_1.dta). If you need to use the variables from both files, you will have to merge the two files. However, before merging two files, you need to make sure that both files are sorted by the identifying variable. This can be done quickly as follows:

```
. use hh_98_1, clear
. sort nh
```

```
. save, replace
. use hh_98_2, clear
. sort nh
. save, replace
```

Now you are ready to merge the two files. One of the files has to be open (it does not matter which file). Open hh_98_1.dta file, and then merge the hh_98_2.dta file with it:

```
. use hh_98_1, clear
. merge nh using hh_98_2
```

In this context, hh_98_1.dta is called the *master file* (the file that remains in the memory before the merging operation) and hh_98_2.dta is called the *using file*. To see how the merge operation went, type the following command:

```
. tab _merge
```

Stata creates this new variable "_merge" during the merging operation. A tab operation to this variable displays different values of "_merge" and thereby status of the merging operation.

_merge	Freq.	Percent	Cum.
3	1129	100.00	100.00
Total	1129	100.00	

Even though in this case "_merge" has only one value (3), it can have up to three possible values, depending on the nature of the merging operation:

- A value of 1 shows the number of observations coming from the *master file* only.
- A value of 2 shows the number of observations coming from the *using file* only.
- A value of 3 shows the number of observations common in both files.

The total number of observations in the resulting data set is the sum of these three "_merge" frequencies. In this example, however, each observation (household) in the hh_98_1.dta file has an exact match in the hh_98_2.dta file, which is why you got "_merge=3" and not 1s or 2s (obviously, because the two files are created from the same file). But in real-life examples, 1s and 2s may remain after merging. Most often, one wants to work with the observations that are common in both files (that is, "_merge=3"). That is done by issuing the following command after the merging operation:

```
. keep if _merge==3
```

In addition, it is good practice to drop the "_merge" variable from the data set after the "_merge" operation. Now you have a data set that is identical to hh_98.dta in content.

Appending Data Sets

Appending data sets is necessary when you need to combine two data sets that have the same (or almost the same) variables, but observation units (households, for example) are mutually exclusive. To demonstrate the append operation, you will again divide the hh_98.dta. This time, however, instead of dropping variables, you will drop a few observations. Open the hh_98.dta file, drop observations 1 to 700, and save this file as hh_98_1.dta:

```
. use hh_98, clear
. drop in 1/700
. save hh_98_1.dta,replace
```

Next, reopen hh_98.dta but keep observations 1 to 700, and save this file as hh_98_2.dta.

```
. use hh_98, clear
. keep in 1/700
. save hh_98_2.dta,replace
```

Now, you have two data sets; both have identical variables but different sets of households. In this situation, you need to append two files. Again, one file has to be in memory (which one does not matter). Open hh_98_1.dta, and then append hh_98_2.dta.

```
. use hh_98_1, clear
. append using hh_98_2
```

Note that individual files do not need to be sorted for the append operation, and Stata does not create any new variable like "_merge" after the append operation. You can verify that the append operation executed successfully by issuing the Stata "count" command, which shows the number of observations in the resulting data set, which must be the sum of the observations in the two individual files (that is, 1,129).

Working with .log and .do Files

This section discusses the use of two types of files that are extremely efficient in Stata applications. One stores Stata commands and results for later review (.log files), and the other stores commands for repeated executions later. The two types of files can work interactively, which is very helpful in debugging commands and in getting a good "feel" for the data.

.log Files

One often wants to save the results of Stata commands and perhaps to print them out. Do this by creating a .log file. Such a file is created by issuing a "log using" command

and closed by a "log close" command; all commands issued in between, as well as corresponding output (except graphs) are saved in the .log file. Use hh_98.dta. Assume that you want to save only the education summary of heads by household gender. Here are the commands:

```
. log using educm.log
. by sexhead, sort:sum educhead
. log close
```

What happens here is that Stata creates a text file named *educm.log* in the current folder and saves the summary output in that file. If you want the .log file to be saved in a folder other than the current folder, you can specify the full path of the folder in the .log creation command. You can also use the File option in the Menu, followed by Log and Begin.

If a .log file already exists, you can either replace it with "log using educm.log" or replace or append new output to it with "log using educm.log, append." If you really want to keep the existing .log file unchanged, then you can rename either this file or the file in the .log creation command. If you want to suppress a portion of a .log file, you can issue a "log off" command before that portion, followed by a "log on" command for the portion that you want to save. You have to close a .log file before opening a new one; otherwise, you will get an error message.

.do Files

You have so far seen interactive use of Stata commands, which is useful for debugging commands and getting a good feel for the data. You type one command line each time, and Stata processes that command, displays the result (if any), and waits for the next command. Although this approach has its own benefits, more advanced use of Stata involves executing commands in a batch—that is, commands are grouped and submitted together to Stata instead one at a time.

If you find yourself using the same set of commands repeatedly, you can save those commands in a file and run them together whenever you need them. These command files are called *.do files*; they are the Stata equivalent of macros. You can create .do files at least three ways:

1. Simply type the commands into a text file, label it "educm.do" (the .do suffix is important), and run the file using "do educm" in the Stata Command window.
2. Right-click anywhere in the Review window to save all the commands that were used interactively. The file in which they were saved can be edited, labeled, and used as a .do file.
3. Use Stata's built-in .do editor. It is invoked by clicking on the icon (the fifth from the right, at the top of the page). Commands may then be typed into the editor.

Run these commands by highlighting them and using the appropriate icon (the second from the right) within the .do editor. With practice, this procedure becomes a very quick and convenient way to work with Stata.

Here is an example of a .do file:

```
log using educm.log
use hh_98
sort nh
save, replace
sort sexhead
by sexhead:sum educhead
log close
```

The main advantages of using .do files instead of typing commands line by line are replicability and repeatability. With a .do file, one can replicate results that were worked on weeks or months before. Moreover, .do files are especially useful when sets of commands need to be repeated—for instance, with different data sets or groups.

Certain commands are useful in a .do file. They are discussed from the following sample .do file:

```
*This is a Stata comment that is not executed
/*****This is a do file that shows some very useful
 commands used in do files. In addition, it creates a
log file and uses some basic Stata commands  ***/

#delimit ;
set more 1;
drop _all;
cap log close;
log using c:\eval\log\try.log, replace;

use c:\eval\data\hh_98.dta ;
describe ;
list in 1/3 ;
list nh famsize educhead if sexhead==0 & agehead<45;
summarize famsize;
summarize famsize, detail;
sum famsize educhead [aw=weight], d;
tab sexhead;
tab educhead sexhead, col row;
tab educhead, summarize(agehead);
label define sexlabel 1 "MALE" 0 "FEMALE";
label values sexhead sexlabel;
tabulate sexhead;
```

```
label variable sexhead "Gender of Head: 1=M, 0=F";
save c:\eval\data\temp.dta, replace;
#delimit cr
use c:\eval\data\hh_91.dta
append using temp
tab year
log close
```

The first line in the file is a comment. Stata treats any line that starts with an asterisk (*) as a comment and ignores it. You can write a multiline comment by using a forward slash and an asterisk (/*) as the start of the comment, and end the comment with an asterisk and forward slash (*/). Comments are very useful for documentation purposes, and you should include at least the following information in the comment of a .do file: the general purpose of the .do file and the last modification time and date. You can include comments anywhere in the .do file, not just at the beginning.

Commands used in the sample .do file are as follows:

`#delimit;`   By default, Stata assumes that each command is ended by the carriage return (that is, by pressing the Enter key). If, however, a command is too long to fit on one line, you can spread it over more than one line. You do that by letting Stata know what the command delimiter is. The command in the example says that a semicolon (;) ends a command. Every command following the "delimit" command has to end with a semicolon. Although for this particular .do file the "#delimit" command is not needed (all commands are short enough), it is done to explain the command.

`set more 1`   Stata usually displays results one screen at a time and waits for the user to press any key. But this process would soon become a nuisance if, after letting a .do file run, you have to press a key for every screen until the program ends. This command displays the whole output, skipping page after page automatically.

`drop _all`   This command clears the memory.

`cap log close`   This command closes any open .log file. If no log file is open, Stata just ignores this command.

Exercise: Run the .do file sample.do, which stores its output in try.log. When you see "end of .do file," open c:\eval\log\try.log in Microsoft Word (or Notepad) and check the results.

.ado Files

The .ado files are Stata programs meant to perform specific tasks. Many Stata commands are implemented as .ado files (for example, the "summarize" command). To run such a program, simply type the name of the program at the command line. Users can write their own .ado programs to meet special requirements. In fact, Stata users and developers are continuously writing such programs, which are often made available to the greater Stata user community on the Internet. You will use such commands throughout the exercises on different impact evaluation techniques. Stata has built-in commands to download and incorporate such commands in Stata. For example, the propensity score matching technique is implemented by an .ado file called *pscore.ado*. To download the latest version of this command, type the following command at the command line:

```
. findit pscore
```

Stata responds with a list of .ado implementations of the program. Clicking on one of them will give its details and present the option to install it. When Stata installs an .ado program, it also installs the help files associated with it.

Follow-up Practice

Look at the 1998 data set that will be used frequently in the impact evaluation exercise.

a. Household characteristics

Look at how different the household characteristics are between the participants and nonparticipants of microfinance programs. Open c:\eval\data\hh_98.dta, which consists of household-level variables. Fill in the following table. You may use the "tabstat" or "table" command in Stata.

```
. tabstat famsize, statistics(mean sd) by(dfmfd)
. table dfmfd, contents(mean famsize sd famsize)
```

	Full sample		Female participants		Households without female participants	
	Mean	Standard deviation	Mean	Standard deviation	Mean	Standard deviation
Average household size	___	___	___	___	___	___
Average household assets	___	___	___	___	___	___
Average household landholding	___	___	___	___	___	___
Average age of household head	___	___	___	___	___	___
Average years of education of household head	___	___	___	___	___	___
Percentage of households with male head	___	___	___	___	___	___

Are the sampled households very different among the full sample, participants, and nonparticipants?

_____

_____

_____

_____

Gender of household heads may also affect household characteristics.

```
. tabstat famsize, statistics(mean sd) by(sexhead)
. table sexhead, contents(mean famsize sd famsize)
```

	Male-headed households		Female-headed households	
	Mean	Standard deviation	Mean	Standard deviation
Average household size	_____	_____	_____	_____
Average years of head schooling	_____	_____	_____	_____
Average head age	_____	_____	_____	_____
Average household assets	_____	_____	_____	_____
Average household landholding	_____	_____	_____	_____

Are the sampled households headed by males very different from those headed by females?

_____

_____

_____

_____

b. Village characteristics

	Mean	Standard deviation
If village is accessible by road	_____	_____
Percentage of village land irrigated	_____	_____

c. Prices

	Full sample		Participants		Nonparticipants	
	Mean	Standard deviation	Mean	Standard deviation	Mean	Standard deviation
Rice	_____	_____	_____	_____	_____	_____
Wheat	_____	_____	_____	_____	_____	_____
Edible oil	_____	_____	_____	_____	_____	_____
Milk	_____	_____	_____	_____	_____	_____
Potato	_____	_____	_____	_____	_____	_____

d. Expenditure

Open c:\eval\data\hh_98.dta. It has household-level consumption expenditure information. Look at the consumption patterns.

	Per capita expenditure		Per capita food expenditure		Per capita nonfood expenditure	
	Mean	Standard deviation	Mean	Standard deviation	Mean	Standard deviation
By head gender						
Male-headed households	___	___	___	___	___	___
Female-headed households	___	___	___	___	___	___
By head education level						
Head has some education	___	___	___	___	___	___
Head has no education	___	___	___	___	___	___
By household size						
Large household (> 5)	___	___	___	___	___	___
Small household (<= 5)	___	___	___	___	___	___
By land ownership						
Large land ownership (> 50/person)	___	___	___	___	___	___
Small land ownership or landless	___	___	___	___	___	___

	Full sample		Female participants		Households without female participants	
	Mean	Standard deviation	Mean	Standard deviation	Mean	Standard deviation
Per capita expenditure	___	___	___	___	___	___
Per capita food expenditure	___	___	___	___	___	___
Per capita nonfood expenditure	___	___	___	___	___	___

Summarize your findings on per capita expenditure comparison.

_____

_____

_____

_____

12. Randomized Impact Evaluation

Randomization works in the ideal scenario where individuals or households are assigned to treatment randomly, eliminating selection bias. In an attempt to obtain an estimate of the impact of a certain program, comparing the same treated individuals over time does not provide a consistent estimate of the program's impact, because other factors besides the program may affect outcomes. However, comparing the outcome of the treated individuals with that of a similar control group can provide an estimate of the program's impact. This comparison works well with randomization because the assignment of individuals or groups to the treatment and comparison groups is random. An unbiased estimate of the impact of the program in the sample will be obtained when the design and implementation of the randomized evaluation are appropriate. This exercise demonstrates randomized impact estimation with different scenarios. In this chapter, the randomization impact evaluation is demonstrated from top down—that is, from program placement to program participation.

Impacts of Program Placement in Villages

Assume that microcredit programs are randomly assigned to villages,[1] and further assume no differences between treated and control villages. You want to ascertain the impact of program placement on household's per capita total annual expenditures.

For this exercise, use the 1998 household data hh_98.dta. The following commands open the data set and create the log form of two variables—outcome ("exptot") and household's land before joining the microcredit program ("hhland," which is changed to acre from decimal by dividing by 100).

```
use ..\data\hh_98;
gen lexptot=ln(1+exptot);
gen lnland=ln(1+hhland/100);
```

Then a dummy variable is created for microcredit program placement in villages. Two program placement variables are created: one for male programs and the other for female programs.

```
gen vill=thanaid*10+villid;
egen progvillm=max(dmmfd), by(vill);
egen progvillf=max(dfmfd), by(vill);
```

First, use the simplest method to calculate average treatment effect of village program placement. It is done by using the Stata "ttest" command, which compares the outcome between treated and control villages. The following command shows the effects of female program placement in the village:

```
ttest lexptot, by(progvillf);
```

The result shows that the difference of outcomes between treated and control villages is significant. That is, female program placement in villages improves per capita expenditure.[2]

```
Two-sample t-test with equal variances

------------------------------------------------------------------------
   Group |    Obs      Mean    Std. Err.  Std. Dev.   [95% Conf. Interval]
---------+--------------------------------------------------------------
       0 |     67   8.328525   .0644093  .5272125    8.199927   8.457122
       1 |   1062   8.458371   .0157201  .5122923    8.427525   8.489217
---------+--------------------------------------------------------------
combined |   1129   8.450665   .0152934  .5138679    8.420659   8.480672
---------+--------------------------------------------------------------
    diff |         -.1298466   .0646421              -.2566789  -.0030142
------------------------------------------------------------------------

Degrees of freedom: 1127

                    Ho: mean(0) - mean(1) = diff = 0

  Ha: diff < 0          Ha: diff != 0           Ha: diff > 0
    t = -2.0087           t = -2.0087             t = -2.0087
P < t =  0.0224      P > |t| = 0.0448       P > t =  0.9776
```

Alternately, you can run the simplest equation that regresses per capita expenditure against the village program dummy:

```
reg lexptot progvillf;
```

The result gives the same effect (0.130), which is significant.

```
   Source |     SS       df       MS              Number of obs =    1129
----------+------------------------------          F( 1, 1127)   =    4.03
    Model | 1.06259118     1 1.06259118           Prob > F       = 0.0448
 Residual | 296.797338  1127 .263351676           R-squared      = 0.0036
----------+------------------------------          Adj R-squared = 0.0027
    Total | 297.85993   1128 .264060221           Root MSE       = .51318
------------------------------------------------------------------------
  lexptot |    Coef.   Std. Err.      t    P>|t|   [95% Conf. Interval]
----------+-------------------------------------------------------------
progvillf |  .1298466  .0646421     2.01   0.045   .0030142   .2566789
    _cons |  8.328525  .0626947   132.84   0.000   8.205513   8.451536
```

The preceding regression estimates the overall impact of the village programs on the per capita expenditure of households. It may be different from the impact on the expenditure after holding other factors constant—that is, specifying the model adjusted for covariates that affect the outcomes of interest. Now, regress the same outcome (log of per capita household expenditures) against the village program dummy plus other factors that may influence the expenditure:

```
reg lexptot progvillf sexhead agehead educhead lnland vaccess pcirr rice
wheat milk oil egg [pw=weight];
```

Adjusting for other covariates, one still finds no significant impacts of program placement on the outcome variable:

```
Regression with robust standard errors        Number of obs =    1129
                                              F( 12, 1116)  =   20.16
                                              Prob > F      = 0.0000
                                              R-squared     = 0.2450
                                              Root MSE      = .46179
```

	Robust					
lexptot	Coef.	Std. Err.	t	P>|t|	[95% Conf.	Interval]
progvillf	-.0455621	.1046759	-0.44	0.663	-.2509458	.1598217
sexhead	-.0373236	.0643335	-0.58	0.562	-.1635519	.0889047
agehead	.0030636	.0012859	2.38	0.017	.0005405	.0055867
educhead	.0486414	.0057184	8.51	0.000	.0374214	.0598614
lnland	.1912535	.0389079	4.92	0.000	.1149127	.2675943
vaccess	-.0358233	.0498939	-0.72	0.473	-.1337197	.0620731
pcirr	.1189407	.0608352	1.96	0.051	-.0004236	.238305
rice	.0069748	.0110718	0.63	0.529	-.0147491	.0286987
wheat	-.029278	.0196866	-1.49	0.137	-.0679049	.009349
milk	.0141328	.0072647	1.95	0.052	-.0001211	.0283867
oil	.0083345	.0038694	2.15	0.031	.0007424	.0159265
egg	.1115221	.0612063	1.82	0.069	-.0085702	.2316145
_cons	7.609248	.2642438	28.80	0.000	7.090777	8.127718

Impacts of Program Participation

Even though microcredit program assignment is random across villages, the participation may not be. Only those households that have fewer than 50 decimals of land can participate in microcredit programs (so-called target groups).

As before, start with the simplest method to calculate average treatment effect of program participation for females. It is done by using the Stata "ttest" command, which compares the outcome between treated and control villages:

```
ttest lexptot, by(dfmfd);
```

The result shows that the difference of outcomes between participants and nonparticipants is insignificant.

```
Two-sample t-test with equal variances

---------------------------------------------------------------------
   Group |   Obs      Mean    Std. Err. Std. Dev. [95% Conf. Interval]
---------+-----------------------------------------------------------
       0 |   534   8.447977   .023202   .5361619   8.402398   8.493555
       1 |   595   8.453079   .0202292  .4934441   8.413349   8.492808
---------+-----------------------------------------------------------
combined |  1129   8.450665   .0152934  .5138679   8.420659   8.480672
---------+-----------------------------------------------------------
    diff |         -.005102   .0306448            -.0652292   .0550253
---------------------------------------------------------------------

Degrees of freedom: 1127

                    Ho: mean(0) - mean(1) = diff = 0

    Ha: diff < 0            Ha: diff != 0            Ha: diff > 0
    t = -0.1665            t = -0.1665              t = -0.1665
  P < t =  0.4339       P > |t| =  0.8678        P > t =  0.5661
```

Again, alternately you can run the simple regression model—outcome against female participation:

```
reg lexptot dfmfd;
```

The regression illustrates that the effect of female participation in microcredit programs is not different from zero.

```
   Source |      SS        df        MS           Number of obs =    1129
----------+-------------------------------         F(1, 1127)    =    0.03
    Model | .007325582      1    .007325582        Prob > F      =  0.8678
 Residual | 297.852604    1127    .264288025        R-squared     =  0.0000
----------+-------------------------------         Adj R-squared = -0.0009
    Total | 297.85993     1128    .264060221        Root MSE      =  .51409
---------------------------------------------------------------------------
  lexptot |    Coef.   Std. Err.     t     P>|t|    [95% Conf. Interval]
----------+----------------------------------------------------------------
    dfmfd | .005102    .0306448    0.17    0.868    -.0550253   .0652292
    _cons | 8.447977   .0222468  379.74    0.000     8.404327   8.491626
---------------------------------------------------------------------------
```

Now, similarly to the regression of village program placement, include other household- and village-level covariates in the female participation equation:

```
reg lexptot dfmfd sexhead agehead educhead lnland vaccess pcirr rice wheat
milk oil egg [pw=weight];
```

Female participation impact to household expenditure has now changed from insignificant to significant (10 percent level).

```
Regression with robust standard errors          Number of obs =    1129

                                                F( 12, 1116)  =  19.72
                                                Prob > F      = 0.0000
                                                R-squared     = 0.2478
                                                Root MSE      = .46093

-----------------------------------------------------------------------
             |               Robust
     lexptot |    Coef.   Std. Err.    t     P>|t|    [95% Conf. Interval]
-------------+---------------------------------------------------------
       dfmfd |  .0654911  .0348852   1.88   0.061   -.0029569   .133939
     sexhead | -.0331386  .0647884  -0.51   0.609   -.1602593   .0939822
     agehead |  .0031133   .001314   2.37   0.018     .000535   .0056915
    educhead |  .0493265  .0060583   8.14   0.000    .0374395   .0612134
      lnland |  .2058408  .0421675   4.88   0.000    .1231043   .2885774
     vaccess | -.0295222  .0501813  -0.59   0.556   -.1279825   .0689381
       pcirr |  .1080647  .0610146   1.77   0.077   -.0116515   .2277809
        rice |  .0057045  .0112967   0.50   0.614   -.0164607   .0278696
       wheat | -.0295285  .0195434  -1.51   0.131   -.0678744   .0088174
        milk |  .0136748  .0073334   1.86   0.062   -.0007139   .0280636
         oil |  .0079069  .0038484   2.05   0.040     .000356   .0154579
         egg |  .1129842  .0612986   1.84   0.066   -.0072893   .2332577
       _cons |  7.560953   .278078  27.19   0.000    7.015339   8.106568
-----------------------------------------------------------------------
```

Capturing Both Program Placement and Participation

The previous two exercises showed in separate regressions the effects of program placement and program participation. However, these two effects can be combined in the same regression, which gives a more unbiased estimate.

```
reg lexptot dfmfd progvillf sexhead agehead educhead lnland vaccess pcirr
rice wheat milk oil egg [pw=weight];
```

The results show no significant effect of program placement but a positive significant effect (7.3 percent) of female program participants ($t = 2.05$).

```
Regression with robust standard errors          Number of obs =    1129
                                                F( 13, 1115)  =  18.34
                                                Prob > F      = 0.0000
                                                R-squared     = 0.2490
                                                Root MSE      = .46079
```

```
-------------------------------------------------------------------------
             |              Robust
     lexptot |    Coef.   Std. Err.     t     P>|t|   [95% Conf. Interval]
-------------+-----------------------------------------------------------
       dfmfd |  .0737423   .0359919    2.05   0.041    .0031228   .1443618
    progvillf | -.0747142    .107158   -0.70   0.486   -.2849682   .1355397
     sexhead | -.0377076   .0641847   -0.59   0.557   -.1636439   .0882288
     agehead |  .0030077   .0012831    2.34   0.019    .0004901   .0055254
    educhead |  .0499607   .0057753    8.65   0.000     .038629   .0612924
      lnland |  .2040906    .040482    5.04   0.000    .1246611   .2835201
     vaccess | -.0348664   .0494669   -0.70   0.481   -.1319252   .0621924
       pcirr |  .1071558   .0609133    1.76   0.079   -.0123617   .2266734
        rice |  .0053896    .011106    0.49   0.628   -.0164013   .0271806
       wheat |  -.028722   .0196859   -1.46   0.145   -.0673476   .0099036
        milk |  .0137693   .0072876    1.89   0.059   -.0005297   .0280683
         oil |  .0077801   .0038339    2.03   0.043    .0002576   .0153025
         egg |  .1137676   .0614016    1.85   0.064   -.0067082   .2342433
       _cons |   7.64048   .2627948   29.07   0.000    7.124852   8.156108
-------------------------------------------------------------------------
```

Impacts of Program Participation in Program Villages

Now, see if program participation matters for households living in program villages. Start with the simple model, and restrict the sample to program villages:

```
reg lexptot dfmfd if progvillf==1 [pw=weight];
```

The result shows that the impact of female participation in microcredit programs on household expenditure in program villages is in fact negative. Female participation lowers per capita expenditure of households in program villages by 7.0 percent.

```
Regression with robust standard errors        Number of obs  =     1062
                                              F(1, 1060)     =     3.57
                                              Prob > F       =   0.0590
                                              R-squared      =   0.0044
                                              Root MSE       =   .51788

             |              Robust
     lexptot |    Coef.   Std. Err.     t     P>|t|   [95% Conf. Interval]
-------------+-----------------------------------------------------------
       dfmfd | -.0700156   .0370416   -1.89   0.059   -.1426987   .0026675
       _cons |  8.519383   .0294207  289.57   0.000    8.461653   8.577112
-------------------------------------------------------------------------
```

Now regress the extended model (that is, including other variables that influence the total expenditures):

```
reg lexptot dfmfd sexhead agehead educhead lnland vaccess pcirr rice wheat
milk oil egg if progvillf==1 [pw=weight];
```

By keeping all other variables constant, you can see that female participation becomes positive and is significant at the 10 percent level.

```
Regression with robust standard errors          Number of obs =    1062
                                                F(12, 1049)   =   18.69
                                                Prob > F      = 0.0000
                                                R-squared     = 0.2567
                                                Root MSE      = .4498
-----------------------------------------------------------------------
              |               Robust
     lexptot  |    Coef.   Std. Err.      t    P>|t|   [95% Conf. Interval]
--------------+--------------------------------------------------------
        dfmfd |  .0670471  .0354779    1.89   0.059   -.0025687   .1366629
      sexhead | -.050392   .0656695   -0.77   0.443   -.1792505   .0784666
      agehead |  .0025747  .001273     2.02   0.043    .0000768   .0050727
     educhead |  .0542814  .0056875    9.54   0.000    .0431212   .0654416
       lnland |  .1641575  .0337974    4.86   0.000    .0978392   .2304758
      vaccess | -.0389844  .0498359   -0.78   0.434   -.1367739   .0588051
        pcirr |  .1246202  .0592183    2.10   0.036    .0084203   .2408201
         rice |  .0006952  .0103092    0.07   0.946   -.0195338   .0209243
        wheat | -.0299271  .0214161   -1.40   0.163   -.0719504   .0120963
         milk |  .0150224  .0068965    2.18   0.030    .0014899   .0285548
          oil |  .0076239  .0038719    1.97   0.049    .0000263   .0152215
          egg |  .105906   .0598634    1.77   0.077   -.0115597   .2233717
        _cons |  7.667193  .2737697   28.01   0.000    7.129995   8.204392
-----------------------------------------------------------------------
```

Measuring Spillover Effects of Microcredit Program Placement

This exercise investigates whether program placement in villages has any impact on nonparticipants. This test is similar to what was done at the beginning, but it excludes program participants. Start with the simple model and restrict the sample to program villages:

```
reg lexptot progvillf if dfmfd==0 [pw=weight];
```

The result does not show any spillover effects.

```
Regression with robust standard errors          Number of obs =     534
                                                F(1,  532)    =    0.00
                                                Prob > F      = 0.9525
                                                R-squared     = 0.0000
                                                Root MSE      = .55686
```

```
-------------------------------------------------------------------
            |              Robust
    lexptot |    Coef.   Std. Err.      t    P>|t|    [95% Conf. Interval]
------------+------------------------------------------------------
   progvillf | -.0074135   .1243228   -0.06   0.952    -.2516373   .2368103
       _cons |  8.526796   .1207848   70.59   0.000     8.289523   8.76407
-------------------------------------------------------------------
```

Next, run the extended model regression.

```
reg lexptot progvillf sexhead agehead educhead lnland vaccess pcirr rice
wheat milk oil egg if dfmfd==0 [pw=weight];
```

As can be seen from the output that follows, program placement in villages shows no spillover effect after other variables are controlled for:

```
Regression with robust standard errors        Number of obs  =      534
                                              F( 12,   521)  =    17.48
                                              Prob > F       =   0.0000
                                              R-squared      =   0.3254
                                              Root MSE       =  .46217
-------------------------------------------------------------------
            |              Robust
    lexptot |    Coef.   Std. Err.      t    P>|t|    [95% Conf. Interval]
------------+------------------------------------------------------
   progvillf | -.0667122   .1048541   -0.64   0.525     -.272701   .1392766
    sexhead | -.0308585   .0919099   -0.34   0.737    -.2114181   .1497011
    agehead |  .0037746   .0017717    2.13   0.034     .0002941   .0072551
   educhead |  .0529039   .0068929    7.68   0.000     .0393625   .0664453
     lnland |  .2384333   .0456964    5.22   0.000     .1486614   .3282053
    vaccess |  .0019065   .0678193    0.03   0.978    -.1313265   .1351394
      pcirr |  .0999683   .0876405    1.14   0.255    -.0722039   .2721405
       rice |  .0118292   .0171022    0.69   0.489    -.0217686   .045427
      wheat | -.0111823   .0263048   -0.43   0.671    -.0628588   .0404942
       milk |  .0084113   .0096439    0.87   0.384    -.0105344   .027357
        oil |  .0077888   .0050891    1.53   0.127    -.0022089   .0177866
        egg |  .1374734   .0815795    1.69   0.093    -.0227918   .2977386
      _cons |  7.347734   .3449001   21.30   0.000     6.670168   8.0253
-------------------------------------------------------------------
```

Further Exercises

Do the same exercise using male participation ("dmmfd"). Discuss the results.

Notes

1. In reality, such random assignment is not done. The assumption is made just to demonstrate the implementation of randomized impact evaluation.
2. Even though the difference is negative in the output, the impact is interpreted as positive. The negative sign simply means that outcome in program villages ("progvillf=1") is more than that in nonprogram villages ("progvillf=0"), implying that the participation impact is in fact positive.

13. Propensity Score Matching Technique

The basic idea behind propensity score matching (PSM) is to match each participant with an identical nonparticipant and then measure the average difference in the outcome variable between the participants and the nonparticipants. This exercise illustrates how to implement PSM in the Stata program.

The estimation command in Stata is "pscore.ado," developed by Becker and Ichino (2002). The "pscore" command estimates the propensity score, which is the probability of getting a treatment for each household, and tests the balancing property—that is, observations with the same propensity score must have the same distribution of observable characteristics independent of treatment status. After balancing is done, different commands can be used to carry out different types of matching and then derive the average treatment effect.

Propensity Score Equation: Satisfying the Balancing Property

The first step in PSM is to determine the propensity score and satisfy the balancing property. It is done using the "pscore" command in Stata. Use the 1998 data, hh_98.dta. Start with the male program participation variable "dmmfd" as the treatment variable. The following command shows the application of the "pscore" command:

```
pscore dmmfd sexhead agehead educhead lnland vaccess pcirr rice
wheat milk oil egg [pw=weight], pscore(ps98) blockid(blockf1)
comsup level(0.001);
```

The results include probit regression output, the estimation and description of the propensity scores, the number of blocks and stratification using propensity scores, and the balancing property test. The area of common support is those propensity scores within the range of the lowest and highest estimated values for households in the treatment group.

The following output shows that the identified region of common support is [.00180123, .50022341], the final number of blocks is 4, and the balancing property is not satisfied. The most important element to look for in the output is the list of variables that cause the balancing property not to be satisfied. The output shows the "egg" variable is not balanced in block 2. The solution to this problem is to use a different set of covariates and rerun the "pscore" command.

```
********************************************
Algorithm to estimate the propensity score
********************************************


The treatment is dmmfd

HH has male  |
microcredit  |
participant  |
 : 1=Y, 0=N  |      Freq.     Percent        Cum.
-------------+-----------------------------------
          0  |       909       80.51       80.51
          1  |       220       19.49      100.00
-------------+-----------------------------------
      Total  |     1,129      100.00
```

Estimation of the propensity score

```
(sum of wgt is  1.1260e+03)
Iteration 0:  log pseudolikelihood = -424.61883
Iteration 1:  log pseudolikelihood = -390.85321
Iteration 2:  log pseudolikelihood = -389.10243
Iteration 3:  log pseudolikelihood = -389.05511
Iteration 4:  log pseudolikelihood = -389.05501
```

```
Probit estimates                        Number of obs   =     1129
                                        Wald chi2(11)   =    64.36
                                        Prob > chi2     =   0.0000
Log pseudolikelihood = -389.05501       Pseudo R2       =   0.0838
-----------------------------------------------------------------------
             |               Robust
      dmmfd  |     Coef.   Std. Err.      z    P>|z|   [95% Conf. Interval]
-------------+---------------------------------------------------------
     sexhead |   .915108    .2432905    3.76   0.000    .4382675    1.391949
     agehead | -.0036952    .0046186   -0.80   0.424   -.0127475     .005357
    educhead |  .0161662    .0170125    0.95   0.342   -.0171777      .04951
      lnland | -.3341691    .1113146   -3.00   0.003   -.5523417   -.1159965
     vaccess | -.0752904    .1770457   -0.43   0.671   -.4222935    .2717128
       pcirr |  .2088394    .1753383    1.19   0.234   -.1348174    .5524961
        rice |   .145771    .0384417    3.79   0.000    .0704268    .2211153
       wheat |  .0465751    .0648087    0.72   0.472   -.0804475    .1735977
        milk | -.0017358     .023861   -0.07   0.942   -.0485026     .045031
         oil | -.0249797    .0135856   -1.84   0.066    -.051607    .0016476
         egg | -.7687454    .2311995   -3.33   0.001   -1.221888   -.3156028
       _cons | -1.188481    .8358266   -1.42   0.155   -2.826671    .4497088
-----------------------------------------------------------------------
```

Note: the common support option has been selected
The region of common support is [.00180123, .50022341]

Description of the estimated propensity score
in region of common support

```
            Estimated propensity score
---------------------------------------------------------------
       Percentiles       Smallest
  1%      .0055359       .0018012
  5%      .0170022       .0020871
 10%      .0346036       .0026732       Obs              1127
 25%       .069733       .0028227       Sum of Wgt.      1127
 50%      .1206795                      Mean         .1339801
                          Largest       Std. Dev.    .0850809
 75%      .1811405       .4698302
 90%      .2527064        .472444       Variance     .0072388
 95%      .2965199       .4735467       Skewness     .8931864
 99%      .3903884       .5002234       Kurtosis     3.942122
```

```
*****************************************************
Step 1: Identification of the optimal number of blocks
Use option detail if you want more detailed output
*****************************************************
```

The final number of blocks is 4

This number of blocks ensures that the mean propensity score
is not different for treated and controls in each blocks

```
*********************************************************
Step 2: Test of balancing property of the propensity score
Use option detail if you want more detailed output
*********************************************************
```

Variable egg is not balanced in block 2

The balancing property is not satisfied

Try a different specification of the propensity score

```
           |       HH has male
 Inferior  |       microcredit
 of block  | participant: 1=Y, 0=N
 of pscore |       0          1  |     Total
-----------+--------------------+----------
        0  |     380         49  |       429
       .1  |     382         97  |       479
       .2  |     140         70  |       210
       .4  |       5          4  |         9
-----------+--------------------+----------
    Total  |     907        220  |     1,127
```

Note: the common support option has been selected

```
********************************************
End of the algorithm to estimate the pscore
********************************************
```

After a few iterations, you will find that dropping "egg" and "lnland" allows the "pscore" command to be rerun with the balancing property satisfied. So "pscore" on "dfmfd" is run again, this time excluding the "egg" and "lnland" variables. Before rerunning the "pscore" command, it is important to drop the "ps98" and "blockf1" variables that were created as a result of the earlier run. Because female program participation is of more interest, the "pscore" command is shown here with female participation only.

```
pscore dfmfd sexhead agehead educhead lnland vaccess pcirr rice
wheat milk oil egg [pw=weight], pscore(ps98) blockid(blockf1)
comsup level(0.001);
```

This time the balancing property is satisfied, as shown here:

```
*******************************************************
Algorithm to estimate the propensity score
*******************************************************

The treatment is dfmfd

      HH has |
      female |
 microcredit |
 participant |
   : 1=Y, 0=N |      Freq.     Percent       Cum.
 ------------+-----------------------------------
          0 |        534       47.30       47.30
          1 |        595       52.70      100.00
 ------------+-----------------------------------
      Total |      1,129      100.00
```

Estimation of the propensity score

```
(sum of wgt is   1.1260e+03)
Iteration 0:   log pseudolikelihood = -750.38718
Iteration 1:   log pseudolikelihood = -682.82636
Iteration 2:   log pseudolikelihood = -680.63459
Iteration 3:   log pseudolikelihood = -680.62452
Iteration 4:   log pseudolikelihood = -680.62452
```

```
Probit estimates                          Number of obs    =      1129
                                          Wald chi2(11)    =     85.21
                                          Prob > chi2      =    0.0000
Log pseudolikelihood = -680.62452         Pseudo R2        =    0.0930
---------------------------------------------------------------------
            |               Robust
      dmmfd |      Coef.  Std. Err.       z    P>|z|   [95% Conf. Interval]
 -----------+---------------------------------------------------------
    sexhead |  -.037986   .1662857   -0.23   0.819     -.3639    .287928
    agehead |  .0013931   .0037305    0.37   0.709  -.0059185   .0087047
   educhead |  -.0465567  .0151559   -3.07   0.002  -.0762618  -.0168516
     lnland |  -.6662184   .101586   -6.56   0.000  -.8653232  -.4671136
    vaccess |  -.1173796    .13358   -0.88   0.380  -.3791916   .1444323
      pcirr |   .4304416   .154365    2.79   0.005   .1278917   .7329915
```

```
    rice |   .0571981    .0307982    1.86   0.063   -.0031652    .1175615
   wheat |  -.0055393     .056959   -0.10   0.923   -.1171769    .1060982
    milk |    .015395    .0184184    0.84   0.403   -.0207044    .0514944
     oil |   .0235048      .01239    1.90   0.058    -.000779    .0477887
     egg |  -.1114687    .1647319   -0.68   0.499   -.4343373    .2113999
   _cons |  -1.483823    .7367316   -2.01   0.044   -2.927791   -.0398558
------------------------------------------------------------------------
```

Note: the common support option has been selected
The region of common support is [.02576077, .71555996]

------------OUTPUT OMITTED----------

****
Step 2: Test of balancing property of the propensity score
Use option detail if you want more detailed output
****

The balancing property is satisfied

------------OUTPUT OMITTED----------

****
End of the algorithm to estimate the pscore
****

With the propensity scores generated, the outcomes of interest (such as total per capita expenditure) between the treatment group and the matched control group are now compared to see whether the microcredit programs affect the outcome of interest. The following sections estimate the treatment effect of microcredit program participation, using different matching techniques that are available.

Average Treatment Effect Using Nearest-Neighbor Matching

The command to estimate the average treatment effect on the treated group using nearest-neighbor matching is "attnd." Following is the application of the "attnd" command to estimate the average treatment effect of female participation in microcredit programs on per capita total expenditure using nearest-neighbor matching:

```
attnd lexptot dfmfd [pweight=weight], pscore(ps98) comsup;
```

Estimating "attnd" with or without weights does not affect the results. Just for the purpose of this exercise, "attnd" was shown with weights estimation.

As the following output shows, female microcredit participation does have a significant impact on household per capita expenditure with the nearest-neighborhood matching method ($t = 3.256$). The average treatment of the treated (ATT) on per capita expenditure for female program participation is 13.6 percent.

```
ATT estimation with Nearest Neighbor Matching method
(random draw version)
Analytical standard errors
------------------------------------------------------------
n. treat.      n. contr.       ATT      Std. Err.        t
------------------------------------------------------------
     595            293       0.136        0.042    3.256
------------------------------------------------------------
```

Note: the numbers of treated and controls refer to actual
nearest-neighbor matches

Average Treatment Effect Using Stratification Matching

The "atts" command calculates the average treatment effect on the treated using stratification matching. To estimate the average treatment effect of female participation on the treated for per capita total expenditure, use the following:

```
atts lexptot dfmfd, pscore(ps98) blockid(blockf1) comsup
```

The result that follows shows a 9.9 percent increase in per capita expenditure because of women's participation in the microcredit programs. The impact is significant at the 5 percent level ($t = 3.320$).

```
ATT estimation with the Stratification method
Analytical standard errors
------------------------------------------------------------
n. treat.      n. contr.       ATT      Std. Err.        t
------------------------------------------------------------
     595            529       0.099        0.030    3.320
------------------------------------------------------------
```

Average Treatment Effect Using Radius Matching

The "attr" command calculates the average treatment effect on the treated using radius matching. Following is a demonstration:

```
. attr lexptot dfmfd, pscore(ps98) radius(0.001) comsup
```

The result shows an increased impact (14.6 percent) with high significance ($t = 3.793$) of women's microcredit participation on per capita expenditure:

```
ATT estimation with the Radius Matching method
Analytical standard errors
------------------------------------------------------------
n. treat.      n. contr.       ATT      Std. Err.        t
------------------------------------------------------------
     478            386       0.146        0.039    3.793
------------------------------------------------------------
```

Note: the numbers of treated and controls refer to actual
matches within radius

Average Treatment Effect Using Kernel Matching

The "attk" command computes the average treatment effect using kernel-based matching. The "reps" option performs the bootstrapping 50 times.

```
attk lexptot dfmfd, pscore(ps98) comsup bootstrap reps(50)
```

Results are consistent with earlier findings. Women's participation increases per capita expenditure by 4 percent at a 5 percent significance level.

```
ATT estimation with the Kernel Matching method
Bootstrapped standard errors
------------------------------------------------------------
n. treat.     n. contr.       ATT      Std. Err.        t
------------------------------------------------------------
    595           529        0.107       0.032        3.331
------------------------------------------------------------
```

Checking Robustness of Average Treatment Effect

There are several ways to check robustness of the findings. One approach is to estimate the propensity score equation and then use the different matching methods previously discussed to compare the results. The findings with different matching techniques are quite consistent.

Another way to check robustness is to apply *direct* nearest-neighbor matching instead of estimating the propensity score equation first. Stata has a command ("nnmatch") to do that. If both methods give similar results, then the findings are assumed to be more reliable.

The following Stata command will estimate the average treatment effect on the outcome of interest using direct nearest-neighbor matching with one match per treatment. The "m" option specifies the number of matches closest to the treated observations.

```
nnmatch lexptot dfmfd sexhead agehead educhead lnland vaccess
pcirr rice wheat milk oil egg, tc(att) m(1);
```

Results are again consistent with earlier findings. A 13.6 percent positive impact of microcredit participation is seen at a 5 percent significance level.

```
Matching estimator: Average Treatment Effect for the Treated

Weighting matrix: inverse variance    Number of obs        =  1129
                                      Number of matches (m) =     1
-------------------------------------------------------------------
  lexptot |    Coef.   Std. Err.     z   P>|z|   [95% Conf. Interval]
----------+--------------------------------------------------------
    SATT  |  .1360462  .0377988   3.60  0.000    .061962   .2101304
-------------------------------------------------------------------

Matching variables: sexhead agehead educhead lnland vaccess pcirr rice
wheat milk oil egg
```

Further Exercises

Do the same exercise using male participation ("dmmfd"). Discuss your results.

Reference

Becker, Sascha, and Andrea Ichino. 2002. "Estimation of Average Treatment Effects Based on Propensity Scores." *Stata Journal* 2 (4): 358–77.

14. Double-Difference Method

The matching methods discussed in previous exercises are meant to reduce bias by choosing the treatment and comparison groups on the basis of observable characteristics. They are usually implemented after the program has been operating for some time and survey data have been collected. Another powerful form of measuring the impact of a program is by using panel data, collected from a baseline survey before the program was implemented and after the program has been operating for some time. These two surveys should be comparable in the questions and survey methods used and must be administered to both participants and nonparticipants. Using the panel data allows elimination of unobserved variable bias, provided that it does not change over time.[1]

This approach, the double-difference (DD, also commonly known as difference-in-difference) method has been popular in nonexperimental evaluations. The DD method estimates the difference in the outcome during the postintervention period between a treatment group and comparison group relative to the outcomes observed during a preintervention baseline survey.

Simplest Implementation: Simple Comparison Using "ttest"

The simplest way of calculating the DD estimator is to manually take the difference in outcomes between treatment and control between the surveys. The panel data hh_9198.dta are used for this purpose. The following commands open the data file and create a new 1991-level outcome variable (per capita expenditure) to make it available in observations of both years. Then, only 1998 observations are kept, and a log of per capita expenditure variable is created; the difference between 1998 and 1991 per capita expenditures (log form) is created.

```
use ..\data\hh_9198;
gen exptot0=exptot if year==0;
egen exptot91=max(exptot0), by(nh);
keep if year==1;
gen lexptot91=ln(1+exptot91);
gen lexptot98=ln(1+exptot);
gen lexptot9891=lexptot98-lexptot91;
```

The following command ("ttest") takes the difference variable of outcomes created earlier ("lexptot9891") and compares it for microcredit participants and nonparticipants. In essence, it creates a second difference of "lexptot9891" for those with dfmfd=1 and those with dfmfd==0. This second difference gives the estimate of the impact of females' microcredit program participation on per capita expenditure.

```
ttest lexptot9891, by(dfmfd);
```

The result shows that microcredit program participation by females increases per capita consumption by 11.1 percent and that this impact is significant at a less than 1 percent level:[2]

```
Two-sample t-test with equal variances

------------------------------------------------------------------------------
   Group |    Obs      Mean    Std. Err.  Std. Dev.   [95% Conf. Interval]
---------+--------------------------------------------------------------------
       0 |    391   .1473188   .0269923   .5337372    .0942502    .2003873
       1 |    435   .2586952    .024194   .5046057    .2111432    .3062472
---------+--------------------------------------------------------------------
combined |    826   .2059734    .018137   .5212616    .1703733    .2415735
---------+--------------------------------------------------------------------
    diff |         -.1113764     .03614               -.1823136   -.0404392
------------------------------------------------------------------------------
Degrees of freedom: 824

                      Ho: mean(0) - mean(1) = diff = 0

    Ha: diff < 0              Ha: diff != 0              Ha: diff > 0
     t = -3.0818               t = -3.0818               t = -3.0818
  P < t =  0.0011         P > |t| =  0.0021           P > t =  0.998
```

Regression Implementation

Instead of manually taking the difference of the outcomes, DD can be implemented using a regression. On the basis of the discussion in Ravallion (2008), the DD estimate can be calculated from the regression

$$Y_{it} = a + DD.T_i t + \beta T_i + \delta t_i + \varepsilon_{it},$$

where T is the treatment variable, t is the time dummy, and the coefficient of the interaction of T and t (DD) gives the estimate of the impact of treatment on outcome Y.

The following commands open the panel data file, create the log of outcome variable, and create a 1998-level participation variable available to both years—that is, those who participate in microcredit programs in 1998 are the assumed treatment group.

```
use hh_9198,clear;
gen lexptot=ln(1+exptot);
gen dfmfd1=dfmfd==1 & year==1;
egen dfmfd98=max(dfmfd1), by(nh);
```

The next command creates the interaction variable of treatment and time dummy (year in this case, which is 0 for 1991 and 1 for 1998).

```
gen dfmfdyr=dfmfd98*year;
```

The next command runs the actual regression that implements the DD method:

```
reg lexptot year dfmfd98 dfmfdyr;
```

The results show the same impact of female participation in microfinance programs on households' annual total per capita expenditures as obtained in the earlier exercise:

```
      Source |       SS       df       MS              Number of obs =    1652
-------------+------------------------------           F(  3,  1648) =   32.18
       Model | 20.2263902        3  6.74213005         Prob > F      =  0.0000
    Residual | 345.321048     1648  .209539471         R-squared     =  0.0553
-------------+------------------------------           Adj R-squared =  0.0536
       Total | 365.547438     1651  .221409714         Root MSE      = .45775
```

```
------------------------------------------------------------------------------
     lexptot |      Coef.   Std. Err.      t    P>|t|     [95% Conf. Interval]
-------------+----------------------------------------------------------------
        year |   .1473188   .0327386     4.50   0.000     .0831052    .2115323
     dfmfd98 |  -.1145671   .0318999    -3.59   0.000    -.1771358   -.0519984
     dfmfdyr |   .1113764   .0451133     2.47   0.014     .0228909    .1998619
       _cons |   8.310481   .0231497   358.99   0.000     8.265075    8.355887
------------------------------------------------------------------------------
```

A basic assumption behind the simple implementation of DD is that other covariates do not change across the years. But if those variables do vary, they should be controlled for in the regression to get the net effect of program participation on the outcome. So the regression model is extended by including other covariates that may affect the outcomes of interest:

```
reg lexptot year dfmfd98 dfmfdyr sexhead agehead educhead
lnland vaccess pcirr rice wheat milk oil egg [pw=weight];
```

By holding other factors constant, one sees that the impact of the microfinance programs has changed from significant to insignificant ($t = 0.97$).

```
Regression with robust standard errors           Number of obs =    1652
                                                 F( 14,  1637) =   24.90
                                                 Prob > F      =  0.0000
                                                 R-squared     =  0.2826
                                                 Root MSE      = .42765
```

```
------------------------------------------------------------------------------
             |               Robust
     lexptot |      Coef.   Std. Err.      t    P>|t|     [95% Conf. Interval]
-------------+----------------------------------------------------------------
        year |   .2768099   .0679939     4.07   0.000     .1434456    .4101741
     dfmfd98 |   .0012122   .0326585     0.04   0.970    -.0628446    .0652691
     dfmfdyr |   .0514655   .0530814     0.97   0.332    -.0526491    .1555802
```

sexhead	-.0455035	.053903	-0.84	0.399	-.1512296	.0602227
agehead	.0017445	.0011041	1.58	0.114	-.0004212	.0039102
educhead	.0385333	.0049841	7.73	0.000	.0287575	.0483092
lnland	.226467	.0309236	7.32	0.000	.165813	.2871209
vaccess	-.011292	.0498495	-0.23	0.821	-.1090674	.0864835
pcirr	.0628715	.0453625	1.39	0.166	-.0261031	.1518461
rice	-.0023961	.0109958	-0.22	0.828	-.0239634	.0191712
wheat	.0071376	.0120905	0.59	0.555	-.0165769	.0308521
milk	.0158481	.005106	3.10	0.002	.0058332	.025863
oil	.0011434	.0031013	0.37	0.712	-.0049395	.0072263
egg	.1458875	.0475718	3.07	0.002	.0525794	.2391956
_cons	7.399387	.2715525	27.25	0.000	6.86676	7.932014

Checking Robustness of DD with Fixed-Effects Regression

Another way to measure the DD estimate is to use a fixed-effects regression instead of ordinary least squares (OLS). Fixed-effects regression controls for household's unobserved and time-invariant characteristics that may influence the outcome variable. The Stata "xtreg" command is used to run fixed-effects regression. In particular, with the "fe" option, it fits fixed-effect models.

Following is the demonstration of fixed-effects regression using the simple model:

```
xtreg lexptot year dfmfd98 dfmfdyr, fe i(nh)
```

The results showed again a significant positive impact of female participation:

```
Fixed-effects (within) regression          Number of obs      =      1652
Group variable (i): nh                     Number of groups   =       826

R-sq: within  = 0.1450                     Obs per group: min =         2
      between = 0.0061                                     avg =       2.0
      overall = 0.0415                                     max =         2
                                           F(2,824)           =      9.90
corr(u_i, Xb) = -0.0379                    Prob > F           =    0.0000

------------------------------------------------------------------------------
   lexptot |    Coef.    Std. Err.      t    P>|t|    [95% Conf. Interval]
-----------+------------------------------------------------------------------
      year |  .1473188   .0262266     5.62   0.000    .0958399    .1987976
   dfmfd98 |  (dropped)
   dfmfdyr |  .1113764    .03614      3.08   0.002    .0404392    .1823136
     _cons |  8.250146   .0127593   646.60   0.000    8.225101    8.27519
-----------+------------------------------------------------------------------
   sigma_u |  .38132289
   sigma_e |  .36670395
       rho |  .51953588   (fraction of variance due to u_i)
------------------------------------------------------------------------------
F test that all u_i=0:   F(825, 824) =      2.11          Prob > F = 0.0000
```

By including other covariates in the regression, the fixed-effects model can be extended in the following way:

```
xtreg lexptot year dfmfd98 dfmfdyr sexhead agehead educhead
lnland vaccess pcirr rice wheat milk oil egg, fe i(nh);
```

Results show that, after controlling for the effects of time-invariant unobserved factors, female participation in microcredit has a 9.1 percent positive impact on household's per capita consumption, and the impact is very significant.

```
Fixed-effects (within) regression          Number of obs      =      1652
Group variable (i): nh                     Number of groups   =       826

R-sq: within= 0.1715                       Obs per group: min =         2
      between= 0.1914                                      avg =       2.0
      overall = 0.1737                                     max =         2
                                           F(13,813)          =     12.95
corr(u_i, Xb) = 0.1222                     Prob > F           =    0.0000


--------------------------------------------------------------------------
   lexptot |    Coef.    Std. Err.      t    P>|t|    [95% Conf. Interval]
-----------+--------------------------------------------------------------
      year |  .2211178    .063087     3.50   0.000    .0972851    .3449504
   dfmfd98 |  (dropped)
   dfmfdyr |  .0906308    .0367358    2.47   0.014    .0185226    .1627391
   sexhead | -.0577238    .0722968   -0.80   0.425   -.1996342    .0841866
   agehead | -.0003766    .0016985   -0.22   0.825   -.0037106    .0029574
  educhead |  .0137419    .0082935    1.66   0.098   -.0025373     .030021
    lnland |  .1381659    .0619682    2.23   0.026    .0165293    .2598025
   vaccess | -.0932955     .053396   -1.75   0.081   -.1981057    .0115147
     pcirr |  .0823594    .0642728    1.28   0.200   -.0438009    .2085196
      rice |  .0107911     .010209    1.06   0.291   -.0092481    .0308303
     wheat | -.0227681    .0123379   -1.85   0.065    -.046986    .0014498
      milk | -.0014743    .0064578   -0.23   0.819   -.0141503    .0112016
       oil |  .0038546    .0031366    1.23   0.219   -.0023022    .0100113
       egg |  .1439482     .047915    3.00   0.003    .0498965        .238
     _cons |  7.853111    .2482708   31.63   0.000    7.365784    8.340439
-----------+--------------------------------------------------------------
   sigma_u |  .34608097
   sigma_e |   .3634207
       rho |  .47557527    (fraction of variance due to u_i)
--------------------------------------------------------------------------
F test that all u_i=0:   F(825, 813) =      1.59          Prob > F = 0.0000
```

Applying the DD Method in Cross-Sectional Data

DD can be applied to cross-sectional data, too, not just panel data. The idea is very similar to the one used in panel data. Instead of a comparison between years, program and nonprogram villages are compared, and instead of a comparison between participants and nonparticipants, target and nontarget groups are compared.

Accordingly, the 1991 data hh_91.dta are used. Create a dummy variable called "target" for those who are eligible to participate in microcredit programs (that is, those who have less than 50 decimals of land). Then, create a village program dummy ("progvill") for those villages that are

```
use ..\data\hh_91,clear;
gen lexptot=ln(1+exptot);
gen lnland=ln(1+hhlanddb/100);
gen target=hhlanddb<50;
gen progvill=thanaid<25;
```

Then, generate a variable interacting the program village and target:

```
gen progtarget=progvill*target
```

Then, calculate the DD estimate by regressing log of total per capita expenditure against program village, target, and their interaction:

```
. reg lexptot progvill target progtarget
```

The results show that the impact of microcredit program placement on the target group is not significant ($t = -0.61$).

Source	SS	df	MS		Number of obs =	826
Model	10.9420259	3	3.64734195		F(3, 822) =	27.38
Residual	109.485295	822	.133193789		Prob > F =	0.0000
					R-squared =	0.0909
					Adj R-squared =	0.0875
Total	120.427321	825	.14597251		Root MSE =	.36496

lexptot	Coef.	Std. Err.	t	P>|t|	[95% Conf. Interval]	
progvill	-.0646577	.0770632	-0.84	0.402	-.2159215	.086606
target	-.2996852	.0815261	-3.68	0.000	-.459709	-.1396614
progtarget	**.0529438**	**.0867976**	**0.61**	**0.542**	**-.1174272**	**.2233147**
_cons	8.485567	.0729914	116.25	0.000	8.342296	8.628839

The coefficient of the impact variable ("progtarget"), which is 0.053, does not give the actual impact of microcredit programs; it has to be adjusted by dividing by the proportion of target households in program villages. The following command can be used to find the proportion:

```
sum target if progvill==1;
```

Of the households in program villages, 68.9 percent belong to the target group. Therefore, the regression coefficient of "progtarget" is divided by this value, giving 0.077, which is the true impact of microcredit programs on the target population, even though it is not significant.

Variable	Obs	Mean	Std. Dev.	Min	Max
target	700	.6885714	.4634087	0	1

As before, the regression model can be specified adjusting for covariates that affect the outcomes of interest:

```
reg lexptot progvill target progtarget sexhead agehead educhead lnland
vaccess pcirr rice wheat milk oil egg [pw=weight];
```

Holding other factors constant, one finds no change in the significance level of microcredit impacts on households' annual total per capita expenditures:

```
Regression with robust standard errors            Number of obs =     826
                                                  F( 14,   811) =   11.03
                                                  Prob > F      =  0.0000
                                                  R-squared     =  0.3236
                                                  Root MSE      = .35757
```

		Robust				
lexptot	Coef.	Std. Err.	t	P>|t|	[95% Conf.	Interval]
progvill	-.001756	.0793878	-0.02	0.982	-.1575857	.1540738
target	.0214491	.0911074	0.24	0.814	-.1573849	.2002832
progtarget	**-.0102772**	**.0895501**	**-0.11**	**0.909**	**-.1860545**	**.1655**
sexhead	-.019398	.0743026	-0.26	0.794	-.1652462	.1264502
agehead	-.0001666	.0014126	-0.12	0.906	-.0029394	.0026062
educhead	.0263119	.0060213	4.37	0.000	.0144927	.0381311
lnland	.268622	.0513087	5.24	0.000	.1679084	.3693356
vaccess	-.0098224	.0695396	-0.14	0.888	-.1463211	.1266764
pcirr	.0007576	.0571461	0.01	0.989	-.1114141	.1129294
rice	-.0082217	.0160899	-0.51	0.610	-.0398044	.023361
wheat	.0206119	.0146325	1.41	0.159	-.0081101	.049334
milk	.0227563	.0059707	3.81	0.000	.0110365	.0344761
oil	-.0067235	.0039718	-1.69	0.091	-.0145196	.0010727
egg	.1182376	.0569364	2.08	0.038	.0064775	.2299978
_cons	7.827818	.3696557	21.18	0.000	7.102223	8.553413

Again, fixed-effects regression can be used instead of OLS to check the robustness of the results. However, with cross-sectional data, household-level fixed effects cannot be run, because each household appears only once in the data. Therefore, a village-level fixed-effects regression is run:

```
xtreg lexptot progvill target progtarget, fe i(vill)
```

This time there is a negative (insignificant) impact of microcredit programs on household per capita expenditure:

```
Fixed-effects (within) regression          Number of obs     =      826
Group variable (i): vill                   Number of groups  =       87

R-sq: within  = 0.1088                     Obs per group: min =        4
      between = 0.0240                                     avg =      9.5
      overall = 0.0901                                     max =       15

                                           F(2,737)          =    44.98
corr(u_i, Xb) = -0.0350                    Prob > F          =   0.0000
```

```
--------------------------------------------------------------------
    lexptot |    Coef.   Std. Err.     t    P>|t|   [95% Conf. Interval]
------------+-------------------------------------------------------
   progvill |  (dropped)
     target | -.2531591   .0801025   -3.16  0.002   -.4104155  -.0959028
 progtarget | -.0134339   .0854701   -0.16  0.875   -.1812278    .15436
      _cons |  8.436668   .0232409  363.01  0.000    8.391041   8.482294
------------+-------------------------------------------------------
    sigma_u |  .16994272
    sigma_e |  .3419746
        rho |  .1980463   (fraction of variance due to u_i)
--------------------------------------------------------------------
F test that all u_i=0:    F(86, 737) =    2.32         Prob > F = 0.0000
```

The same fixed-effects regression is run after including other covariates:

```
xtreg lexptot progvill target progtarget sexhead agehead educh-
ead lnland, fe i(vill)
```

Again, no change is seen in the significance level:

```
Fixed-effects (within) regression        Number of obs      =        826
Group variable (i): vill                 Number of groups   =         87

R-sq:  within  = 0.2258                   Obs per group: min =          4
       between = 0.0643                                  avg =        9.5
       overall = 0.1887                                  max =         15

                                          F(6,733)           =      35.62
corr(u_i, Xb)  = -0.0497                  Prob > F           =     0.0000
--------------------------------------------------------------------
    lexptot |    Coef.   Std. Err.     t    P>|t|   [95% Conf. Interval]
------------+-------------------------------------------------------
   progvill |  (dropped)
     target |  .0326157   .0818661    0.40  0.690   -.1281043   .1933357
 progtarget | -.0081697     .07999   -0.10  0.919   -.1652066   .1488671
    sexhead | -.0051257   .0568657   -0.09  0.928   -.1167648   .1065134
    agehead |  .0001635   .0010231    0.16  0.873   -.0018451   .0021721
   educhead |  .0229979   .0039722    5.79  0.000    .0151997   .0307962
     lnland |  .2732536   .0385588    7.09  0.000    .1975548   .3489523
      _cons |  8.072129   .0806635  100.07  0.000     7.91377   8.230488
------------+-------------------------------------------------------
    sigma_u |  .16666988
    sigma_e |  .3196088
        rho |  .21380081  (fraction of variance due to u_i)
--------------------------------------------------------------------
F test that all u_i=0:    F(86, 733) =    2.55         Prob > F = 0.0000
```

Taking into Account Initial Conditions

Even though DD implementation through regression (OLS or fixed effects) controls for household- and community-level covariates, the initial conditions during the baseline survey may have a separate influence on the subsequent changes in outcome or assignment to the treatment. Ignoring the separate effect of initial conditions therefore may bias the DD estimates.

Including the initial conditions in the regression is tricky, however. Because the baseline observations in the panel sample already contain initial characteristics, extra variables for initial conditions cannot be added directly. One way to add initial conditions is to take into account an alternate implementation of the fixed-effects regression. In this implementation, difference variables are created for all variables (outcome and covariates) between the years, and then these difference variables are used in regression instead of the original variables. In this modified data set, initial condition variables can be added as extra regressors without a colinearity problem.

The following commands create the difference variables from the panel data hh_9198:

```
sort nh year;
by nh: gen dlexptot=lexptot[2]-lexptot[1];
by nh: gen ddmfd98= dmfd98[2]- dmfd98[1];
by nh: gen ddmmfd98= dmmfd98[2]- dmmfd98[1];
by nh: gen ddfmfd98= dfmfd98[2]- dfmfd98[1];
by nh: gen ddmfdyr= dmfdyr[2]- dmfdyr[1];
by nh: gen ddmmfdyr= dmmfdyr[2]- dmmfdyr[1];
by nh: gen ddfmfdyr= dfmfdyr[2]- dfmfdyr[1];
by nh: gen dsexhead= sexhead[2]- sexhead[1];
by nh: gen dagehead= agehead[2]- agehead[1];
by nh: gen deduchead= educhead[2]- educhead[1];
by nh: gen dlnland= lnland[2]- lnland[1];
by nh: gen dvaccess= vaccess[2]- vaccess[1];
by nh: gen dpcirr= pcirr[2]- pcirr[1];
by nh: gen drice= rice[2]- rice[1];
by nh: gen dwhtflr= whtflr[2]- whtflr[1];
by nh: gen dmilk= milk[2]- milk[1];
by nh: gen dmustoil= mustoil[2]- mustoil[1];
by nh: gen dhenegg= henegg[2]- henegg[1];
```

Stata creates these difference variables for both years. Then an OLS regression is run with the difference variables plus the original covariates as additional regressors, restricting the sample to the baseline year (year = 0). This is done because the baseline year contains both the difference variables and the initial condition variables.

```
reg dlexptot ddfmfd98 ddfmfdyr dsexhead dagehead deduchead
dlnland dvaccess dpcirr drice dwhtflr dmilk dmustoil dhenegg
sexhead agehead educhead lnland vaccess pcirr rice whtflr milk
mustoil henegg if year==0 [pw=weight];
```

The results show that, after controlling for the initial conditions, the impact of microcredit participation disappears ($t = 1.42$):

```
Regression with robust standard errors    Number of obs =      826
                                          F( 23,  802) =     2.93
                                          Prob > F      =   0.0000
                                          R-squared     =   0.0917
                                          Root MSE      =  .51074
```

dlexptot	Coef.	Robust Std. Err.	t	P>|t|	[95% Conf. Interval]	
ddfmfd98	(dropped)					
ddfmfdyr	**.0619405**	**.0435103**	**1.42**	**0.155**	**-.0234671**	**.1473481**
dsexhead	-.0615416	.0871488	-0.71	0.480	-.2326083	.1095251
dagehead	.0013583	.0023165	0.59	0.558	-.0031889	.0059055
deduchead	.0153497	.0117889	1.30	0.193	-.0077909	.0384904
dlnland	.1260302	.0701158	1.80	0.073	-.011602	.2636624
dvaccess	-.1365889	.0702504	-1.94	0.052	-.2744853	.0013075
dpcirr	.1042085	.1124156	0.93	0.354	-.1164551	.3248721
drice	.0065267	.0147616	0.44	0.659	-.0224493	.0355027
dwheat	-.04828	.0261598	-1.85	0.065	-.0996297	.0030697
dmilk	-.0071707	.0143637	-0.50	0.618	-.0353656	.0210241
doil	.0137635	.0062199	2.21	0.027	.0015542	.0259727
degg	.1991899	.101613	1.96	0.050	-.0002689	.3986486
sexhead	-.1157563	.0844686	-1.37	0.171	-.281562	.0500494
agehead	.0054212	.002046	2.65	0.008	.001405	.0094375
educhead	.0230352	.008891	2.59	0.010	.0055828	.0404876
lnland	-.0690961	.0545822	-1.27	0.206	-.1762369	.0380448
vaccess	-.1142214	.1065896	-1.07	0.284	-.323449	.0950062
pcirr	.1471455	.109057	1.35	0.178	-.0669254	.3612164
rice	-.0047485	.0317983	-0.15	0.881	-.0671661	.0576691
wheat	-.0337045	.0306002	-1.10	0.271	-.0937705	.0263614
milk	-.0047502	.0129723	-0.37	0.714	-.0302138	.0207134
oil	.0205757	.0083353	2.47	0.014	.0042142	.0369373
egg	.1015795	.1273284	0.80	0.425	-.1483568	.3515158
_cons	-.704969	.5861648	-1.20	0.229	-1.855567	.4456292

The DD Method Combined with Propensity Score Matching

The DD method can be refined in a number of ways. One is by using propensity score matching (PSM) with the baseline data to make certain the comparison group is similar to the treatment group and then applying double differences to the matched sample. This way, the observable heterogeneity in the initial conditions can be dealt with.

Using the "pscore" command, the participation variable in 1998/99 (which is created here as "dfmfd98" for both years) is regressed with 1991/92 exogenous variables to obtain propensity scores from the baseline data. These commands are as follows:

```
use ..\data\hh_9198,clear;
gen lnland=ln(1+hhland/100);
gen dfmfd1=dfmfd==1 & year==1;
egen dfmfd98=max(dfmfd1), by(nh);
keep if year==0;
pscore dfmfd98 sexhead agehead educhead lnland vaccess
   pcirr rice wheat milk oil egg [pw=weight], pscore(ps98)
   blockid(blockf1) comsup level(0.001);
```

The balancing property of the PSM has been satisfied, which means that households with the same propensity scores have the same distributions of all covariates for all five blocks. The region of common support is [.06030439, .78893426], and 26 observations have been dropped:

```
******************************************************
Algorithm to estimate the propensity score
******************************************************

The treatment is dfmfd98

     dfmfd98 |      Freq.     Percent        Cum.
-------------+-----------------------------------
           0 |        391       47.34       47.34
           1 |        435       52.66      100.00
-------------+-----------------------------------
       Total |        826      100.00

Estimation of the propensity score

(sum of wgt is  8.2233e+02)
Iteration 0:   log pseudolikelihood = -554.25786
Iteration 1:   log pseudolikelihood = -480.05123
Iteration 2:   log pseudolikelihood = -475.25432
Iteration 3:   log pseudolikelihood = -475.17443
Iteration 4:   log pseudolikelihood =  -475.1744

Probit estimates                          Number of obs =       826
                                          Wald chi2(11) =     78.73
                                          Prob > chi2   =    0.0000
Log pseudolikelihood = -475.1744          Pseudo R2     =    0.1427
--------------------------------------------------------------------------
             |              Robust
     dfmfd98 |     Coef.    Std. Err.      z    P>|z|    [95% Conf. Interval]
-------------+------------------------------------------------------------
     sexhead | -.1512794    .2698723    -0.56   0.575   -.6802194    .3776605
     agehead | -.0073102    .0046942    -1.56   0.119   -.0165106    .0018903
    educhead | -.0261142    .018235     -1.43   0.152   -.0618542    .0096257
      lnland | -.9010234    .137662     -6.55   0.000   -1.170836   -.6312109
     vaccess |  .2894359    .2626682     1.10   0.271   -.2253843    .804256
       pcirr |  .0367083    .1999013     0.18   0.854   -.3550911    .4285077
        rice |  .1682276    .0606261     2.77   0.006    .0494028    .2870525
       wheat |  .0603593    .0500646     1.21   0.228   -.0377655    .1584841
        milk | -.0472819    .0205877    -2.30   0.022    -.087633   -.0069309
         oil |  .009133     .0141985     0.64   0.520   -.0186954    .0369615
         egg | -.2991866    .184372     -1.62   0.105    -.660549    .0621759
       _cons | -1.002465    1.241022    -0.81   0.419   -3.434823    1.429894
--------------------------------------------------------------------------

Note: the common support option has been selected
The region of common support is [.06030439, .78893426]

Description of the estimated propensity score
in region of common support

            Estimated propensity score
-------------------------------------------------------------
      Percentiles       Smallest
 1%      .0800224       .0603044
 5%      .1415098       .061277
10%      .2124288       .0622054        Obs                800
25%      .3583033       .0647113        Sum of Wgt.        800
```

```
50%        .481352                        Mean         .4579494
                          Largest        Std. Dev.    .1612539
75%        .570064        .7616697
90%        .6600336       .7650957        Variance     .0260028
95%        .688278        .7716357        Skewness    -.4881678
99%        .7515092       .7889343        Kurtosis     2.637857
```

```
**********************************************************
Step 1: Identification of the optimal number of blocks
Use option detail if you want more detailed output
**********************************************************

The final number of blocks is 4

This number of blocks ensures that the mean propensity score
is not different for treated and controls in each blocks

**********************************************************
Step 2: Test of balancing property of the propensity score
Use option detail if you want more detailed output
**********************************************************

The balancing property is satisfied

This table shows the inferior bound, the number of treated,
and the number of controls for each block

 Inferior |
 of block |        dfmfd98
 of pscore |        0            1 |       Total
----------+----------------------+-----------
 .0603044 |        53           16 |          69
       .2 |       110           70 |         180
       .4 |       151          250 |         401
       .6 |        51           99 |         150
----------+----------------------+-----------
    Total |       365          435 |         800

Note: the common support option has been selected

*********************************************
End of the algorithm to estimate the pscore
*********************************************
```

The following commands keep the matched households in the baseline year and merge them with panel data to keep only the matched households in the panel sample:

```
keep if blockf1!=.;
keep nh;
sort nh;
merge nh using ..\data\hh_9198;
keep if _merge==3;
```

The next step is to implement the DD method as before. For this exercise, only the fixed-effects implementation is shown:

```
xtreg lexptot year dfmfd98 dfmfdyr sexhead agehead educhead
lnland vaccess pcirr rice wheat milk oil egg, fe i(nh);
```

The results show that applying PSM to DD retains the original positive impact of female participation in microcredit programs on household expenditure:

```
Fixed-effects (within) regression        Number of obs      =     1600
Group variable (i): nh                   Number of groups   =      800

R-sq: within  =   0.1791                 Obs per group: min =        2
      between =   0.1237                              avg =      2.0
      overall =   0.1434                              max =        2

                                         F(13,787)          =    13.21
corr(u_i, Xb)  = 0.0414                  Prob > F           =   0.0000
-------------------------------------------------------------------------
   lexptot |      Coef.   Std. Err.     t    P>|t|    [95% Conf. Interval]
-----------+-------------------------------------------------------------
      year |    .222509   .0639108    3.48   0.001    .0970532    .3479647
    dfmfd98 |   (dropped)
    dfmfdyr |   .0925741   .0371517    2.49   0.013     .019646    .1655023
    sexhead |   -.084584   .0739679   -1.14   0.253   -.2297818    .0606138
    agehead |  -.0003225    .001732   -0.19   0.852   -.0037223    .0030773
   educhead |   .0132322   .0084471    1.57   0.118   -.0033494    .0298138
     lnland |   .2003341   .0778701    2.57   0.010    .0474766    .3531917
    vaccess |  -.0857169   .0542065   -1.58   0.114   -.1921234    .0206896
      pcirr |    .083983   .0644159    1.30   0.193   -.0424644    .2104303
       rice |   .0131877   .0102657    1.28   0.199   -.0069638    .0333392
      wheat |  -.0272757   .0123259   -2.21   0.027   -.0514712   -.0030802
       milk |  -.0015386   .0064937   -0.24   0.813   -.0142857    .0112084
        oil |   .0047885   .0031592    1.52   0.130    -.001413    .0109899
        egg |   .1400882   .0485296    2.89   0.004    .0448254    .2353509
      _cons |   7.815588   .2504303   31.21   0.000    7.323998    8.307179
-----------+-------------------------------------------------------------
    sigma_u |  .33642591
    sigma_e |  .36009944
        rho |  .46605118   (fraction of variance due to u_i)
-------------------------------------------------------------------------
F test that all u_i=0:     F(799, 787) =     1.58     Prob > F = 0.0000
```

Notes

1. Panel data are not strictly needed for double-difference estimation. How this technique can be applied to cross-sectional data is shown later.
2. The negative sign in output means that outcome of participants (dfmfd = 1) is greater than that of nonparticipants (dfmfd = 0), thus implying that the participation impact is in fact positive.

Reference

Ravallion, Martin. 2008. "Evaluating Anti-poverty Programs." In *Handbook of Development Economics*, vol. 4, ed. T. Paul Schultz and John Strauss, 3787–846. Amsterdam: North-Holland.

15. Instrumental Variable Method

Another way of measuring the impact of the program when treatment has not been randomly assigned is by using the instrumental variable (IV) method. The IV estimation regards the treatment variable (in this case, participation in microfinance programs) as endogenous. The idea is to find an observable exogenous variable or variables (instruments) that influence the participation variable but do not influence the outcome of the program if participating. Thus, one would want at least one instrument that is not in the covariates and that satisfies the preceding requirements. IV estimation is a two-step process. First, the treatment variable is run against all covariates, including the instruments. Then, the predicted value of the treatment—instead of the actual value—is used in the second stage.

IV Implementation Using the "ivreg" Command

The first step in IV implementation is to find an instrument. In the example, a household's choice to participate in the microcredit program is used as the instrument variable. The household's choice depends on two factors: availability of microcredit programs in the village and the household's eligibility to participate (which is determined by its landholding). Even though program placement in the village may be endogenous, a household's eligibility is not, and the combination of these two factors is therefore exogenous.

Using the 1998 data (hh_98.dta), create a village program variable for females and then a female program choice variable at the household level.[1] As mentioned in earlier exercises, a household is eligible to participate in microcredit programs if it has fewer than 50 decimals of land.

```
egen villfmf=max(dmmfd), by(vill);
gen fchoice=villfmf==1 & hhland<50;
```

Next, create additional instruments by interacting the choice variable with all covariates. The Stata "for" command is used to do so in one command:

```
for var agehead-educhead lnland vaccess pcirr rice-oil: gen
fchX=fchoice*X;
```

The next step is the IV implementation, which uses the Stata "ivreg" command. The first-stage equation appears within parentheses in the syntax, and the first option displays the first-stage results:

```
ivreg lexptot agehead-educhead lnland vaccess pcirr rice-oil
(dfmfd= agehead-educhead lnland vaccess pcirr rice-oil fch*),
first;
```

The output shows the first-stage results first and then the second-stage results. According to the first-stage output, household head's education and household's land asset negatively influence microcredit program participation; so do the instruments. The second-stage results show that after controlling for the endogeneity of program participation, female participation in microcredit programs has a significant impact (32.6 percent) on household's per capita expenditure ($t = 2.28$).

First-stage regressions

Source	SS	df	MS		Number of obs =	1129
Model	31.9544747	23	1.38932499		F(23, 1105) =	6.15
Residual	249.471566	1105	.225766123		Prob > F =	0.0000
					R-squared =	0.1135
Total	281.426041	1128	.249491171		Adj R-squared =	.0951
					Root MSE =	.47515

dfmfd	Coef.	Std. Err.	t	P>|t|	[95% Conf. Interval]	
agehead	-.0017996	.001853	-0.97	0.332	-.0054354	.0018362
sexhead	-.090353	.0949407	-0.95	0.341	-.2766374	.0959314
educhead	-.0111658	.006549	-1.70	0.088	-.0240157	.0016841
lnland	-.0743253	.0463394	-1.60	0.109	-.1652485	.0165979
vaccess	-.1696796	0699002	-2.43	0.015	-.3068316	-.0325275
pcirr	-.0459691	0831373	-0.55	0.580	-.2090939	.1171558
rice	.0085986	.0155203	0.55	0.580	-.0218539	.0390511
wheat	.0102826	.0292563	0.35	0.725	-.0471216	.0676869
milk	-.0211565	.0104327	-2.03	0.043	-.0416267	-.0006864
potato	(dropped)					
egg	.0043442	.0934236	0.05	0.963	-.1789635	.1876519
oil	.0017818	.0065519	0.27	0.786	-.0110737	.0146373
fchoice	-.97571	.4857339	-2.01	0.045	-1.928775	-.022645
fchagehead	.0062515	.0023876	2.62	0.009	.0015669	.0109362
fchsexhead	.1562665	.1116846	1.40	0.162	-.0628713	.3754043
fcheduchead	-.0083186	.0088998	-0.93	0.350	-.0257811	.0091439
fchlnland	-.0028382	.1781701	-0.02	0.987	-.3524282	.3467517
fchvaccess	.1823573	.084952	2.15	0.032	.0156719	.3490427
fchpcirr	.1830853	.1025273	1.79	0.074	-.0180849	.3842554
fchrice	-.0253889	.019694	-1.29	0.198	-.0640307	.0132529
fchwheat	-.019292	.0365608	-0.53	0.598	-.0910284	.0524444
fchmilk	.0319648	.0126207	2.53	0.011	.0072016	.056728
fchegg	.0802827	.1110378	0.72	0.470	-.137586	.2981513
fchoil	.0097549	.007933	1.23	0.219	-.0058106	.0253203
_cons	.7880826	.3962508	1.99	0.047	.0105937	1.565571

```
Instrumental variables (2SLS) regression
```

Source	SS	df	MS		Number of obs =	1129
					F(12, 1116) =	22.94
Model	48.1621199	12	4.01350999		Prob > F =	0.0000
Residual	249.69781	1116	.223743557		R-squared =	0.1617
					Adj R-squared =	0.1527
Total	297.85993	1128	.264060221		Root MSE =	.47302

lexptot	Coef.	Std. Err.	t	P>|t|	[95% Conf. Interval]	
dfmfd	.3255436	.1426528	2.28	0.023	.0456457	.6054415
agehead	.0030299	.0011679	2.59	0.010	.0007383	.0053214
sexhead	-.0566001	.0494292	-1.15	0.252	-.1535847	.0403844
educhead	.0533665	.0048684	10.96	0.000	.0438142	.0629188
lnland	.2210422	.0408664	5.41	0.000	.1408586	.3012258
vaccess	-.0030504	.0403496	-0.08	0.940	-.08222	.0761193
pcirr	.1389462	.0496316	2.80	0.005	.0415644	.2363281
rice	.0054628	.009462	0.58	0.564	-.0131025	.0240281
wheat	-.0401031	.0173472	-2.31	0.021	-.0741399	-.0060664
milk	.0207911	.0058035	3.58	0.000	.0094042	.032178
potato	(dropped)					
egg	.1005972	.0508165	1.98	0.048	.0008905	.2003039
oil	.0081386	.0038401	2.12	0.034	.0006041	.0156732
_cons	7.407985	.2280463	32.48	0.000	6.960537	7.855433

```
Instrumented:  dfmfd
Instruments:   agehead sexhead educhead lnland vaccess pcirr rice
               wheat milk
               potato egg oil fchoice fchagehead fchsexhead
               fcheduchead
               fchlnland fchvaccess fchpcirr fchrice fchwheat
               fchmilk fchegg
               fchoil
```

Testing for Endogeneity: OLS versus IV

A few tests can be used to determine whether an ordinary least squares (OLS) or IV is more appropriate. Stata has a command "ivendog" that performs an F-test and chi-square test following methodologies called the Wu-Hausman test and the Durbin-Wu-Hausman test, respectively. The null hypothesis is that OLS is consistent (in this case, it implies treatment is exogenous). If the null hypothesis is not rejected, an OLS should suffice; otherwise an IV method should be used. The "ivendog" command is used after the "ivreg" command:

```
ivendog;
```

The results show that the null hypothesis is rejected at the 10 percent level, implying that IV is a better model than OLS:

```
Tests of endogeneity of: dfmfd
H0: Regressor is exogenous
    Wu-Hausman F test:                 3.01281   F(1,1115)    P-value = 0.08289
    Durbin-Wu-Hausman chi-sq test:     3.04242   Chi-sq(1)    P-value = 0.08111
```

IV Method for Binary Treatment: "treatreg" Command

The preceding IV estimation methods apply when the endogenous regressor is continuous. When the endogenous regressor is binary (participant/nonparticipant), using a linear model in the first stage of the IV procedure may or may not be appropriate. Another method that fits a treatment-effects model when the endogenous regressor is binary is the "treatreg" command in Stata. The "treatreg" command fits a treatment-effects model using either the full maximum likelihood or the two-step consistent estimator. The "treatreg" command takes into account the effect of the binary endogenous variable on the outcome of interests conditional on the two sets of exogenous variables. The command estimates two regressions simultaneously. The first equation is estimated using probit regression to predict the probability of treatment. The second is either a linear or probit regression for the outcome variables. The two error terms are assumed to be jointly normally distributed.

Following is an example of how the "treatreg" command is used with the Bangladesh 1998 data. Its syntax is very similar to that of the "ivreg" command:

```
treatreg lexptot agehead-educhead lnland vaccess pcirr
rice-oil, treat (dfmfd= agehead-educhead lnland vaccess pcirr
rice-oil fch*);
```

Following is the treatment-effect method using maximum likelihood estimation. It shows that women's participation does have a positive significant impact on household's expenditure ($t = 3.49$):

```
Treatment effects model -- MLE           Number of obs   =     1129
                                          Wald chi2(12)   =   271.45
Log likelihood = -1427.6651               Prob > chi2     =   0.0000
```

	Coef.	Std. Err.	z	P>|z|	[95% Conf. Interval]	
lexptot						
agehead	.0028983	.0011858	2.44	0.015	.0005742	.0052225
sexhead	-.0558392	.0504364	-1.11	0.268	-.1546927	.0430142
educhead	.0547403	.0048088	11.38	0.000	.0453152	.0641654
lnland	.2386945	.0384969	6.20	0.000	.163242	.3141469
vaccess	.0026497	.0408488	0.06	0.948	-.0774125	.0827118
pcirr	.1305888	.0500755	2.61	0.009	.0324427	.228735
rice	.0060323	.0096418	0.63	0.532	.0128654	.02493
wheat	-.0404817	.017699	-2.29	0.022	-.0751711	-.0057923
milk	.0208849	.0059217	3.53	0.000	.0092787	.0324912
egg	.0944399	.0515543	1.83	0.067	-.0066047	.1954846
oil	.0074181	.0038636	1.92	0.055	-.0001545	.0149906
dfmfd	**.4168906**	**.1196073**	**3.49**	**0.000**	**.1824647**	**.6513166**
_cons	7.391633	.2322404	31.83	0.000	6.93645	7.846816
dfmfd						
agehead	-.004252	.0050252	-0.85	0.397	-.0141012	.0055973
sexhead	-.1799594	.2534342	-0.71	0.478	-.6766813	.3167625

```
    educhead |  -.0453168   .0184985   -2.45   0.014   -.0815733   -.0090604
     lnland |  -.1791062   .1315339   -1.36   0.173   -.4369079    .0786956
    vaccess |  -.5458849   .1822059   -3.00   0.003   -.9030019   -.1887679
      pcirr |   -.121319   .2202852   -0.55   0.582   -.5530702    .3104321
       rice |   .0093552   .0406836    0.23   0.818   -.0703831    .0890935
      wheat |   .0082867   .0782386    0.11   0.916   -.1450581    .1616316
       milk |  -.0605588   .0294469   -2.06   0.040   -.1182737    -.002844
        egg |   .0366651   .2578851    0.14   0.887   -.4687804    .5421107
        oil |  -.0017389   .0177263   -0.10   0.922   -.0364818     .033004
    fchoice |  -3.391314   1.291503   -2.63   0.009   -5.922613   -.8600159
  fchagehead |   .0156243   .0063892    2.45   0.014    .0031018    .0281468
  fchsexhead |   .3432873   .2937005    1.17   0.242   -.2323551    .9189296
 fcheduchead |   .0056506   .0247551    0.23   0.819   -.0428685    .0541698
   fchlnland |  -.2419577   .4632756   -0.52   0.601   -1.149961    .6660458
   fchvaccess |   .6105495   .2173745    2.81   0.005    .1845032    1.036596
    fchpcirr |   .4829752   .2662667    1.81   0.070    -.038898    1.004848
     fchrice |  -.0446986    .050703   -0.88   0.378   -.1440747    .0546775
    fchwheat |  -.0191072   .0959983   -0.20   0.842   -.2072604     .169046
     fchmilk |   .0866831   .0345121    2.51   0.012    .0190407    .1543255
      fchegg |   .1975426    .297008    0.67   0.506   -.3845824    .7796676
      fchoil |   .0345253   .0207377    1.66   0.096   -.0061198    .0751704
       _cons |   1.309823   1.095342    1.20   0.232   -.8370069    3.456653
-----------+----------------------------------------------------------------
     /athrho |  -.4622307   .1677019   -2.76   0.006   -.7909205    -.133541
     /lnsigma |  -.7283617   .0440104  -16.55   0.000   -.8146205    -.642103
-----------+----------------------------------------------------------------
        rho |  -.4319006   .1364191                    -.6589302   -.1327528
       sigma |   .4826991   .0212438                     .4428074    .5261847
      lambda |   -.208478   .0740375                    -.3535888   -.0633673
----------------------------------------------------------------------------
LR test of indep. eqns. (rho = 0): chi2(1) = 5.14 Prob > chi2 = 0.0234
----------------------------------------------------------------------------
```

IV with Fixed Effects: Cross-Sectional Estimates

Instrumental variable regression can be combined with fixed effects. Here a demonstration using cross-sectional data is shown. The command to use is "xtivreg" with the "fe" option. A village-level fixed-effects regression is run using the same hh_98.dta. Here is the command for women's participation in microcredit:

```
xtivreg lexptot year agehead-educhead lnland vaccess pcirr
rice-oil (dfmfd= agehead-educhead lnland vaccess pcirr rice-oil
mch*), fe i(vill);
```

Next, run a village-level fixed-effects regression with the same hh_98.dta. Using village-level fixed effects causes the participation impacts to disappear:

```
Fixed-effects (within) IV regression      Number of obs      =        1129
Group variable: vill                      Number of groups   =         104

R-sq: within  = 0.1550                    Obs per group: min =           4
      between = 0.2246                                    avg =        10.9
      overall = 0.1618                                    max =          19

                                          Wald chi2(5)       =   453021.37
corr(u_i, Xb) = 0.0511                     Prob > chi2        =      0.0000
```

```
-----------------------------------------------------------------------
  lexptot |     Coef.    Std. Err.     z      P>|z|    [95% Conf. Interval]
----------+------------------------------------------------------------
    dfmfd |    .1901029    .1956837    0.97    0.331     -.19343    .5736359
  agehead |    .0020665    .0011244    1.84    0.066   -.0001373    .0042703
  sexhead |   -.0352392    .0472055   -0.75    0.455   -.1277602    .0572818
 educhead |    .0433888    .0056147    7.73    0.000    .0323842    .0543934
   lnland |    .2283189    .0470498    4.85    0.000    .1361029    .3205349
  vaccess |   (dropped)
    pcirr |   (dropped)
     rice |   (dropped)
    wheat |   (dropped)
     milk |   (dropped)
      egg |   (dropped)
      oil |   (dropped)
    _cons |    8.10043     .1268782   63.84    0.000    7.851754    8.349107
----------+------------------------------------------------------------
  sigma_u |   .24105185
  sigma_e |   .42196914
      rho |   .24604092    (fraction of variance due to u_i)
-----------------------------------------------------------------------
F test that all u_i=0:    F(103,1020) =     3.04         Prob > F  = 0.0000
-----------------------------------------------------------------------
Instrumented:  dfmfd
Instruments:   agehead sexhead educhead lnland vaccess pcirr rice wheat
milk egg oil mchoice mchagehead mchsexhead mcheduchead mchlnland mchvaccess
mchpcirr mchrice mchwheat mchmilk mchegg mchoil
```

IV with Fixed Effects: Panel Estimates

An implementation of "xtivreg" using panel data is now shown with the panel data hh_9198.dta. After creating necessary variables as before, issue the "xtivreg" command.

```
xtivreg lexptot year agehead-educhead lnland vaccess pcirr
rice-oil (dfmfd= agehead-educhead lnland vaccess pcirr rice-oil
mch*), fe i(nh);
```

The results do not show any participation impact on expenditure.

```
Fixed-effects (within) IV regression      Number of obs     =      1652
Group variable: nh                        Number of groups  =       826

R-sq: within  = 0.1667                    Obs per group: min =        2
      between = 0.1924                                    avg =      2.0
      overall = 0.1733                                    max =        2

                                          Wald chi2(14)     = 866855.47
corr(u_i, Xb) = 0.1215                    Prob > chi2       =    0.0000
-----------------------------------------------------------------------
  lexptot |     Coef.    Std. Err.     z      P>|z|    [95% Conf. Interval]
----------+------------------------------------------------------------
    dfmfd |    .0430727    .124483     0.35    0.729   -.2009096     .287055
     year |    .2360629    .0707606    3.34    0.001    .0973747    .3747511
  agehead |    .000021     .0017636    0.01    0.990   -.0034355    .0034775
  sexhead |   -.0536457    .0727231   -0.74    0.461   -.1961803     .088889
 educhead |    .0136537    .008419     1.62    0.105   -.0028472    .0301546
```

```
      lnland |    .1362576    .0629346     2.17    0.030     .0129079    .2596072
      vaccess |   -.0991489      .05371    -1.85    0.065    -.2044186    .0061207
       pcirr |    .0954609    .0642934     1.48    0.138    -.0305519    .2214737
        rice |    .0199218    .0131231     1.52    0.129     -.005799    .0456426
       wheat |   -.0244967    .0128117    -1.91    0.056    -.0496072    .0006138
        milk |   -.0028403    .0065394    -0.43    0.664    -.0156572    .0099766
      potato |      -.0199    .0165334    -1.20    0.229    -.0523049    .0125048
         egg |    .1703499    .0483323     3.52    0.000     .0756203    .2650795
         oil |    .0045626    .0031518     1.45    0.148    -.0016148      .01074
       _cons |    7.833876    .2515847    31.14    0.000     7.340779    8.326973
-------------+----------------------------------------------------------------
     sigma_u |   .34559734
     sigma_e |   .36468826
         rho |   .47314159    (fraction of variance due to u_i)
------------------------------------------------------------------------------
F test that all u_i=0:     F(825,812) =     1.57            Prob > F    = 0.0000
------------------------------------------------------------------------------
Instrumented: dfmfd
Instruments:   year agehead sexhead educhead lnland vaccess pcirr rice wheat
milk potato egg oil fchoice fchagehead fchsexhead fcheduchead fchlnland
fchvaccess fchpcirr fchrice fchwheat fchmilk fchpotato fchegg fchoil
```

Note

1. By 1998, all sample villages had microcredit programs, but for purposes of demonstrating the process of creating the variable, this exercise creates the village program variable.

16. Regression Discontinuity Design

When treatment is assigned exclusively on the basis of a cutoff value, then regression discontinuity (RD) design is a suitable alternative to randomized experiments or other quasi-experimental designs. Unlike randomized design, an eligible group need not be excluded from treatment just for the sake of impact assessment. Impact assessment can be implemented with RD design using the Bangladesh data because participation in microcredit programs is officially determined by a household's landholding; that is, a household is eligible to participate only if it has fewer than 50 decimals of land. Therefore, the cutoff point of 50 decimals in land assets fulfills the RD design criterion.

Impact Estimation Using RD

The impact assessment of RD is based on the idea that the sample in the neighborhood of the cutoff point (above and below) represents features of randomized design, because households in treatment and control groups are very similar in their characteristics and they vary only in their treatment status. So a difference in mean outcomes of treated and control groups restricted to the vicinity of the cutoff point (that is, local to the discontinuity) gives the impact of intervention. RD has two versions. In one, called *sharp discontinuity*, the cutoff point deterministically establishes treatment status. That is, everyone eligible gets the treatment, and no one ineligible gets it. In the other type of discontinuity, called *fuzzy discontinuity*, treatment status does not jump abruptly from zero to one as households become eligible from ineligible. This scenario is more realistic, particularly in this case, because some eligible households decide (for one reason or another) not to participate in microcredit, whereas some ineligible households do participate. In good RD design, eligible nonparticipants and ineligible participants remain low. The impact of microcredit participation, using RD design, can be given by following expression:

$$I = (y^+ - y^-)/(s^+ - s^-),\qquad(16.1)$$

where, y^+ is the mean outcome for microcredit participants whose landholding is in the vicinity of 50 decimals, y^- is the mean outcome for microcredit nonparticipants whose landholding is in the vicinity of 50 decimals, s^+ is the mean treatment status for eligible households whose landholding is in the vicinity of 50 decimals, and s^- is the mean treatment status for ineligible households whose landholding is in the vicinity of 50 decimals.

In sharp discontinuity, $s^+ = 1$ and $s^- = 0$, and the difference in mean outcomes of participants and nonparticipants gives the impact.

In reality, instead of directly calculating means of outcome and treatment, one estimates their values from local linear (or kernel) regressions that are implemented in both sides of the cutoff point. Then these values are plugged into equation 16.1 to get estimated impacts.

Implementation of Sharp Discontinuity

Bangladesh data hh_91.dta or hh_98.dta do not satisfy the conditions to fulfill sharp discontinuity design because program participation is not deterministic based on the landholding cutoff point. In other words, some eligible households (land asset < 50 decimals) do not participate, and some ineligible households (land asset >= 50 decimals) do participate. Therefore, to demonstrate sharp discontinuity, hh_98.dta are adjusted by dropping these two types of households:

```
use ..\data\hh_98,clear;
gen lexptot=ln(1+exptot);
gen lnland=ln(1+hhland/100);

drop if (hhland<50 & (dmmfd==0|dfmfd==0))|(hhland>=50 &
(dmmfd==1|dfmfd==1));
```

The next step is to run the local linear regression for outcome (household per capita expenditure) against household's landholding for both eligible (participants) and ineligible (nonparticipants) households. As a result of the previous operation of dropping some households, eligible households are now deterministically participants and ineligibles deterministically nonparticipants. Local polynomial regression allows estimated outcomes to be stored for both participants and nonparticipants. The next step is to take means of those outcomes at the cutoff point. Because the cutoff point is a single value (50 decimals), it is better to specify a range of landholding values and take means of outcomes for households that are within that range. That range is set from 45 to 50 decimals for participants and from 50 to 55 for nonparticipants. With the means of outcomes computed, their difference can be taken to get estimated impacts of microcredit participation on per capita expenditure in the neighborhood of the cutoff point. This whole process is coded as follows within a Stata program called *rd_sharp*:

```
prog rd_sharp, rclass;
  version 8.2;
  args outcome;
  confirm var `outcome';
  tempname outrd1 outrd0 outcome1 outcome0;
  locpoly `outcome' lnland if hhland<50, gen(`outrd1')
at(lnland) nogr tri w(3) d(1);
```

```
locpoly `outcome' lnland if hhland>=50, gen(`outrd0')
at(lnland) nogr tri w(3) d(1);
  sum `outrd1' if hhland>=45 & hhland<50, meanonly;
  scalar `outcome1'=r(mean);
  sum `outrd0' if hhland>=50 & hhland<55, meanonly;
  scalar `outcome0'=r(mean);
  return scalar diff_outcome=`outcome1'-`outcome0';
end;
```

Although estimated impacts can be calculated this way, this process does not give a standard error that is used to calculate t-statistics. Standard error can be calculated by bootstrapping the preceding program. Bootstrapping runs a command (or set of commands) repeatedly by randomly drawing observations (with replacement) from the data, stores estimation results for each run, and then calculates standard error from the saved estimations. Each command need not be bootstrapped separately. Instead, the program that includes all the needed commands can be bootstrapped. For this reason, when multiple commands need to be bootstrapped together, writing a Stata program is extremely convenient. Programming also allows the same program to be run using different parameters. Look at different options of the "locpoly" command in the rd_sharp program, which runs the local linear regression of generic outcome variable against log of household land for both participants and nonparticipants:

gen()   stores the result of the estimation, that is, estimated value of outcome

at()   specifies a variable that contains the values at which the smooth of kernel regression should be evaluated

tri   specifies that the kernel type for local linear regression is triangle

w   specifies the half-width of the kernel, the bandwidth of the smoothing window around each point

nogr   suppresses graphs for each bandwidth

d()   specifies degree of polynomial to be used in the smoothing (1 implies linear regression)

In local linear regression, different bandwidths can produce different estimates, so testing with more than one bandwidth is recommended. Choice of kernel is less important, although trying different types can help check the robustness of estimates. An important observation to make here is that the rd_sharp program has no parameter to indicate microcredit program participation. That is because microcredit program participation has been made deterministic by landholding (by, as mentioned before, the "drop" command).

The following commands set a seed for random drawing for the bootstrapping and then do the bootstrapping. Bootstrapping is done by executing the Stata "bootstrap" command, which is followed by the command to be bootstrapped in double quotes (" ") and then the statistics or expression to be estimated. Here the "bootstrap" command runs the previously defined rd_sharp program with the "lexptot" argument, which replaces the generic argument "outcome" with lexptot (log of per capita annual expenditure). Consequently, lexptot is run against lnland (log of household landholding) using local linear regressions. At the end of execution, program rd_sharp returns the difference of means of lexptot (estimated impact), which the "bootstrap" command stores in a variable called "impact_sharp." Finally, "bootstrap" executes the rd_sharp program 100 times.

```
set seed 12345;
bootstrap "rd_sharp lexptot" impact_sharp=r(diff_outcome),
reps(100) nowarn;
```

The output of the "bootstrap" command is as follows. It shows that microcredit program participation has a negative impact on per capita expenditure (−12.6 percent) and standard error is 0.112:

```
command:      rd_sharp lexptot
statistic:    impact_s~p = r(diff_outcome)

Bootstrap statistics                              Number of obs  =      243
                                                  Replications   =      100
-----------------------------------------------------------------------------
Variable     | Reps  Observed   Bias    Std. Err. [95% Conf. Interval]
-------------+---------------------------------------------------------------
impact_sharp |  92  -.1264224  .0023491  .1116639  -.3482292 .0953843   (N)
             |                                     -.3132059 .0937947   (P)
             |                                     -.3132059 .125849    (BC)
-----------------------------------------------------------------------------

Note: N  = normal
      P  = percentile
      BC = bias-corrected
```

The following commands create the *t*-statistics of the estimated impact and display them:

```
gen t_impact_sharp=_b[impact_sharp]/_se[impact_sharp];
sum t_impact_sharp;
```

After executing these commands, one can see that estimated impact is not significant ($t = -1.132$).

```
    Variable |  Obs    Mean    Std. Dev.    Min        Max
-------------+---------------------------------------------------------------
t_impact_s~p |  243  -1.132169      0     -1.132169  -1.132169
```

Implementation of Fuzzy Discontinuity

Unlike the implementation of sharp discontinuity, implementation of fuzzy discontinuity does not require dropping observations for eligible households' nonparticipation or ineligible households' participation. The program to estimate impacts for fuzzy discontinuity is very similar to the one used for sharp discontinuity. Here local polynomial regressions for treatment are included in addition to those for outcomes. Estimated impact is calculated using the formula specified in equation 16.1. The program to calculate fuzzy discontinuity follows:

```
prog rd_fuzzy, rclass;
  version 8.2;
  args treatment outcome;
  confirm var `treatment';
  confirm var `outcome';
  tempname treatrd1 treatrd0 outrd1 outrd0 treat1 treat0 out-
come1 outcome0;
  locpoly `treatment' lnland if hhland<50, gen(`treatrd1')
at(lnland) nogr tri w(3) d(1);
  locpoly `treatment' lnland if hhland>=50, gen(`treatrd0')
at(lnland) nogr tri w(3) d(1);
  locpoly `outcome' lnland if hhland<50, gen(`outrd1')
at(lnland) nogr tri w(3) d(1);
  locpoly `outcome' lnland if hhland>=50, gen(`outrd0')
at(lnland) nogr tri w(3) d(1);
  sum `treatrd1' if hhland>=45 & hhland<=55, meanonly;
  scalar `treat1'=r(mean);
  sum `treatrd0' if hhland>=45 & hhland<=55, meanonly;
  scalar `treat0'=r(mean);
  sum `outrd1' if hhland>=45 & hhland<=55, meanonly;
  scalar `outcome1'=r(mean);
  sum `outrd0' if hhland>=45 & hhland<=55, meanonly;
  scalar `outcome0'=r(mean);
  return scalar impact=(`outcome1'-`outcome0')/(`treat1'-
`treat0');
end;
```

The rd_fuzzy program, as opposed to rd_sharp, takes two arguments—one for treatment and one for outcome. Therefore, to estimate impacts of female microcredit participation on households' per capita expenditure, the "bootstrap" command executes the program rd_fuzzy with two arguments: dfmfd (women's microcredit participation) and lexptot (per capita annual expenditure). Here are the codes that run the relevant "bootstrap" command:

```
set seed 123;
bootstrap "rd_fuzzy dfmfd lexptot" impact_fuzzy_f=r(impact),
reps(100) nowarn;
```

The output of the "bootstrap" command shows that the sign of estimated impact is still negative:

```
command:     rd_fuzzy dfmfd lexptot
statistic:   impact_f~f = r(impact)
```

```
Bootstrap statistics                          Number of obs  =      1129
                                              Replications   =       100
----------------------------------------------------------------------
Variable     | Reps  Observed    Bias     Std. Err.  [95% Conf. Interval]
-------------+--------------------------------------------------------
impact_fuz~f | 100  -1.702198  1.92124   3.571683  -8.789193   5.384796  (N)
             |                                     -10.52238   9.24404   (P)
             |                                     -13.93708  -.0473376  (BC)
----------------------------------------------------------------------

Note: N  = normal
      P  = percentile
      BC = bias-corrected
```

The following commands create and display the t-statistics of the estimated impact:

```
gen t_impact_fuzzy_f=_b[impact_fuzzy_f]/_se[impact_fuzzy_f];
sum t_impact_fuzzy_f;
```

After executing these commands, one sees that estimated impact is insignificant ($t = -0.477$):

```
    Variable |  Obs      Mean    Std. Dev.      Min        Max
-------------+--------------------------------------------------
t_impact_f~f |  1129  -.4765815      0      -.4765815  -.4765815
```

Exercise

Estimate male program participation impacts on household per capita expenditure using fuzzy discontinuity design. Discuss your results.

Answers to Chapter Questions

Chapter 2

1. b

2. d

3. c

4. a

5. b

6. c

Chapter 3

1. b

2. c

3. c

4. d

5. a

6. b

Chapter 4

1. a

2. a

3. c

4. d

5. b

Chapter 5

1. c

2. c

3. c

4. e

5. b

Chapter 6

1. b

2. a

3. a

4. d

5. d

Chapter 7

1. d

2. b

3. c

4. c

5. c

Appendix: Programs and .do Files for Chapter 12–16 Exercises

Chapter 12

```
capture log close
log using ..\log\random.log,replace

drop _all
set more 1
set mem 50m

#delimit ;
use ..\data\hh_98;
gen lexptot=ln(1+exptot);
gen lnland=ln(1+hhland/100);
gen vill=thanaid*10+villid;
egen progvillm=max(dmmfd), by(vill);
egen progvillf=max(dfmfd), by(vill);

***Impacts of program placement;
****t-test;
ttest lexptot, by(progvillm);
ttest lexptot, by(progvillf);

****Regression implementation;
reg lexptot progvillm;
reg lexptot progvillf;

****Expanded regression
reg lexptot progvillm sexhead agehead educhead lnland vaccess
pcirr rice wheat
   milk oil egg [pw=weight];
reg lexptot progvillf sexhead agehead educhead lnland vaccess
pcirr rice wheat
   milk oil egg [pw=weight];

***Impacts of program participation;
****t-test;
ttest lexptot, by(dmmfd);
ttest lexptot, by(dfmfd);
```

```
****Regression implementation;
reg lexptot dmmfd;
reg lexptot dfmfd;

****Expanded regression;
reg lexptot dmmfd sexhead agehead educhead lnland vaccess pcirr
rice wheat
    milk oil egg [pw=weight];
reg lexptot dfmfd sexhead agehead educhead lnland vaccess pcirr
rice wheat
    milk oil egg [pw=weight];

****Expanded regression: capturing both program placement and
participation;
reg lexptot dmmfd progvillm sexhead agehead educhead lnland
vaccess pcirr rice
    wheat milk oil egg [pw=weight];
reg lexptot dfmfd progvillf sexhead agehead educhead lnland
vaccess pcirr rice
    wheat milk oil egg [pw=weight];

***Impacts of program participation in program villages;
reg lexptot dmmfd if progvillm==1 [pw=weight];
reg lexptot dfmfd if progvillf==1 [pw=weight];
reg lexptot dmmfd sexhead agehead educhead lnland vaccess pcirr
rice wheat milk
    oil egg if progvillm==1 [pw=weight];
reg lexptot dfmfd sexhead agehead educhead lnland vaccess pcirr
rice wheat milk
    oil egg if progvillf==1 [pw=weight];

***Spillover effects of program placement;
reg lexptot progvillm if dmmfd==0 [pw=weight];
reg lexptot progvillf if dfmfd==0 [pw=weight];
reg lexptot progvillm sexhead agehead educhead lnland vaccess
pcirr rice wheat
    milk oil egg if dmmfd==0 [pw=weight];
reg lexptot progvillf sexhead agehead educhead lnland vaccess
pcirr rice wheat
    milk oil egg if dfmfd==0 [pw=weight];

log close
```

Chapter 13

```
capture log close
log using ..\log\psm.log,replace
```

```
drop _all
set more 1
set mem 50m
use ..\data\hh_98
gen lexptot=ln(1+exptot)
gen lnland=ln(1+hhland/100)

#delimit ;
****Impacts of program participation;

***Male participants;
****pscore equation;
pscore dmmfd sexhead agehead educhead lnland vaccess pcirr rice
wheat milk oil egg [pw=weight],
    pscore(ps98) blockid(blockf1) comsup level(0.001);
drop ps98 blockf1;
pscore dmmfd sexhead agehead educhead vaccess pcirr rice wheat
milk oil [pw=weight],
    pscore(ps98) blockid(blockf1) comsup level(0.001);

****Nearest-Neighbor Matching;
attnd lexptot dmmfd [pweight=weight], pscore(ps98) comsup;

****Stratification Matching;
atts lexptot dmmfd, pscore(ps98) blockid(blockf1) comsup;

****Radius Matching;
attr lexptot dmmfd, pscore(ps98) radius(0.001) comsup;

****Kernel Matching;
attk lexptot dmmfd, pscore(ps98) comsup bootstrap reps(50);

drop ps98 blockf1;

***Female participants;
****pscore equation;
pscore dfmfd sexhead agehead educhead lnland vaccess pcirr rice
wheat milk oil egg [pw=weight],
    pscore(ps98) blockid(blockf1) comsup level(0.001);

****Nearest-Neighbor Matching;
attnd lexptot dfmfd [pweight=weight], pscore(ps98) comsup;

****Stratification Matching;
atts lexptot dfmfd, pscore(ps98) blockid(blockf1) comsup;

****Radius Matching;
attr lexptot dfmfd, pscore(ps98) radius(0.001) comsup;
```

```
****Kernel Matching;
attk lexptot dfmfd, pscore(ps98) comsup bootstrap reps(50);

****Direct Matching using Nearest Neighbor;
nnmatch lexptot dmmfd sexhead agehead educhead lnland vaccess
pcirr rice wheat milk oil egg [pw=weight], tc(att) m(1);
nnmatch lexptot dfmfd sexhead agehead educhead lnland vaccess
pcirr rice wheat milk oil egg [pw=weight], tc(att) m(1);

log close;
```

Chapter 14

```
capture log close
log using ..\log\dd.log,replace
****DD IMPLEMENTATION;

drop _all
set more 1
set mem 50m

#delimit ;
***Simplest implementation;
use ..\data\hh_9198;
gen exptot0=exptot if year==0;
egen exptot91=max(exptot0), by(nh);
keep if year==1;
gen lexptot91=ln(1+exptot91) if year==1;
gen lexptot98=ln(1+exptot) if year==1;
gen lexptot9891=lexptot98-lexptot91;

ttest lexptot9891 if year==1, by(dmmfd);
ttest lexptot9891 if year==1, by(dfmfd);

***Regression implementation;
use ..\data\hh_9198,clear;
gen lexptot=ln(1+exptot);
gen lnland=ln(1+hhland/100);
gen dmmfd1=dmmfd==1 & year==1;
egen dmmfd98=max(dmmfd1), by(nh);
gen dfmfd1=dfmfd==1 & year==1;
egen dfmfd98=max(dfmfd1), by(nh);
gen dmmfdyr=dmmfd98*year;
gen dfmfdyr=dfmfd98*year;

***Basic model;
reg lexptot year dmmfd98 dmmfdyr;
reg lexptot year dfmfd98 dfmfdyr;
```

```
****Full model;
reg lexptot year dmmfd98 dmmfdyr sexhead agehead educhead
lnland vaccess pcirr rice wheat milk oil egg [pw=weight];
reg lexptot year dfmfd98 dfmfdyr sexhead agehead educhead
lnland vaccess pcirr rice wheat milk oil egg [pw=weight];

****Fixed effects: Basic;
xtreg lexptot year dmmfd98 dmmfdyr, fe i(nh);
xtreg lexptot year dfmfd98 dfmfdyr, fe i(nh);

****Fixed effects: Full Model;
xtreg lexptot year dmmfd98 dmmfdyr sexhead agehead educhead
lnland vaccess pcirr rice wheat milk oil egg, fe i(nh);
xtreg lexptot year dfmfd98 dfmfdyr sexhead agehead educhead
lnland vaccess pcirr rice wheat milk oil egg, fe i(nh);

***DD in cross-sectional data;
use ..\data\hh_91,clear;
gen vill=thanaid*10+villid;
gen lexptot=ln(1+exptot);
gen lnland=ln(1+hhland/100);
gen target=hhland<50;
gen progvill=thanaid<25;
gen progtarget=progvill*target;

sum target if progvill==1;

reg lexptot progvill target progtarget;
reg lexptot progvill target progtarget sexhead agehead educhead
lnland vaccess pcirr rice wheat milk oil egg [pw=weight];
xtreg lexptot progvill target progtarget, fe i(vill);
xtreg lexptot progvill target progtarget sexhead agehead
educhead lnland, fe i(vill);

****Taking into account initial conditions;
use ..\data\hh_9198,clear;

gen lexptot=ln(1+exptot);
gen lnland=ln(1+hhland/100);
gen dmmfd1=dmmfd==1 & year==1;
egen dmmfd98=max(dmmfd1), by(nh);
gen dfmfd1=dfmfd==1 & year==1;
egen dfmfd98=max(dfmfd1), by(nh);
gen dmmfdyr=dmmfd98*year;
gen dfmfdyr=dfmfd98*year;
drop dmmfd1 dfmfd1;

sort nh year;
by nh: gen dlexptot=lexptot[2]-lexptot[1];
```

```
by nh: gen ddmmfd98= dmmfd98[2]- dmmfd98[1];
by nh: gen ddfmfd98= dfmfd98[2]- dfmfd98[1];
by nh: gen ddmmfdyr= dmmfdyr[2]- dmmfdyr[1];
by nh: gen ddfmfdyr= dfmfdyr[2]- dfmfdyr[1];
by nh: gen dsexhead= sexhead[2]- sexhead[1];
by nh: gen dagehead= agehead[2]- agehead[1];
by nh: gen deduchead= educhead[2]- educhead[1];
by nh: gen dlnland= lnland[2]- lnland[1];
by nh: gen dvaccess= vaccess[2]- vaccess[1];
by nh: gen dpcirr= pcirr[2]- pcirr[1];
by nh: gen drice= rice[2]- rice[1];
by nh: gen dwheat= wheat[2]- wheat[1];
by nh: gen dmilk= milk[2]- milk[1];
by nh: gen doil= oil[2]- oil[1];
by nh: gen degg= egg[2]- egg[1];

reg dlexptot ddmmfd98 ddmmfdyr dsexhead dagehead deduchead dln-
land dvaccess dpcirr drice dwheat dmilk doil degg
     sexhead agehead educhead lnland vaccess pcirr rice wheat
milk oil egg if year==0 [pw=weight];
reg dlexptot ddfmfd98 ddfmfdyr dsexhead dagehead deduchead dln-
land dvaccess dpcirr drice dwheat dmilk doil degg
     sexhead agehead educhead lnland vaccess pcirr rice wheat
milk oil egg if year==0 [pw=weight];

****DD with PSM;
****Male participants;
use ..\data\hh_9198,clear;
gen lnland=ln(1+hhland/100);
gen dmmfd1=dmmfd==1 & year==1;
egen dmmfd98=max(dmmfd1), by(nh);
keep if year==0;
pscore dmmfd98 sexhead agehead educhead lnland vaccess pcirr
rice wheat milk oil egg [pw=weight],
   pscore(ps98) blockid(blockf1) comsup level(0.001);
keep if blockf1!=.;
keep nh;
sort nh;
merge nh using ..\data\hh_9198;
keep if _merge==3;
gen lexptot=ln(1+exptot);
gen lnland=ln(1+hhland/100);
gen dmmfd1=dmmfd==1 & year==1;
egen dmmfd98=max(dmmfd1), by(nh);
gen dmmfdyr=dmmfd98*year;

xtreg lexptot year dmmfd98 dmmfdyr sexhead agehead educhead
lnland vaccess pcirr rice wheat milk oil egg, fe i(nh);
```

```
****Female participants;
use ..\data\hh_9198,clear;
gen lnland=ln(1+hhland/100);
gen dfmfd1=dfmfd==1 & year==1;
egen dfmfd98=max(dfmfd1), by(nh);
keep if year==0;

pscore dfmfd98 sexhead agehead educhead lnland vaccess pcirr
rice wheat milk oil egg [pw=weight],
     pscore(ps98) blockid(blockf1) comsup level(0.001);
keep if blockf1!=.;
keep nh;
sort nh;
merge nh using ..\data\hh_9198;
keep if _merge==3;
gen lexptot=ln(1+exptot);
gen lnland=ln(1+hhland/100);
gen dfmfd1=dfmfd==1 & year==1;
egen dfmfd98=max(dfmfd1), by(nh);
gen dfmfdyr=dfmfd98*year;

xtreg lexptot year dfmfd98 dfmfdyr sexhead agehead educhead
lnland vaccess pcirr rice wheat milk oil egg, fe i(nh);

log close;
```

Chapter 15

```
capture log close
log using ..\log\iv.log,replace

drop _all
set more 1
set mem 50m

#delimit ;
****IV using ivreg implementation;
use ..\data\hh_98,clear;
gen lexptot=ln(1+exptot);
gen lnland=ln(1+hhland/100);
gen vill=thanaid*10+villid;
egen villmmf=max(dmmfd), by(vill);
gen mchoice=villmmf==1 & hhland<50;
for var agehead-educhead lnland vaccess pcirr rice-oil: gen
mchX=mchoice*X;
egen villfmf=max(dfmfd), by(vill);
gen fchoice=villfmf==1 & hhland<50;
```

```
for var agehead-educhead lnland vaccess pcirr rice-oil: gen
fchX=fchoice*X;

****Male participation;
ivreg lexptot agehead-educhead lnland vaccess pcirr rice-oil
(dmmfd= agehead-educhead
      lnland vaccess pcirr rice-oil mch*);
****Test for endogeneity;
ivendog;

****Female participation;
ivreg lexptot agehead-educhead lnland vaccess pcirr rice-oil
(dfmfd= agehead-educhead
      lnland vaccess pcirr rice-oil fch*), first;
****Test for endogeneity;
ivendog;

****IV using treatreg implementation;
treatreg lexptot agehead-educhead lnland vaccess pcirr rice-
oil, treat (dmmfd= agehead-educhead
    lnland vaccess pcirr rice-oil mch*);
treatreg lexptot agehead-educhead lnland vaccess pcirr rice-
oil, treat (dfmfd= agehead-educhead
    lnland vaccess pcirr rice-oil fch*);

****IV with FE implementation in cross-sectional data;
use ..\data\hh_98,clear;
gen lexptot=ln(1+exptot);
gen lnland=ln(1+hhland/100);
gen vill=thanaid*10+villid;
egen villmmf=max(dmmfd), by(vill year);
gen mchoice=villmmf==1 & hhland<50;
for var agehead-educhead lnland vaccess pcirr rice-oil: gen
mchX=mchoice*X;
egen villfmf=max(dfmfd), by(vill year);
gen fchoice=villfmf==1 & hhland<50;
for var agehead-educhead lnland vaccess pcirr rice-oil: gen
fchX=fchoice*X;
xtivreg lexptot year agehead-educhead lnland vaccess pcirr
rice-oil (dmmfd= agehead-educhead
    lnland vaccess pcirr rice-oil mch*), fe i(vill);
****Test for endogeneity;
dmexogxt;
xtivreg lexptot year agehead-educhead lnland vaccess pcirr
rice-oil (dfmfd= agehead-educhead
    lnland vaccess pcirr rice-oil mch*), fe i(vill);
****Test for endogeneity;
dmexogxt;
```

```
****IV with FE implementation in panel data;
use ..\data\hh_9198,clear;
gen lexptot=ln(1+exptot);
gen lnland=ln(1+hhland/100);
gen vill=thanaid*10+villid;
egen villmmf=max(dmmfd), by(vill year);
gen mchoice=villmmf==1 & hhland<50;
for var agehead-educhead lnland vaccess pcirr rice-oil: gen
mchX=mchoice*X;
egen villfmf=max(dfmfd), by(vill year);
gen fchoice=villfmf==1 & hhland<50;
for var agehead-educhead lnland vaccess pcirr rice-oil: gen
fchX=fchoice*X;

xtivreg lexptot year agehead-educhead lnland vaccess pcirr
rice-oil (dmmfd= agehead-educhead
     lnland vaccess pcirr rice-oil mch*), fe i(nh);

****Test for endogeneity;
dmexogxt;
xtivreg lexptot year agehead-educhead lnland vaccess pcirr
rice-oil (dfmfd= agehead-educhead
     lnland vaccess pcirr rice-oil fch*), fe i(nh);
****Test for endogeneity;
dmexogxt;
log close;
```

Chapter 16

```
capture log close
log using ..\log\rd.log,replace

****IMPLEMENTATION OF REGRESSION DISCONTINUITY;
drop _all
set more 1
set mem 50m

#delimit ;
use ..\data\hh_98,clear;
gen lexptot=ln(1+exptot);
gen lnland=ln(1+hhland/100);

*****Program for Sharp Discontinuity;
drop if (hhland<50 & (dmmfd==0|dfmfd==0))|(hhland>=50 &
(dmmfd==1|dfmfd==1));
capture prog drop rd_sharp;
prog rd_sharp, rclass;
```

```
    version 8.2;
    args outcome;
    confirm var `outcome';
    tempname outrd1 outrd0 outcome1 outcome0;
    locpoly `outcome' lnland if hhland<50, gen(`outrd1')
at(lnland) nogr tri w(3) d(1);
    locpoly `outcome' lnland if hhland>=50, gen(`outrd0')
at(lnland) nogr tri w(3) d(1);
    sum `outrd1' if hhland>=45 & hhland<50, meanonly;
    scalar `outcome1'=r(mean);
    sum `outrd0' if hhland>=50 & hhland<55, meanonly;
    scalar `outcome0'=r(mean);
    return scalar diff_outcome=`outcome1'-`outcome0';
end;


****Participation;
set seed 12345;
bootstrap "rd_sharp lexptot" impact_sharp=r(diff_outcome),
reps(100) nowarn;
gen t_impact_sharp=_b[impact_sharp]/_se[impact_sharp];
sum t_impact_sharp;


use ..\data\hh_98,clear;
gen lexptot=ln(1+exptot);
gen lnland=ln(1+hhland/100);
*****Program for Fuzzy Discontinuity;
capture prog drop rd_fuzzy;
prog rd_fuzzy, rclass;
    version 8.2;
    args treatment outcome;
    confirm var `treatment';
    confirm var `outcome';
    tempname treatrd1 treatrd0 outrd1 outrd0 treat1 treat0 out-
come1 outcome0;
    locpoly `treatment' lnland if hhland<50, gen(`treatrd1')
at(lnland) nogr tri w(3) d(1);
    locpoly `treatment' lnland if hhland>=50, gen(`treatrd0')
at(lnland) nogr tri w(3) d(1);
    locpoly `outcome' lnland if hhland<50, gen(`outrd1')
at(lnland) nogr tri w(3) d(1);
    locpoly `outcome' lnland if hhland>=50, gen(`outrd0')
at(lnland) nogr tri w(3) d(1);
    sum `treatrd1' if hhland>=45 & hhland<=55, meanonly;
    scalar `treat1'=r(mean);
    sum `treatrd0' if hhland>=45 & hhland<=55, meanonly;
    scalar `treat0'=r(mean);
    sum `outrd1' if hhland>=45 & hhland<=55, meanonly;
    scalar `outcome1'=r(mean);
```

```
    sum `outrd0' if hhland>=45 & hhland<=55, meanonly;
    scalar `outcome0'=r(mean);

    return scalar impact=(`outcome1'-`outcome0')/(`treat1'-
`treat0');
end;
***Male participation;
set seed 12345;
bootstrap "rd_fuzzy dmmfd lexptot" impact_fuzzy_m=r(impact),
reps(100) nowarn;
gen t_impact_fuzzy_m=_b[impact_fuzzy_m]/_se[impact_fuzzy_m];
sum t_impact_fuzzy_m;

***Female participation;
set seed 123;
bootstrap "rd_fuzzy dfmfd lexptot" impact_fuzzy_f=r(impact),
reps(100) nowarn;
gen t_impact_fuzzy_f=_b[impact_fuzzy_f]/_se[impact_fuzzy_f];
sum t_impact_fuzzy_f;

log close;
```

Index

Boxes, figures, notes, and tables are indicated by *b*, *f*, *n*, and *t*, respectively.

ECO-AUDIT
Environmental Benefits Statement

The World Bank is committed to preserving endangered forests and natural resources. The Office of the Publisher has chosen to print *Handbook on Impact Evaluation* on recycled paper with 30 percent postconsumer fiber in accordance with the recommended standards for paper usage set by the Green Press Initiative, a nonprofit program supporting publishers in using fiber that is not sourced from endangered forests. For more information, visit www.greenpressinitiative.org.

Saved:
- 9 trees
- 3 million BTUs of total energy
- 874 lbs. of CO_2 equivalent of greenhouse gases
- 4,212 gallons of wastewater
- 256 lbs. of solid waste

CPSIA information can be obtained at www.ICGtesting.com
Printed in the USA
LVOW052027011211

257409LV00014BA/28/P